W9-BXW-308

YOUR **PERSONAL HOROSCOPE**
2022

JOSEPH POLANSKY

YOUR PERSONAL
HOROSCOPE
2022

Month-by-month
forecast for every sign

Thorsons

Thorsons
An Imprint of HarperCollins*Publishers*
1 London Bridge Street
London SE1 9GF

www.harpercollins.co.uk

HarperCollins*Publishers*
1st Floor, Watermarque Building, Ringsend Road
Dublin 4, Ireland

First published by Thorsons 2021

5 7 9 10 8 6 4

© Star ★ Data, Inc. 2021

Star ★ Data assert the moral right to be
identified as the authors of this work

A catalogue record for this book is
available from the British Library

ISBN 978-0-00-843847-0

Printed and Bound in the UK using 100%
Renewable Electricity at CPI Group (UK) Ltd

All rights reserved. No part of this publication may be
reproduced, stored in a retrieval system, or transmitted,
in any form or by any means, electronic, mechanical,
photocopying, recording or otherwise, without the
prior written permission of the publishers.

MIX
Paper from
responsible sources
FSC™ C007454

This book is produced from independently certified FSC™ paper
to ensure responsible forest management.

For more information visit: www.harpercollins.co.uk/green

The author is grateful to the people of STAR ★ DATA, who truly fathered this book and without whom it could not have been written.

Contents

Introduction

Welcome to the fascinating and intricate world of astrology!

For thousands of years the movements of the planets and other heavenly bodies have intrigued the best minds of every generation. Life holds no greater challenge or joy than this: knowledge of ourselves and the universe we live in. Astrology is one of the keys to this knowledge.

Your Personal Horoscope 2022 gives you the fruits of astrological wisdom. In addition to general guidance on your character and the basic trends of your life, it shows you how to take advantage of planetary influences so you can make the most of the year ahead.

The section on each sign includes a Personality Profile, a look at general trends for 2022, and in-depth month-by-month forecasts. The Glossary (see page 5) explains some of the astrological terms you may be unfamiliar with.

One of the many helpful features of this book is the 'Best' and 'Most Stressful' days listed at the beginning of each monthly forecast. Read these sections to learn which days in each month will be good overall, good for money, and good for love. Mark them on your calendar – these will be your best days. Similarly, make a note of the days that will be most stressful for you. It is best to avoid booking important meetings or taking major decisions on these days, as well as on those days when important planets in your horoscope are retrograde (moving backwards through the zodiac).

The Major Trends section for your sign lists those days when your vitality is strong or weak, or when relationships with your co-workers or loved ones may need a bit more effort on your part. If you are going through a difficult time, take a look at the colour, metal, gem and scent listed in the 'At a Glance' section of your Personality Profile. Wearing a piece of jewellery that contains your metal and/or gem will strengthen your vitality, just as wearing clothes or decorating your room or office in the colour ruled by your sign, drinking teas made from the herbs ruled by your sign or wearing the scents associated with your sign will sustain you.

Another important virtue of this book is that it will help you to know not only yourself but those around you: your friends, co-workers, partners and/or children. Reading the Personality Profile and forecasts for their signs will provide you with an insight into their behaviour that you won't get anywhere else. You will know when to be more tolerant of them and when they are liable to be difficult or irritable.

In this edition we have included foot reflexology charts as part of the health section. So many health problems could perhaps be avoided or alleviated if we understood which organs were most vulnerable and what we could do to protect them. Though there are many natural and drug-free ways to strengthen vulnerable organs, these charts show a valid way to proceed. The vulnerable organs for the year ahead are clearly marked in the charts. It's very good to massage the whole foot on a regular basis, as the feet contain reflexes to the entire body. Try to pay special attention to the specific areas marked in the charts. If this is done diligently, health problems can be avoided. And even if they can't be completely avoided, their impact can be softened considerably.

I consider you – the reader – my personal client. By studying your Solar Horoscope I gain an awareness of what is going on in your life – what you are feeling and striving for and the challenges you face. I then do my best to address these concerns. Consider this book the next best thing to having your own personal astrologer!

It is my sincere hope that *Your Personal Horoscope* 2022 will enhance the quality of your life, make things easier, illuminate the way forward, banish obscurities and make you more aware of your personal connection to the universe. Understood properly and used wisely, astrology is a great guide to knowing yourself, the people around you and the events in your life – but remember that what you do with these insights – the final result – is up to you.

A Note on the 'New Zodiac'

Recently an article was published that postulated two things: the discovery of a new constellation – Ophiuchus – making a thirteenth constellation in the heavens and thus a thirteenth sign, and the statement that because the Earth has shifted relative to the constellations in the past few thousand years, all the signs have shifted backwards by one sign. This has caused much consternation, and I have received a stream of letters, emails and phone calls from people saying things like: 'I don't want to be a Taurus, I'm happy being a Gemini', 'What's my real sign?' or 'Now that I finally understand myself, I'm not who I think I am!'

All of this is 'much ado about nothing'. The article has some partial truth to it. Yes, in two thousand years the planets have shifted relative to the constellations in the heavens. This is old news. We know this and Hindu astrologers take this into account when casting charts. This shift doesn't affect Western astrologers in North America and Europe. We use what is called a 'tropical' zodiac. This zodiac has nothing to do with the constellations in the heavens. They have the same names, but that's about it. The tropical zodiac is based on the Earth's revolution around the Sun. Imagine the circle that this orbit makes, then divide this circle by twelve and you have our zodiac. The Spring Equinox is always 0 degrees (Aries), and the Autumn Equinox is always 0 degrees Libra (180 degrees from Aries). At one time a few thousand years ago, these tropical signs coincided with the actual constellations; they were pretty much interchangeable, and it didn't matter what zodiac you used. But in the course of thousands of years the planets have shifted relative to these constellations. Here in the West it doesn't affect our practice one iota. You are still the sign you always were.

In North America and Europe there is a clear distinction between an astrological sign and a constellation in the heavens. This issue is more of a problem for Hindu astrologers. Their zodiac is based on the actual constellations – this is called the 'sidereal' zodiac. And Hindu astrologers have been accounting for this shift all the time. They keep close tabs on it. In two thousand years there is a shift of 23 degrees, and they subtract this from the Western calculations. So in their system many a Gemini would be a Taurus and this is true for all the signs. This is nothing new – it is all known and accounted for, so there is no bombshell here.

The so-called thirteenth constellation, Ophiuchus, is also not a problem for the Western astrologer. As we mentioned, our zodiac has nothing to do with the constellations. It could be more of a problem for the Hindus, but my feeling is that it's not a problem for them either. What these astronomers are calling a new constellation was probably considered a part of one of the existing constellations. I don't know this as a fact, but I presume it is so intuitively. I'm sure we will soon be getting articles by Hindu astrologers explaining this.

Glossary of Astrological Terms

Ascendant

We experience day and night because the Earth rotates on its axis once every 24 hours. It is because of this rotation that the Sun, Moon and planets seem to rise and set. The zodiac is a fixed belt (imaginary, but very real in spiritual terms) around the Earth. As the Earth rotates, the different signs of the zodiac seem to the observer to rise on the horizon. During a 24-hour period every sign of the zodiac will pass this horizon point at some time or another. The sign that is at the horizon point at any given time is called the Ascendant, or rising sign. The Ascendant is the sign denoting a person's self-image, body and self-concept – the personal ego, as opposed to the spiritual ego indicated by a person's Sun sign.

Aspects

Aspects are the angular relationships between planets, the way in which one planet stimulates or influences another. If a planet makes a harmonious aspect (connection) to another, it tends to stimulate that planet in a positive and helpful way. If, however, it makes a stressful aspect to another planet, this disrupts that planet's normal influence.

Astrological Qualities

There are three astrological qualities: *cardinal, fixed* and *mutable*. Each of the 12 signs of the zodiac falls into one of these three categories.

Cardinal Signs

Aries, Cancer, Libra and Capricorn

The cardinal quality is the active, initiating principle. Those born under these four signs are good at starting new projects.

Fixed Signs

Taurus, Leo, Scorpio and Aquarius

Fixed qualities include stability, persistence, endurance and perfectionism. People born under these four signs are good at seeing things through.

Mutable Signs

Gemini, Virgo, Sagittarius and Pisces

Mutable qualities are adaptability, changeability and balance. Those born under these four signs are creative, if not always practical.

Direct Motion

When the planets move forward through the zodiac – as they normally do – they are said to be going 'direct'.

Grand Square

A Grand Square differs from a normal Square (usually two planets separated by 90 degrees) in that four or more planets are involved. When you look at the pattern in a chart you will see a whole and complete square. This, though stressful, usually denotes a new manifestation in the life. There is much work and balancing involved in the manifestation.

Grand Trine

A Grand Trine differs from a normal Trine (where two planets are 120 degrees apart) in that three or more planets are involved. When you look at this pattern in a chart, it takes the form of a complete triangle – a Grand Trine. Usually (but not always) it occurs in one of the four elements: Fire, Earth, Air or Water. Thus the particular element in which it occurs will be highlighted. A Grand Trine in Water is not the same as a Grand Trine in Air or Fire, etc. This is a very fortunate and happy aspect, and quite rare.

Houses

There are 12 signs of the zodiac and 12 houses of experience. The 12 signs are personality types and ways in which a given planet expresses itself; the 12 houses show 'where' in your life this expression takes place. Each house has a different area of interest. A house can become potent and important – a house of power – in different ways: if it contains the Sun, the Moon or the 'ruler' of your chart; if it contains more than one planet; or if the ruler of that house is receiving unusual stimulation from other planets.

1st House
Personal Image and Sensual Delights

2nd House
Money/Finance

3rd House
Communication and Intellectual Interests

4th House
Home and Family

5th House
Children, Fun, Games, Creativity, Speculations and Love Affairs

6th House
Health and Work

7th House
Love, Marriage and Social Activities

8th House
Transformation and Regeneration

9th House
Religion, Foreign Travel, Higher Education and Philosophy

10th House
Career

11th House
Friends, Group Activities and Fondest Wishes

12th House
Spirituality

Karma

Karma is the law of cause and effect which governs all phenomena. We are all where we find ourselves because of karma – because of actions we have performed in the past. The universe is such a balanced instrument that any act immediately sets corrective forces into motion – karma.

Long-term Planets

The planets that take a long time to move through a sign show the long-term trends in a given area of life. They are important for forecasting the prolonged view of things. Because these planets stay in one sign for so long, there are periods in the year when the faster-moving (short-term) planets will join them, further activating and enhancing the importance of a given house.

Jupiter
stays in a sign for about 1 year

Saturn
2½ years

Uranus
7 years

Neptune
14 years

Pluto
15 to 30 years

Lunar

Relating to the Moon. See also 'Phases of the Moon', below.

Natal

Literally means 'birth'. In astrology this term is used to distinguish between planetary positions that occurred at the time of a person's birth (natal) and those that are current (transiting). For example, Natal Sun refers to where the Sun was when you were born; transiting Sun refers to where the Sun's position is currently at any given moment – which usually doesn't coincide with your birth, or Natal, Sun.

Out of Bounds

The planets move through the zodiac at various angles relative to the celestial equator (if you were to draw an imaginary extension of the Earth's equator out into the universe, you would have an illustration of this celestial equator). The Sun – being the most dominant and powerful influence in the Solar system – is the measure astrologers use as a standard. The Sun never goes more than approximately 23 degrees north or south of the celestial equator. At the winter solstice the Sun reaches its maximum southern angle of orbit (declination); at the summer solstice it reaches its maximum northern angle. Any time a planet exceeds this Solar boundary – and occasionally planets do – it is said to be 'out of bounds'. This means that the planet exceeds or tres-passes into strange territory – beyond the limits allowed by the Sun, the ruler of the Solar system. The planet in this condition becomes more emphasized and exceeds its authority, becoming an important influence in the forecast.

Phases of the Moon

After the full Moon, the Moon seems to shrink in size (as perceived from the Earth), gradually growing smaller until it is virtually invisible to the naked eye – at the time of the next new Moon. This is called the waning Moon phase, or the waning Moon.

After the new Moon, the Moon gradually gets bigger in size (as perceived from the Earth) until it reaches its maximum size at the time of the full Moon. This period is called the waxing Moon phase, or waxing Moon.

Retrogrades

The planets move around the Sun at different speeds. Mercury and Venus move much faster than the Earth, while Mars, Jupiter, Saturn, Uranus, Neptune and Pluto move more slowly. Thus there are times when, relative to the Earth, the planets appear to be going backwards. In reality they are always going forward, but relative to our vantage point on Earth they seem to go backwards through the zodiac for a period of time. This is called 'retrograde' motion and tends to weaken the normal influence of a given planet.

Short-term Planets

The fast-moving planets move so quickly through a sign that their effects are generally of a short-term nature. They reflect the immediate, day-to-day trends in a horoscope.

Moon
stays in a sign for only 2½ days

Mercury
20 to 30 days

Sun
30 days

Venus
approximately 1 month

Mars
approximately 2 months

T-square

A T-square differs from a Grand Square (see page 6) in that it is not a complete square. If you look at the pattern in a chart it appears as 'half a complete square', resembling the T-square tools used by architects and designers. If you cut a complete square in half, diagonally, you have a T-square. Many astrologers consider this more stressful than a Grand Square, as it creates tension that is difficult to resolve. T-squares bring learning experiences.

Transits

This term refers to the movements or motions of the planets at any given time. Astrologers use the word 'transit' to make the distinction between a birth, or Natal, planet (see 'Natal', page 9) and the planet's current movement in the heavens. For example, if at your birth Saturn was in the sign of Cancer in your 8th house, but is now moving through your 3rd house, it is said to be 'transiting' your 3rd house. Transits are one of the main tools with which astrologers forecast trends.

YOUR PERSONAL HOROSCOPE 2022

Aries

♈

THE RAM

Birthdays from
21st March to
20th April

Personality Profile

ARIES AT A GLANCE

Element – Fire

Ruling Planet – Mars
　　Career Planet – Saturn
　　Love Planet – Venus
　　Money Planet – Venus
　　Planet of Fun, Entertainment, Creativity and Speculations – Sun
　　Planet of Health and Work – Mercury
　　Planet of Home and Family Life – Moon
　　Planet of Spirituality – Neptune
　　Planet of Travel, Education, Religion and Philosophy – Jupiter

Colours – carmine, red, scarlet

Colours that promote love, romance and social harmony – green, jade green

Colour that promotes earning power – green

Gem – amethyst

Metals – iron, steel

Scent – honeysuckle

Quality – cardinal (= activity)

Quality most needed for balance – caution

Strongest virtues – abundant physical energy, courage, honesty, independence, self-reliance

Deepest need – action

Characteristics to avoid – haste, impetuousness, over-aggression, rashness

Signs of greatest overall compatibility – Leo, Sagittarius

Signs of greatest overall incompatibility – Cancer, Libra, Capricorn

Sign most helpful to career – Capricorn

Sign most helpful for emotional support – Cancer

Sign most helpful financially – Taurus

Sign best for marriage and/or partnerships – Libra

Sign most helpful for creative projects – Leo

Best Sign to have fun with – Leo

Signs most helpful in spiritual matters – Sagittarius, Pisces

Best day of the week – Tuesday

Understanding an Aries

Aries is the activist *par excellence* of the zodiac. The Aries need for action is almost an addiction, and those who do not really understand the Aries personality would probably use this hard word to describe it. In reality 'action' is the essence of the Aries psychology – the more direct, blunt and to-the-point the action, the better. When you think about it, this is the ideal psychological makeup for the warrior, the pioneer, the athlete or the manager.

Aries likes to get things done, and in their passion and zeal often lose sight of the consequences for themselves and others. Yes, they often try to be diplomatic and tactful, but it is hard for them. When they do so they feel that they are being dishonest and phoney. It is hard for them even to understand the mindset of the diplomat, the consensus builder, the front office executive. These people are involved in endless meetings, discussions, talks and negotiations – all of which seem a great waste of time when there is so much work to be done, so many real achievements to be gained. An Aries can understand, once it is explained, that talk and negotiations – the social graces – lead ultimately to better, more effective actions. The interesting thing is that an Aries is rarely malicious or spiteful – even when waging war. Aries people fight without hate for their opponents. To them it is all good-natured fun, a grand adventure, a game.

When confronted with a problem many people will say, 'Well, let's think about it, let's analyse the situation.' But not an Aries. An Aries will think, 'Something must be done. Let's get on with it.' Of course, neither response is the total answer. Sometimes action is called for, sometimes cool thought. But an Aries tends to err on the side of action.

Action and thought are radically different principles. Physical activity is the use of brute force. Thinking and deliberating require one not to use force – to be still. It is not good for the athlete to be deliberating the next move; this will only slow down his or her reaction time. The athlete must act instinctively and instantly. This is how Aries people tend to behave in life. They are quick, instinctive decision-makers and their decisions tend to be translated into action almost immediately. When their intuition is sharp and well tuned, their actions are powerful and successful. When their intuition is off, their actions can be disastrous.

Do not think this will scare an Aries. Just as a good warrior knows that in the course of combat he or she might acquire a few wounds, so too does an Aries realize – somewhere deep down – that in the course of being true to yourself you might get embroiled in a disaster or two. It is all part of the game. An Aries feels strong enough to weather any storm.

There are many Aries people who are intellectual. They make powerful and creative thinkers. But even in this realm they tend to be pioneers – outspoken and blunt. These types of Aries tend to elevate (or sublimate) their desire for physical combat in favour of intellectual, mental combat. And they are indeed powerful.

In general, Aries people have a faith in themselves that others could learn from. This basic, rock-solid faith carries them through the most tumultuous situations in life. Their courage and self-confidence make them natural leaders. Their leadership is more by way of example than by actually controlling others.

Finance

Aries people often excel as builders or estate agents. Money in and of itself is not as important as are other things – action, adventure, sport, etc. They are motivated by the need to support and be well-thought-of by their partners. Money as a way of attaining pleasure is another important motivation. Aries function best in their own businesses or as managers of their own departments within a large business or corporation. The fewer orders they have to take from higher up, the better. They also function better out in the field rather than behind a desk.

Aries people are hard workers with a lot of endurance; they can earn large sums of money due to the strength of their sheer physical energy.

Venus is their money planet, which means that Aries need to develop more of the social graces in order to realize their full earning potential. Just getting the job done – which is what an Aries excels at – is not enough to create financial success. The co-operation of others needs to be attained. Customers, clients and co-workers need to be made to feel comfortable; many people need to be treated properly in order for success to happen. When Aries people develop these abilities – or hire someone to do this for them – their financial potential is unlimited.

Career and Public Image

One would think that a pioneering type would want to break with the social and political conventions of society. But this is not so with the Aries-born. They are pioneers within conventional limits, in the sense that they like to start their own businesses within an established industry.

The sign of Capricorn is on the cusp of the 10th house of career of Aries' solar horoscope. Saturn is the planet that rules their life's work and professional aspirations. This tells us some interesting things about the Aries character. First off, it shows that, in order for Aries people to reach their full career potential, they need to develop some qualities that are a bit alien to their basic nature: they need to become better administrators and organizers; they need to be able to handle details better and to take a long-range view of their projects and their careers in general. No one can beat an Aries when it comes to achieving short-range objectives, but a career is long term, built over time. You cannot take a 'quickie' approach to it.

Some Aries people find it difficult to stick with a project until the end. Since they get bored quickly and are in constant pursuit of new adventures, they prefer to pass an old project or task on to somebody else in order to start something new. Those Aries who learn how to put off the search for something new until the old is completed will achieve great success in their careers and professional lives.

In general, Aries people like society to judge them on their own merits, on their real and actual achievements. A reputation acquired by 'hype' feels false to them.

Love and Relationships

In marriage and partnerships Aries like those who are more passive, gentle, tactful and diplomatic – people who have the social grace and skills they sometimes lack. Our partners always represent a hidden part of ourselves – a self that we cannot express personally.

An Aries tends to go after what he or she likes aggressively. The tendency is to jump into relationships and marriages. This is especially true if Venus is in Aries as well as the Sun. If an Aries likes you, he or she will have a hard time taking no for an answer; many attempts will be made to sweep you off your feet.

Though Aries can be exasperating in relationships – especially if they are not understood by their partners – they are never consciously or wilfully cruel or malicious. It is just that they are so independent and sure of themselves that they find it almost impossible to see somebody else's viewpoint or position. This is why an Aries needs as a partner someone with lots of social graces.

On the plus side, an Aries is honest, someone you can lean on, someone with whom you will always know where you stand. What he or she lacks in diplomacy is made up for in integrity.

Home and Domestic Life

An Aries is of course the ruler at home – the Boss. The male will tend to delegate domestic matters to the female. The female Aries will want to rule the roost. Both tend to be handy round the house. Both like large families and both believe in the sanctity and importance of the family. An Aries is a good family person, although he or she does not especially like being at home a lot, preferring instead to be roaming about.

Considering that they are by nature so combative and wilful, Aries people can be surprisingly soft, gentle and even vulnerable with their children and partners. The sign of Cancer, ruled by the Moon, is on the cusp of their solar 4th house of home and family. When the Moon is well aspected – under favourable influences – in the birth chart, an Aries will be tender towards the family and will want a family life that is nurturing and supportive. Aries likes to come home after a hard day on the battlefield of life to the understanding arms of their partner and the unconditional love and support of their family. An Aries feels that there is enough 'war' out in the world – and he or she enjoys participating in that. But when Aries comes home, comfort and nurturing are what's needed.

Horoscope for 2022

Major Trends

Things started to get easier for you late in 2020 and 2021, Aries. Health and energy are vastly improved, and this continues in the year ahead. More on this later.

The year ahead is happy in other ways too. Jupiter will enter your sign this year. This will happen on May 11. He will then retrograde out of your sign on October 29 and re-enter on December 21. (Jupiter's behaviour is a bit unusual this year – he spends approximately half the year in your 12th house and half the year in your 1st house. Usually he will spend most of the year in just one of your houses.) Jupiter's move into your own sign will bring personal pleasure, fun, good fortune, foreign travel and overall happiness and success. (You will have more of this next year as well.) Women of childbearing age are very fertile in the year ahead. This is also a wonderful transit for college-level students, and especially for those who are applying to colleges. You seem in demand. Colleges are seeking you rather than vice versa. There will also be good fortune in your legal affairs – if you're involved with those things.

The year ahead also bodes well for students not yet at college. Mars (the ruler of your Horoscope) will spend an unusual amount of time in your 3rd house of communication and intellectual interests. He will be there for more than four months, from August 20 onwards. This shows focus and focus brings success.

Finances will be good this year, but I like 2023 even better. More on finance later.

Pluto has been in your 10th house of career for many, many years now. He will still be there this year but is getting ready to move on. This will happen next year. So, for many years, you have been dealing with death and issues to do with death. Parents or parent figures in your life have had many a crisis – perhaps undergoing surgery and having near-death kinds of experiences. Your career path has been transformed (this is Pluto's job). You are entering the career of your dreams very shortly.

Neptune has been in your 12th house for many years. So, you have been under very strong spiritual influences. This year, with Jupiter also in your 12th house of spirituality, the spiritual life is even more important and happier. Important spiritual breakthroughs are happening – and these will lead to worldly, practical breakthroughs as well. More on this later.

Your most important interests this year will be the body, image and personal appearance (from May 11 to October 29 and from December 21 onwards); finance; communication and intellectual interests (from August 20 onwards); career; friends, groups and group activities; and spirituality (all year, but especially from January 1 to May 11 and from October 29 to December 21).

Your paths of greatest fulfilment will be finance (from January 19 onwards); spirituality (from January 1 to May 11 and from October 29 to the December 21); and the body, image and personal appearance (from May 11 to October 29 and from December 21 onwards).

Health

(Please note that this is an astrological perspective on health and not a medical one. In days of yore there was no difference, both these perspectives were identical. But these days there could be quite a difference. For a medical perspective, please consult your doctor or health practitioner.)

Health and energy have been getting better and better over the years. This year there is only one long-term planet – Pluto – in stressful alignment with you, and even here, most of you are not feeling it; only those of you born late in the sign of Aries (from April 15 to the 20th) are noticeably affected. All the other long-term planets are either in harmonious aspect with you or leaving you alone. So, health and energy will be good this year. If you have pre-existing conditions, they seem in abeyance these days and not as severe as they usually are.

Health is good this year but, even so, there will be periods where your health and energy are less good than usual. These things come from the transits of the short-term planets and are not trends for the year. When these difficult transits pass, your normal good health and energy return.

Your empty 6th house of health and work is also a positive health signal. You have no need to be overly focused here. 'If it ain't broke,' the saying goes, 'don't fix it.'

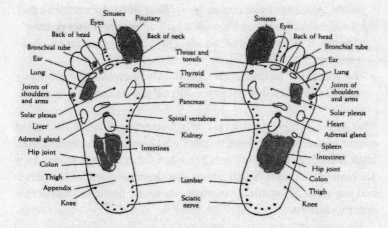

Important foot reflexology points for the year ahead

Try to massage all of the foot on a regular basis – the top of the foot as well as the bottom – but pay extra attention to the points highlighted on the chart. When you massage, be aware of 'sore spots' as these need special attention. It's also a good idea to massage the ankles and below them.

Jupiter, as we mentioned, will spend (on and off) half the year in your sign. This brings heightened fertility for women of childbearing age. For others it can bring weight gain (too much of the good life). So, there will be a need to watch the weight.

Good though your health is, you can make it better. Give more attention to the following – the vulnerable areas of your Horoscope this year (the reflex points are shown in the chart above):

- The head, face and scalp. These are always important areas for you, Aries, so regular scalp and face massages will be wonderful. Craniosacral therapy will also be good.
- The arms, shoulders, lungs, bronchial tubes, small intestine and respiratory system. These too are always important for Aries. Regular arm and shoulder massages will be very beneficial, as tension tends to collect in the shoulders and needs to be released.
- The musculature. This too is an important area for you, so it is important to have good muscle tone. You don't need to be a body

builder, just have good muscle tone. Weak or flabby muscles can knock the spine and skeleton out of alignment and this will cause all kinds of other problems. So vigorous physical exercise is important – according to your age and stage in life.

- The adrenals. The important thing here is to avoid anger and fear, the two emotions that stress the adrenal glands out.

Your health planet, Mercury, is a very fast-moving planet. During the course of the year he moves through all 12 signs and houses of your chart (and this year he will move through Capricorn twice). So, there are many short-term health trends that depend on where Mercury is and the kinds of aspects he receives. These are best dealt with in the monthly reports.

Mercury goes retrograde three times a year. These are times to avoid making important health decisions and having procedures or tests done. The likelihood of error is greatly increased at these times. This year Mercury will be retrograde from January 14 to February 3, May 10 to June 2, and September 10 to October 1. This last Mercury retrograde will be a lot stronger in its effect than the earlier ones because many other planets will also be retrograde at the time and this creates a cumulative effect.

Home and Family

Your 4th house of home and family is not prominent this year. Only short-term planets will move through there on a temporary basis. This I read as a good sign: it tends to the status quo. You have no pressing need to make important changes here. Also, since last year when two important planets moved out of your 10th house (where they were in stressful alignment to your 4th house) things should be easier at home this year. You will find it easier to balance your career and family goals.

Keep in mind that we will have two lunar eclipses this year, one on May 16 and the other on November 8. Since the Moon rules your 4th house, every lunar eclipse has an impact on the home and family, and you get these things twice (and sometimes three times) a year. The eclipses can bring dramas in the lives of family members. They tend to bring out long-repressed feelings (usually negative) in family members and personally. Often repairs are needed in the home. But, as was mentioned, you get this twice a year and so, by now, you know how to handle these things. These dramas tend to be short lived.

If you're planning major renovations to your home you might be better off waiting until next year. Mars, which rules these things, will not visit your 4th house this year. However, if you are redecorating or improving the home in a cosmetic kind of way, June 21 to August 12 would be a good time. It will also be a good time to buy objects of beauty for the home. If you're planning to buy entertainment or sports equipment for the home, June 21 to July 23 would be good.

Parents and parent figures have had many personal dramas over the past twenty years – surgeries and perhaps near-death experiences. In some cases there will have been actual physical death. But most of this is now over with, as was mentioned earlier.

Parents and parent figures can benefit from regular foot massage and spiritual healing and, later in the year, from scalp and face massages. One of the parents or parent figures in your life seems very focused on finance and is likely to have a good financial year. (You seem involved with this from March 6 to April 15.) A move is likely for this parent after May 11 – and this could happen next year too.

Children and children figures in your life are having a stable home and family year. A move is not likely. If they are married their marriages are being tested. There is severe stress here. It doesn't necessarily mean a break-up – just that a lot more work is needed to keep things together. If they are single, marriage is not likely this year.

Grandchildren, if you have them (or those who play that role in your life), are likely to move. In the latter part of the year they become more fertile than usual. They are having a good year.

Siblings and sibling figures are having a stable home and family year. From August 20 onwards they need to be more mindful on the physical plane.

Finance and Career

Finance is prominent in your Horoscope this year. (This has been the case for many years now.) Uranus in your money house has done many things (and this will continue). He has brought a need to experiment and innovate in finance. You throw out all the rule books – the do's and don'ts – and learn through trial, error and experimentation what works for you. Things that work for others might not work for you; things that you are told to avoid could benefit you. There's only one way to find out, and that is to try – to experiment. Not all experiments are successful. But no matter, at least you learned what not to do.

Uranus is the generic ruler of the 11th house of friends, technology, science, astrology and astronomy. (In your chart he is the actual ruler of these things as well.) So, all these areas are interesting as jobs, businesses or investments. The online world seems very important financially too. There are all kinds of online companies out there and they are interesting as investments or for work. Your technological expertise is very important in your finances, so it is good to keep up to date. You're spending more on technology, but you earn from it as well. These expenditures seem like good investments.

Your social contacts seem important financially as well. You have rich friends this year and they provide opportunities.

Uranus in the money house makes the finances very exciting. There's never a dull moment. Money and opportunities can come at any time or from any place, and often in ways you never expected. Earnings can also be more erratic these days (this has been the case for some years now). At times they can spike beyond your imagination, but there can be dry spells as well. So it's a good idea to put aside some money from the high times to cover the low times. If you run your own business you will need to 'smooth out' your earnings.

Though 2023 will be more prosperous than 2022, the year ahead is going to be good financially. Jupiter will move into your own sign on May 11 and stays there for almost half the year. (He makes a return to Pisces from October 29 to December 11.) Jupiter in your sign signals the good life – the high life. Regardless of your actual earnings you will live on a higher standard. People will see you as prosperous and you will dress the part. You will be travelling and enjoying all the pleasures of the senses. Jupiter will see to it that you can afford this life. He brings with him a feeling of optimism and a 'can do' spirit. Thus, there is a feeling that you are more than sufficient for any of the challenges that arise.

With regards to career, you've had a few years of intense – very intense – career activity. Last year, however, things eased up, and this is the situation in the year ahead too. You've paid your dues. You've earned your success. Now you're enjoying the fruits of your success. You are mixing with new friends – and high-status ones. You're involved with people who can help you careerwise. Who you know is perhaps just as important as your own professional skills.

You've been very experimental in financial affairs and we see this same tendency in your approach to management. You're willing to try out new things and approaches. You're ready to innovate. You seem less controlling in management. In addition, in the past few years you've had very controlling and difficult to please bosses; this eases up now.

Technology is important in your finances and seems just as important in your career. Your technological expertise boosts the career. You have the chart of someone with a career in the tech or the online world. These kinds of companies and jobs call to you.

Love and Social Life

This is not a particularly strong love and social year, Aries. First off, your 7th house of love is empty: only short-term planets will move through there this year. In addition, *all* the long-term planets are in the independent, Eastern sector of your chart. This has been the case for a few years now, but it is even more pronounced this year. Though your Western social sector will get stronger later in the year, it will never be dominant.

So, the year ahead is a 'me' year. It's about getting your body and personal desires in order. It's more about self-fulfilment than the fulfilment of others. If you're happy, others will be happy (eventually). Take care of number one.

For singles, there is nothing against marriage this year. But there is nothing especially supporting it either. You just don't seem that interested. Of course, you will date and socialize, but the fire in the belly is not there. For those of you already married or in a relationship, the year ahead is stable. Finance, career and your spiritual life seem much more important to you than the social life. Some years are like that.

Venus is your love planet. As our regular readers know, she is a fast-moving planet and will move through all the signs and houses of your chart during the year. (This year, in fact, she will move through your 10th house twice.) So there are many short-term trends in love depending on where Venus is and the kinds of aspects that she receives. These are best discussed in the monthly reports.

Venus will be retrograde from January 1 to 28. This will further complicate the love life. Relationships seem to go backwards instead of forwards. The social grace and judgement are not up to their usual standard. It is not a good idea to make important love (or financial) decisions during that period.

The marriage of the parents or parent figures is easier this year. It has been tested over the past few years. Single siblings or sibling figures will have an improved social life after May 11. There are opportunities in the online dating and social media worlds.

Children and children figures, as we mentioned, are having their relationships tested this year. Singles are not likely to marry. Grandchildren (or those who play that role in your life) are not likely to marry this year either. There is nothing against it, but nothing that especially supports it.

Though romance is not a big deal this year, the area of friendships seems very important and happy. As we mentioned earlier, you're socializing with important and successful people. Wealth and success are turn-ons. You meet friends as you pursue your career and financial goals. You find people involved with your finances and career alluring.

Self-improvement

As we've said above, the year ahead is very spiritual – much more so than in previous years. Not only is Neptune in your spiritual 12th house but Jupiter as well. Spiritual Neptune in the 12th house favours mysticism. It shows how one transcends the material world and sees things from a higher perspective. This mere ability to rise above things is often the solution to many problems. Things that seem insurmountable while you're on the ground are seen as 'no issue' when viewed from above, like from a hot-air balloon. From a balloon you can see that the traffic jam that has you worried or stymied is nothing – a mere blip – it clears up shortly. You can see it from a different, higher perspective.

Jupiter in the 12th house is a bit different. It's not just about transcendence but about the discernment of the spiritual laws. There is some rationality about it. The understanding of the spiritual laws helps you to apply them. Where Neptune is not at all concerned with any specific religion – Neptune is above all religion – Jupiter is religious. Every true religion is based on spiritual laws and they attempt to codify them in the behaviour of their followers. So, in the year ahead you're going to get a deeper insight into all religions – and especially the one that you were born into.

Where the Neptune influence can lead a person to reject *all* religions, the Jupiter influence leads people to understand the spiritual and mystical origins of their religion. Every religion has its mystical side, and this is a year to discover it.

Your spiritual practice is on steroids this year. The dream life is hyperactive and very revelatory. You should keep a dream journal. Much of what you see will only be understood later on, but dreams are highly significant these days. In fact, the dream life is so active – and so interesting – there could be a danger of ignoring everyday life; the dream life, where there are no physical limitations or boundaries, is so much more alluring. However, Aries likes action – physical action – so the danger for you is minimal.

Your spiritual faculties – ESP, intuition, psychic abilities – are much stronger than in previous years. This is a year for supernatural types of experiences – synchronicities, precognitions, miraculous types of protection, and the like. The spiritual world is active on your behalf and letting you know that it is around.

Most of you are already on a spiritual path, but if not, this is a year to embark on one. For more information about this subject you can visit my blog at www.spiritual-stories.com.

Month-by-month Forecasts

January

Best Days Overall: 1, 8, 9, 18, 19, 27, 28
Most Stressful Days Overall: 2, 3, 16, 17, 23, 24, 29, 30
Best Days for Love: 2, 3, 11, 12, 21, 22, 23, 24, 29, 30
Best Days for Money: 2, 3, 6, 11, 12, 16, 21, 22, 25, 29, 30
Best Days for Career: 2, 3, 4, 5, 13, 14, 23, 24, 29, 30, 31

This is a successful but complicated month. You are in the midst of a yearly career peak until the 20th – and for many of you it will continue to peak even afterwards. Your 10th house of career is full of planets, indicating that this is where your focus needs to be. Your 4th house of home and family, by contrast, is empty – only the Moon will move through there on the 16th and 17th. You serve your family best by being successful in your external life. Outer success will lead to emotional harmony and wellness.

Mars, the ruler of your Horoscope, enters your 10th house on the 25th. This is also showing success, but in a more personal way. Your success is not just about your professional skills, but also about who you are – your personal appearance and overall demeanour are big factors too. You are a celebrity in your world this month.

Here are the complications, however. Mars goes 'out of bounds' from the 12th. Thus, you are operating outside your normal sphere. Probably there are no answers in your normal orbit and you must go outside it to find them. This tends to insecurity. You're outside your comfort zone.

Venus, who rules both finance and love in your Horoscope, is retrograde until the 28th. This introduces glitches and delays in both areas of life. It will not be advisable to make important love or financial decisions during this period. Study things further. Things are not as they seem. Gain clarity.

In spite of Venus's retrograde, the month ahead should be prosperous. Venus is strongly positioned – in your 10th house – and this often shows pay rises, official or unofficial, and the financial favour of bosses, parents and elders. But there can be delays involved with this.

Health needs some monitoring this month. On a long-term level health is good, but this is not your best period. There will be some improvement after the 20th, but you still need to pace yourself and rest and relax more. Your health planet, Mercury, goes into retrograde motion from the 14th onwards. This is not a good time to take medical tests or have procedures done. Either have them done before the 14th or wait until next month.

February

Best Days Overall: 5, 6, 14, 15, 24, 25
Most Stressful Days Overall: 12, 13, 19, 20, 26, 27
Best Days for Love: 7, 8, 17, 18, 19, 20, 27
Best Days for Money: 2, 3, 7, 8, 12, 13, 17, 18, 21, 22, 27
Best Days for Career: 1, 9, 10, 11, 19, 20, 26, 27, 28

Health and energy improve this month but still need watching. Your health planet, Mercury, will move forward on the 4th. Back and knee massage will enhance the health until the 15th. After then, ankle and calf massage will be good. Until the 15th you seem very conservative in health matters. But this will change afterwards. You become more experimental and more open to alternative therapies. Make sure to get enough fresh air, especially after the 15th. And, as always, rest when you feel tired. Listen to the messages of your body.

A lot of the complications of last month are dissolving this month. For a start, after the 4th all the planets are moving forward. Thus there is clarity and movement, in the world and in your personal affairs. The pace of life quickens – just the way that you like it, Aries. Mars is still 'out of bounds' early in the month, but comes back on track on the 10th. This gives a feeling of security. You feel on more solid ground.

Though your career peak is technically over, career is still important and you still seem very successful. Mars, the ruler of your Horoscope, spends the month in your career house. People look up to you. You seem above everyone in your world.

Venus spends the month in your 10th house as well. You seem practical in love. Down to earth. You are attracted to the powerful – to people of status and position – and you're meeting these kinds of people. Your career is advanced by social means as well as through your overall image and demeanour. For singles there is an interesting love encounter from the 25th to the 28th as Mars and Venus travel together. It is also an excellent financial period.

Finances are good this month. Pay rises – official or unofficial – can still happen. Bosses, parents and elders are favourably disposed to your financial goals. Furthermore, Venus in Capricorn indicates sound financial judgement and a long-term perspective on wealth. You are adopting the image of wealth these days.

March

Best Days Overall: 4, 5, 14, 15, 23, 24
Most Stressful Days Overall: 11, 12, 13, 18, 19, 25, 26
Best Days for Love: 9, 18, 19, 27, 28
Best Days for Money: 2, 3, 6, 7, 8, 9, 18, 19, 11, 12, 21, 22, 27, 28, 30, 31
Best Days for Career: 1, 9, 10, 18, 19, 25, 26, 27, 28

A very happy and prosperous month, Aries, enjoy! There are so many wonderful things happening. The temporary stresses of the short-term planets are abating. By the 6th there will be only one long-term planet in stressful alignment; all the others will be either in harmonious alignment or leaving your alone. So health and energy are excellent. If you like, you can enhance it even further through ankle and calf massage until the 10th; through foot massage from the 10th to the 27th; and through scalp and face massage from the 27th onwards. Spiritual healing techniques are extremely powerful from the 10th to the 27th, and especially from the 20th to the 23rd. If you feel under the weather, see a spiritual healer.

You have energy too. All the planets are moving forward this month. When the Sun moves into your sign on the 20th, you are in the best starting energy of the year. However, it would be best to wait until your birthday or afterwards to launch those new projects or products into the world. You will then have both the universal solar cycle and your personal social cycle in waxing mode.

You are an independent kind of person by nature. But right now, even more so than usual. All the planets are in the Eastern, independent sector of your chart this month. After the 20th you will have the maximum Eastern energy, so this is the time to create your own happiness. Take the bull by the horns and make the changes that need to be made. If you are happy there is that much less suffering in the world.

The month ahead is also very spiritual. You can expect important spiritual breakthroughs and all kinds of supernatural experiences. The dream life will be active and revelatory.

Mars travels with Pluto from the 2nd to the 4th. This is a very dynamic transit. Watch your temper, avoid confrontations and don't be in a rush. Perhaps surgery will be recommended to you. There might also be a psychological confrontation with death – although generally not a literal death. Detox regimes are especially powerful now.

April

Best Days Overall: 1, 2, 10, 11, 19, 20, 28, 29
Most Stressful Days Overall: 8, 9, 15, 16, 21, 22
Best Days for Love: 8, 15, 16, 17, 18, 25, 26, 27
Best Days for Money: 3, 4, 8, 9, 17, 18, 25, 26, 27, 30
Best Days for Career: 5, 6, 15, 16, 21, 22, 23, 24

Another happy and prosperous month ahead, Aries. Even the solar eclipse on the 30th will not do much to dim your happiness. It will just add some spice to life and keep things interesting.

Last month, on the 20th, you began one of your yearly personal pleasure peaks. This continues until the 20th of this month. This is a great month to pamper the body and enjoy all the sensual delights. Children and children figures in your life seem devoted to you. You're in a happy-go-lucky kind of month. Personal independence is at its maximum for the year. So, if you haven't yet made the changes that need to be made for your happiness, now is the time.

Starting new projects or launching new products is still favoured this month – especially from your birthday onwards. Not only are you in the best starting energy of the year, but all the planets are moving forward until the 29th, ensuring that there will be a lot of cosmic help to your efforts. The Moon's waxing phase from the 1st to the 16th will add even more cosmic momentum to your efforts.

On the 20th, the Sun enters your money house and you begin a yearly financial peak. Earnings should increase. You seem lucky in speculations. You make money in happy ways and spend on happy things. You're in a period of 'happy money'.

The solar eclipse of the 30th occurs in your money house, indicating a need to make financial changes and course corrections in your financial life. The events of the eclipse will show where your financial assumptions are awry, thus enabling you to correct them.

Every solar eclipse has an impact on the children and children figures in your life, and this one is no different. They should reduce their schedule over this period. There can be dramas in the lives of the money people in your life. It is not a good idea to speculate during the eclipse period.

Health is good this month, and you can enhance it further with head, face and scalp massages until the 11th. Afterwards, neck massage will be beneficial. Don't let financial ups and downs impact your health. You are more than your bank balance.

May

Best Days Overall: 7, 8, 9, 16, 17, 25, 26
Most Stressful Days Overall: 5, 6, 12, 13, 19
Best Days for Love: 7, 8, 12, 13, 16, 17
Best Days for Money: 1, 6, 7, 8, 16, 17, 25, 27, 28
Best Days for Career: 3, 4, 13, 19, 21, 22, 31

The lunar eclipse of the 16th occurs in your 8th house of regeneration. So take it nice and easy over this period and avoid risk-taking activities. This kind of eclipse often brings psychological confrontations with death. Often there are dreams of death or the death (or near death) of people you know. Perhaps family members. Every lunar eclipse (and you get them twice a year on average) impacts on the home and family and this one is no different. Often repairs are needed in the home. Family members tend to be more temperamental and you need more patience with them. Siblings and sibling figures are forced to make financial course corrections.

These psychological confrontations with death are not meant to harm or punish you. It is only the Cosmos's way to remind you that life is short and can end at any time. No more dilly-dallying – do the work that you came here to do.

The month ahead is prosperous, as you are still in a yearly financial peak until the 21st. When the Sun travels with Uranus on the 4th and 5th sudden money can come to you – something out of the blue. Sometimes this transit can bring a sudden expense too, but the money to cover it will also come.

Prosperity is seen in other ways. Jupiter moves into your own house on the 11th – a classic signal for prosperity. Venus, your financial planet, crosses your Ascendant on the 13th and also enters your 1st house. This brings financial windfalls to you. It's as if money is chasing you rather than the other way around. Probably personal accessories or clothing will come to you too. This is a good period for spending on these kinds of things as well. You spend on yourself these days. You adopt the image of prosperity. People see you this way. Personal appearance is a big factor in earnings.

The same situation holds for love. Love chases you. There is nothing special that you need to do: just go about your daily business. Those already in a relationship will find that your spouse, partner or current love is more devoted than usual.

Health is excellent this month.

June

Best Days Overall: 4, 5, 13, 14, 21, 22
Most Stressful Days Overall: 1, 2, 3, 9, 10, 15, 16, 28, 29, 30
Best Days for Love: 6, 7, 9, 10, 16, 26
Best Days for Money: 4, 6, 7, 13, 16, 21, 23, 24, 25, 26
Best Days for Career: 2, 3, 10, 15, 16, 18, 29, 30

On May 11, Jupiter enters your sign – a very positive and happy transit. He will be in your sign all month (and beyond). Mars also enters your sign, on May 25, and will remain there all this month. These are great aspects for your health and energy. Self-esteem and confidence are high. Personal independence is also strongly indicated. You have loads of energy and you get things done quickly. Mars and Jupiter travelling together (near each other) show a month of positive achievements. Health is good this month, and although the Sun moves into a stressful alignment with you after the 21st, it is not enough to cause problems.

Retrograde activity increases this month. We are far from the maximum for the year, but it is still increased over last month.

The month ahead seems prosperous. Mars travelling with Jupiter indicates financial increase and good fortune. You're catching the financial lucky breaks. You're travelling more – and it looks like happy travel, pleasurable travel. Jupiter in your sign (and Mars near Jupiter) is a great aspect for college-level students or those applying to colleges. You will be pleasantly surprised. Chances are colleges are recruiting you, pursuing you.

Prosperity is seen in other ways too. Venus, your financial planet, remains in the money house until the 23rd. She is powerful here in her own sign and house. Earnings should increase. Venus will travel with Uranus on the 10th and 11th. This can bring sudden money. It indicates the financial favour of friends – they bring financial opportunity. You may need to make some financial adjustments. Venus in the money house often shows a partnership or joint venture. On the 23rd Venus will move into your 3rd house of communication. This would show earnings from sales, marketing, teaching, writing and trading. Investors should look at telecommunications, transportation and media companies. Retailing also seems interesting. Your gift of the gab is your fortune from the 23rd onwards.

Love is down to earth and practical this month, at least until the 23rd. Love is shown in material kinds of ways. This is how you show love and how you feel loved. Singles find romantic opportunities as they pursue their financial goals or with people involved in their finances.

July

Best Days Overall: 1, 2, 10, 11, 18, 19, 20, 28, 29
Most Stressful Days Overall: 6, 7, 12, 13, 26, 27
Best Days for Love: 6, 7, 15, 26
Best Days for Money: 1, 2, 6, 7, 10, 11, 15, 18, 19, 21, 22, 26, 28, 29
Best Days for Career: 7, 12, 13, 15, 24

Health and energy need more attention this month. There is nothing serious afoot, just short-term stresses caused by short-term planets. You will see a dramatic improvement after the 23rd, but in the meantime make sure to get enough rest. You can enhance your health with arm and shoulder massage until the 5th. Deep breathing and fresh air will also be a help. From the 5th to the 19th, diet becomes important. Massage of the stomach reflex will also help things. Good emotional health – positive moods and feelings – is important. After the 19th, massage of the heart reflex and chest massage will be good.

Retrograde activity increases still further this month, though we are still far from the maximum of the year: 30 per cent of the planets are retrograde until the 28th; 40 per cent afterwards.

The planetary power this month is below the horizon of your chart – the night side. Your 4th house of home and family is easily the strongest in your chart. So the focus should be on the home, family and domestic situation – more importantly on emotional healing. This is a month where you build up the internal forces for a future career push, which will happen in a few months' time.

Mars will enter your money house on the 5th and stay there for the rest of the month, which is a positive signal for earnings. It shows focus. Jupiter is still in your sign all month – very near the Ascendant. So the month ahead is prosperous.

Venus, your love and financial planet, will be in Gemini, your 3rd house, until the 18th. Thus, like last month, earnings come from your communication skills. This transit still favours writing, teaching, blogging, sales, marketing, retailing and trading. Whatever you actually do, good advertising and PR is very important.

Love can be found in your neighbourhood until the 18th. There will be no need to travel far and wide in search of it. There are romantic opportunities for singles in educational-type settings – schools, lectures, seminars and even bookstores. After the 18th love opportunities happen through the family and family connections.

August

Best Days Overall: 7, 8, 15, 16, 25, 26
Most Stressful Days Overall: 2, 3, 9, 10, 22, 23, 29, 30
Best Days for Love: 2, 3, 4, 5, 15, 25, 26, 29, 30
Best Days for Money: 4, 5, 7, 15, 17, 18, 25, 26
Best Days for Career: 3, 9, 10, 12, 21, 30

Planetary retrograde activity increases even further this month. After the 24th half the planets are moving backwards. The main lesson for you, Aries, is patience. You like things in a hurry – you like speed – but this is not a month for that. Slower is faster. Be perfect in all that you do. There are no short cuts now.

Health and energy are much, much better – vastly better – than last month. This translates to a happy month. Your challenge is to use this gift of energy, this gift of life force, in a positive way. Most people are not suffering from 'lack of power' but from the misuse of the power that they already have.

Last month on the 23rd you began a yearly personal pleasure peak. This will continue (and be even stronger) until the 23rd of this month. This is a time to explore your personal creativity and to enjoy leisure activities. Take a vacation from your cares and worries and explore the rapture of life. When you drop your cares, you very often find that insoluble problems are solved, naturally and normally.

Mars travels with Uranus on the 1st and 2nd. This is a very dynamic aspect. Be more mindful on the physical plane. Watch your temper and drive more carefully. On the other hand, this aspect brings a closeness with friends. You probably want to test your body, but be sure to do it mindfully and safely.

Mars remains in your money house until the 20th, so the month ahead is prosperous (Jupiter is still in your sign all month as well).

Those of you looking for work have two job opportunities this month. The new Moon of the 27th will further clarify the job situation as the month progresses into September.

Love is happy, although you seem moody in love. Getting into the right mood seems the main challenge. Things change on the 12th as Venus moves into your 5th house of fun and creativity. This is not a transit for marriage, but more for love affairs. Love has to be fun. Never mind the hard times – you'll deal with that when the time comes. Those who can show you a good time are the most alluring right now.

September

Best Days Overall: 3, 4, 11, 12, 21, 22, 30
Most Stressful Days Overall: 5, 6, 18, 19, 20, 26, 27
Best Days for Love: 4, 5, 13, 14, 15, 26, 27
Best Days for Money: 3, 4, 5, 11, 13, 14, 15, 21, 30
Best Days for Career: 5, 6, 7, 8, 16, 17, 26, 27

Retrograde activity increases even further this month, with 60 per cent of the planets travelling backwards after the 10th. (This is the maximum extent this year.) So, like last month, the keyword is patience, patience, patience. There are no short cuts these days. Short cuts are illusions and can actually cause more delays. Slow down and be perfect in all that you do. This will minimize – though not eliminate – glitches and delays.

With all these retrogrades (including the retrograde of your health planet Mercury from the 10th onwards) this is not a good time for any surgery, medical tests or procedures. If you have some option in the matter, reschedule them for a later time.

Health is good this month but does need watching after the 23rd. The good news is that you are focused and paying attention to your health – until the 23rd – and this will stand you in good stead for later. There is nothing seriously amiss here, just short-term stress caused by the short-term planets. Still, with less overall energy pre-existing conditions can start acting up. Enhance the health with more rest and massage of the lower abdomen until the 24th and with hip massage afterwards. The kidney reflex (see page 23) should be massaged after the 24th.

Venus, your love and financial planet, is having her solstice from September 30 to October 3. This means she pauses in the heavens (in her latitudinal motion) and then changes direction. So, this happens financially and socially too. It is a pause that refreshes.

We have two rare Grand Trines this month – one in the Earth signs (that began last month) and the other in the Air signs. Now one Grand Trine is rare enough. This month we have two of them. This is good news. In spite of the delays and retrogrades, nice things are happening. Your communication and management skills are much enhanced.

On the 23rd the Sun enters your 7th house of love and stays there for the rest of the month. You begin a yearly love and social peak. You attend more parties and go out more. Singles have many romantic opportunities.

October

Best Days Overall: 1, 9, 10, 18, 19, 27, 28
Most Stressful Days Overall: 2, 3, 16, 17, 23, 24, 30
Best Days for Love: 4, 5, 13, 14, 23, 24, 25
Best Days for Money: 4, 5, 8, 9, 11, 12, 13, 14, 18, 25, 26, 27
Best Days for Career: 2, 3, 4, 5, 13, 14, 23, 24, 30

Retrograde activity is still intense, but lessening compared to last month (a maximum of 40 per cent of the planets). Perhaps the most important of these retrogrades is the retrograde of Mars which begins on the 30th. Mars is the ruler of your Horoscope and thus a very important planet for Aries. His retrograde shows a need to gain clarity on your personal goals, on the kind of image and appearance that you want to project to others. You might feel a lack of direction. You might feel that you're going backwards instead of forwards. Though love is there for you, you're not sure what you want. So, work to gain clarity here.

You're still in a yearly love and social peak until the 23rd. There are plenty of romantic opportunities for singles. The problem, as we mentioned above, is you. You could be backing away from serious romance from the 20th.

Health still needs watching, but this is a short-term blip. By the 23rd you will see dramatic improvement. Perhaps credit will go to some therapist, pill or potion, but the reality is that the planets shifted in your favour; they were only the means that the Cosmos used to improve things. In the meantime, you can enhance health further with massage of the lower abdomen until the 11th and hip massage from the 11th to the 30th. It would be good to massage the kidney reflex after the 11th as well. Good health for you means good social health from the 11th to the 30th. So, if health problems arise restore harmony with friends and the beloved as quickly as possible.

A solar eclipse on the 25th occurs in your 8th house. This eclipse isn't that strong. It is a partial eclipse and doesn't impact on other planets. Still, it won't hurt to reduce your schedule. This eclipse can bring psychological encounters with death. These are love letters from the Cosmos to remind you to get more serious about life. The spouse, partner or current love has to make important financial changes. Children and children figures have personal dramas. They should take it easy over this period too.

Three planets have their solstice this month, which is highly unusual: Venus, Mercury and Jupiter. They pause in the heavens (in their latitudinal motion) and then change direction. So there is a pause and change of direction in legal issues and higher education (Jupiter) from the 1st to the 16th; a pause in health and work issues (Mercury) from the 13th to the 16th; and a pause in love and financial issues (Venus) from the 1st to the 3rd.

November

Best Days Overall: 5, 6, 15, 16, 24, 25
Most Stressful Days Overall: 12, 13, 19, 20, 26, 27
Best Days for Love: 3, 4, 13, 19, 20, 23, 24
Best Days for Money: 3, 4, 7, 8, 13, 14, 23, 24
Best Days for Career: 1, 2, 10, 11, 19, 20, 26, 27, 28, 29

On October 29 Jupiter travelled out of your sign and back into Pisces, your 12th house. So, spirituality has become important again. A lot of nice things are getting ready to happen and you need to be mentally and spiritually prepared. Focus on your spiritual practice.

We have a lunar eclipse on the 8th that occurs in your money house. This eclipse seems to be very powerful. Firstly, it is a total eclipse. (The Native Americans refer to it as a 'Blood Moon'.) More important than that is the fact that it impacts three other planets – Mercury, Uranus and Venus. So many areas of your life are affected here. Take a nice easy schedule over that period, for a few days before and after the 8th. Things that need to be done should be done. But non-essentials are better off re-scheduled. (This eclipse is another good reason to focus on your spiritual practice – it is the best way to go through something like this.)

Thus there are financial shake-ups. Your financial thinking – your assumptions – are not realistic and need to be refined. Usually some event reveals this. There are dramas in the lives of friends – life-changing kinds of dramas, which will test friendships. Your high-tech equipment gets tested and can behave erratically. Make sure important files are backed up and that your anti-virus and anti-hacking software is up to date. Don't open suspicious emails. The love life also gets tested. You're coming out of a very strong social period and many of you are in relationships. Now they get tested to see how real they are. The impact of the eclipse on Mercury indicates job changes and disruptions at the workplace. You will be making important changes to your health regime in the coming months. Every lunar eclipse affects the home and family; hidden flaws in the home can be revealed under this kind of eclipse. Though not pleasant, this is a good thing. You have the opportunity to correct these flaws. There are dramas in the lives of family members and especially of a parent or parent figure.

December

Best Days Overall: 2, 3, 12, 13, 21, 22, 29, 30
Most Stressful Days Overall: 9, 10, 11, 17, 18, 23, 24
Best Days for Love: 2, 3, 14, 17, 18, 23, 24
Best Days for Money: 1, 2, 3, 4, 5, 6, 11, 14, 20, 21, 23, 24, 29
Best Days for Career: 7, 8, 17, 18, 23, 24, 25, 26

Retrograde activity is much less this month. In fact, the planetary power is overwhelmingly forward – 80 per cent of the planets are moving forward. So blocked projects move forward again. The pace of life speeds up – just the way you like it.

Mars has not only been retrograde since October 30 but has been 'out of bounds' too. This is the case in the month ahead. You're outside your normal lane – out of your normal element – and it's understandable that you would feel a little insecure.

In spite of this, you are successful this month. Your 10th career house is powerful all month, and especially from the 22nd. You are in a yearly career peak. Much progress will be made.

Jupiter will move back into your sign on the 21st – another signal of success. Foreign travel is likely this month. (Your 9th house, which rules such things, is powerful until the 22nd and Jupiter, the planet that rules travel, crosses your Ascendant on the 21st.) There is good fortune for those seeking college admissions and in legal matters.

Three planets are 'out of bounds' this month. We have discussed Mars, but Venus and Mercury are also 'out of bounds': Venus from the 2nd to the 24th and Mercury from the 1st to the 22nd. Almost all month! So, you are not only outside your lane personally but in love, finance and health as well. You're in a period where you seek answers outside your normal sphere. You seem forced to think and act 'outside the box'.

Health needs more attention from the 22nd. As always, make sure to get enough rest. You need to keep your energy levels as high as possible. You can enhance the health with thigh massage and massage of the liver reflex until the 7th. After then, back and knee massage will be beneficial.

Taurus

♉

THE BULL

Birthdays from
21st April to
20th May

Personality Profile

TAURUS AT A GLANCE

Element – Earth

Ruling Planet – Venus
  Career Planet – Uranus
  Love Planet – Pluto
  Money Planet – Mercury
  Planet of Health and Work – Venus
  Planet of Home and Family Life – Sun
  Planet of Spirituality – Mars
  Planet of Travel, Education, Religion and Philosophy – Saturn

Colours – earth tones, green, orange, yellow

Colours that promote love, romance and social harmony – red-violet, violet

Colours that promote earning power – yellow, yellow-orange

Gems – coral, emerald

Metal – copper

Scents – bitter almond, rose, vanilla, violet

Quality – fixed (= stability)

Quality most needed for balance – flexibility

Strongest virtues – endurance, loyalty, patience, stability,
    a harmonious disposition

Deepest needs – comfort, material ease, wealth

Characteristics to avoid – rigidity, stubbornness, tendency to be overly
    possessive and materialistic

Signs of greatest overall compatibility – Virgo, Capricorn

Signs of greatest overall incompatibility – Leo, Scorpio, Aquarius

Sign most helpful to career – Aquarius

Sign most helpful for emotional support – Leo

Sign most helpful financially – Gemini

Sign best for marriage and/or partnerships – Scorpio

Sign most helpful for creative projects – Virgo

Best Sign to have fun with – Virgo

Signs most helpful in spiritual matters – Aries, Capricorn

Best day of the week – Friday

Understanding a Taurus

Taurus is the most earthy of all the Earth signs. If you understand that Earth is more than just a physical element, that it is a psychological attitude as well, you will get a better understanding of the Taurus personality.

A Taurus has all the power of action that an Aries has. But Taurus is not satisfied with action for its own sake. Their actions must be productive, practical and wealth-producing. If Taurus cannot see a practical value in an action they will not bother taking it.

Taurus's forte lies in their power to make real their own or other people's ideas. They are generally not very inventive but they can take another's invention and perfect it, making it more practical and useful. The same is true for all projects. Taurus is not especially keen on starting new projects, but once they get involved they bring things to completion. Taurus carries everything through. They are finishers and will go the distance, so long as no unavoidable calamity intervenes.

Many people find Taurus too stubborn, conservative, fixed and immovable. This is understandable, because Taurus dislikes change – in the environment or in their routine. They even dislike changing their minds! On the other hand, this is their virtue. It is not good for a wheel's axle to waver. The axle must be fixed, stable and unmovable. Taurus is the axle of society and the heavens. Without their stability and so-called stubbornness, the wheels of the world (and especially the wheels of commerce) would not turn.

Taurus loves routine. A routine, if it is good, has many virtues. It is a fixed – and, ideally, perfect – way of taking care of things. Mistakes can happen when spontaneity comes into the equation, and mistakes cause discomfort and uneasiness – something almost unacceptable to a Taurus. Meddling with Taurus's comfort and security is a sure way to irritate and anger them.

While an Aries loves speed, a Taurus likes things slow. They are slow thinkers – but do not make the mistake of assuming they lack intelligence. On the contrary, Taurus people are very intelligent. It is just that they like to chew on ideas, to deliberate and weigh them up.

Only after due deliberation is an idea accepted or a decision taken. Taurus is slow to anger – but once aroused, take care!

Finance

Taurus is very money-conscious. Wealth is more important to them than to many other signs. Wealth to a Taurus means comfort and security. Wealth means stability. Where some zodiac signs feel that they are spiritually rich if they have ideas, talents or skills, Taurus only feels wealth when they can see and touch it. Taurus's way of thinking is, 'What good is a talent if it has not been translated into a home, furniture, car and holidays?'

These are all reasons why Taurus excels in estate agency and agricultural industries. Usually a Taurus will end up owning land. They love to feel their connection to the Earth. Material wealth began with agriculture, the tilling of the soil. Owning a piece of land was humanity's earliest form of wealth: Taurus still feels that primeval connection.

It is in the pursuit of wealth that Taurus develops intellectual and communication ability. Also, in this pursuit Taurus is forced to develop some flexibility. It is in the quest for wealth that they learn the practical value of the intellect and come to admire it. If it were not for the search for wealth and material things, Taurus people might not try to reach a higher intellect.

Some Taurus people are 'born lucky' – the type who win any gamble or speculation. This luck is due to other factors in their horoscope; it is not part of their essential nature. By nature they are not gamblers. They are hard workers and like to earn what they get. Taurus's innate conservatism makes them abhor unnecessary risks in finance and in other areas of their lives.

Career and Public Image

Being essentially down-to-earth people, simple and uncomplicated, Taurus tends to look up to those who are original, unconventional and inventive. Taurus people like their bosses to be creative and original – since they themselves are content to perfect their superiors' brainwaves. They admire people who have a wider social or political consciousness and they feel that someday (when they have all the comfort and security they need) they too would like to be involved in these big issues.

In business affairs Taurus can be very shrewd – and that makes them valuable to their employers. They are never lazy; they enjoy working and getting good results. Taurus does not like taking unnecessary risks and they do well in positions of authority, which makes them good managers and supervisors. Their managerial skills are reinforced by their natural talents for organization and handling details, their patience and thoroughness. As mentioned, through their connection with the earth, Taurus people also do well in farming and agriculture.

In general a Taurus will choose money and earning power over public esteem and prestige. A position that pays more – though it has less prestige – is preferred to a position with a lot of prestige but lower earnings. Many other signs do not feel this way, but a Taurus does, especially if there is nothing in his or her personal birth chart that modifies this. Taurus will pursue glory and prestige only if it can be shown that these things have a direct and immediate impact on their wallet.

Love and Relationships

In love, the Taurus-born likes to have and to hold. They are the marrying kind. They like commitment and they like the terms of a relationship to be clearly defined. More importantly, Taurus likes to be faithful to one lover, and they expect that lover to reciprocate this fidelity. When this doesn't happen, their whole world comes crashing down. When they are in love Taurus people are loyal, but they are also very possessive. They are capable of great fits of jealousy if they are hurt in love.

Taurus is satisfied with the simple things in a relationship. If you are involved romantically with a Taurus there is no need for lavish entertainments and constant courtship. Give them enough love, food and comfortable shelter and they will be quite content to stay home and enjoy your company. They will be loyal to you for life. Make a Taurus feel comfortable and – above all – secure in the relationship, and you will rarely have a problem.

In love, Taurus can sometimes make the mistake of trying to control their partners, which can cause great pain on both sides. The reasoning behind their actions is basically simple: Taurus people feel a sense of ownership over their partners and will want to make changes that will increase their own general comfort and security. This attitude is OK when it comes to inanimate, material things – but is dangerous when applied to people. Taurus needs to be careful and attentive to this possible trait within themselves.

Home and Domestic Life

Home and family are vitally important to Taurus. They like children. They also like a comfortable and perhaps glamorous home – something they can show off. They tend to buy heavy, ponderous furniture – usually of the best quality. This is because Taurus likes a feeling of substance in their environment. Their house is not only their home but their place of creativity and entertainment. The Taurus's home tends to be truly their castle. If they could choose, Taurus people would prefer living in the countryside to being city-dwellers. If they cannot do so during their working lives, many Taurus individuals like to holiday in or even retire to the country, away from the city and closer to the land.

At home a Taurus is like a country squire – lord (or lady) of the manor. They love to entertain lavishly, to make others feel secure in their home and to encourage others to derive the same sense of satisfaction as they do from it. If you are invited for dinner at the home of a Taurus you can expect the best food and best entertainment. Be prepared for a tour of the house and expect to see your Taurus friend exhibit a lot of pride and satisfaction in his or her possessions.

Taurus people like children but they are usually strict with them. The reason for this is they tend to treat their children – as they do most things in life – as their possessions. The positive side to this is that their children will be well cared for and well supervised. They will get every material thing they need to grow up properly. On the down side, Taurus can get too repressive with their children. If a child dares to upset the daily routine – which Taurus loves to follow – he or she will have a problem with a Taurus parent.

Horoscope for 2022

Major Trends

Saturn is still in adverse aspect to you this year, so energy levels will need to be watched. Happily, he is the only long-term planet in stressful alignment to you, so health should be good. More on this later.

You've been in a strong career cycle for many years now and it is still going on, although this year you need to work harder to achieve your goals. Saturn in your 10th house of career suggests that you need to succeed by actually being the best at what you do. Social contacts and cronyism can open doors for you, but in the end you have to produce the goods. More details later.

Uranus has been in your sign for a number of years now, and he will be there for another few to come. So, you are experiencing many – and sudden – dramatic personal changes. You're changing your self-concept, your image, the way that you want others to see you. This has been going on for some years and continues in the year ahead. A lot of these changes have to do with your career and outer ambitions; these changes are forcing you to alter your image.

Learning to make friends with change is perhaps the major life lesson these days. It's not always comfortable, but in the end it is good.

Pluto has been in your 9th house for many, many years, and he'll remain there in the year ahead. But he is now getting ready to leave. Thanks to Pluto you have been experiencing a complete transformation of your religious and philosophical beliefs (this was his purpose), and now have healthier belief systems.

Pluto is also your love planet, so many of the trends in love that we've written about over the past years are still in effect. You seem cautious about love. Conservative. You favour settled kinds of people – perhaps older people. This will change next year, and there's more on this later.

Jupiter will spend approximately half the year in your 11th house and half the year in your 12th house. So, at the beginning of the year you are making new friends, buying high-tech equipment and getting more involved with social media. These new friends seem very spiritual and seem to play a big role in your spiritual life.

On May 11 Jupiter will move into your 12th house and this will energize the spiritual life. There will be spiritual breakthroughs and many spiritual – supernatural – experiences. You will learn, as Thoreau said, 'that there is more to me than what's beneath my hat'.

Your most important interests this year will be the body, image and personal appearance; religion, philosophy, higher education and foreign travel; career; friends, groups, group activities and technology; spirituality (from May 11 to October 29 and from December 21 onwards); and finance (from August 20th onwards).

Your paths of greatest fulfilment this year will be the body, image and personal appearance; friends, groups and group activities (until May 11 and from October 29 to December 21); and spirituality (from May 11 to October 29 and from December 21 onwards).

Health

(Please note that this is an astrological perspective on health and not a medical one. In days of yore there was no difference, both these perspectives were identical. But these days there could be quite a difference. For a medical perspective, please consult your doctor or health practitioner.)

Health, as we mentioned above, will be good. Only Saturn is in stressful alignment with you this year. Of course, short-term planets will sometimes make stressful aspects, but these are not trends for the year but only short-term blips. When these short-term stresses move away, health and energy return.

Good though your health is you can make it better. Give more attention to the following – the vulnerable areas of your Horoscope this year (the reflex points are shown in the chart opposite):

- The heart only became an important area last year, when Saturn moved into stressful alignment with you, and the reflex point is shown above. Chest massage – especially of the breastbone and upper rib cage – is also beneficial. The important thing with the heart, according to many spiritual healers, is to avoid worry and

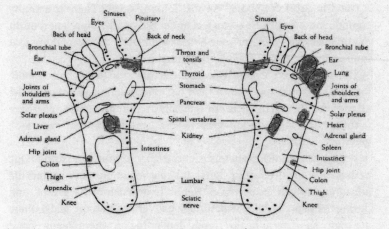

Important foot reflexology points for the year ahead

Try to massage all of the foot on a regular basis – the top of the foot as well as the bottom – but pay extra attention to the points highlighted on the chart. When you massage, be aware of 'sore spots' as these need special attention. It's also a good idea to massage the ankles and below them.

anxiety, the two emotions that stress it out. Replace worry with faith. Meditation will be a big help here.

- The neck and throat. These areas are always important for Taurus. Regular neck massage will be wonderful and should be part of your normal health regime. Tension tends to collect there and needs to be released. Craniosacral therapy is excellent for the neck, as are chiropractic and yoga.
- The kidneys and hips. These too are always important for Taurus, and the reflex points are shown above. Regular hip massage will be very beneficial. This will not only strengthen the kidneys but the lower back as well (an added benefit).

Since Venus, the planet of love, is your health planet, good health for you means good social health – healthy friendships and a healthy marriage and love life. Problems here could impact on your feeling of wellness. So if, God forbid, problems arise, restore harmony here as quickly as possible.

Good health for you also means 'looking good'. There is a vanity component to health. So if you feel under the weather, buy a new outfit or some accessory, or get your hair or nails done. Do something that improves your image. You will feel much better.

The other message of the Horoscope is that good health will do more for your personal appearance than hosts of lotions and potions. The state of your health impacts dramatically on your personal appearance (although this is not so for everyone). So, stay healthy and you'll look good.

Venus, your health planet, is also the ruler of your Horoscope. This of itself is a positive health signal. It shows its importance in your life and that you give it attention. Venus is a fast-moving planet, and during the year she will move through your entire Horoscope. So, there are many short-term health trends depending on where Venus is and the kinds of aspects she receives. These are best dealt with in the monthly reports.

Venus will make one of her rare retrogrades at the beginning of the year, from January 1 to January 28. This is not a time for surgery, tests or procedures if they can be avoided; the chances of error or misdiagnosis increase. This is also not a period to make important changes to the diet or health regime.

Home and Family

Your 4th house of home and family is not prominent this year, it is not a house of power. This, as our regular readers know, tends to the status quo. The year ahead will pretty much be like last year. It shows a sense of contentment with things as they are and that you have no need to make major changes.

Add to this that the upper, day side of your Horoscope is much stronger than the night side. Thus, the focus is more on the career and outer objectives than on the domestic life and family. Though the night side of your chart will get stronger as the year progresses, it will never dominate. With the exception of Uranus, only short-term planets will move through the night side of the chart. The same holds true for your 4th house. Some years are like that. The Cosmos aims for a balanced development. Different qualities and interests take priority in given years. This is a much stronger career and spiritual year than a family year.

Sure, there will be a few dramas here. There are two solar eclipses this year, and since the Sun is your family planet, these are sure to bring some family dramas or disruption in the home. But you go through these things twice a year and by now know how to deal with them.

Mars, the planet that rules construction and major repairs and renovations, won't enter your 4th house this year. So, if you're planning these things it's probably better to wait till next year.

If you're redecorating on a cosmetic level – painting or wallpapering – or buying objects of beauty for the home, August 12 to September 5 should be a good time for this.

One of the parents or parent figures in your life has been restless for many years now. There could have been multiple moves – and this trend continues in the year ahead. Sometimes they don't literally move, but they stay in different places for long periods of time.

Children and children figures in your life are having a stable home and family year, but the love life seems very active and happy. If they are of appropriate age marriage could happen. If they are younger, they are making many new friends – significant ones. They might not move this year, but they could be making renovations in the home.

Siblings and sibling figures are having a stable home and family year too. Those of appropriate age have had their marriages or relationships severely tested in past years (2018 and 2019 especially), but things look easier in the year ahead.

Finance and Career

The financial acumen of Taurus is legendary. They are naturals when it comes to business and making money. They love the whole thing. It is rare to find a Taurus really in a state of lack or poverty. They will often complain about finance – but if you listen to the complaints you can see that they are not poor. You will often hear them say, 'Oh my God, I'm in a real crisis! I'm down to my last million!' Or, 'Last year was terrible financially, my company's profits were down to 10 million. The year before we made 15 million!' So, Taurus is always interested

in finance. But this year less so than usual. Career – status and position
– seem more important than mere money. I read this as basically a
good thing. It tends to the status quo. It shows a sense of contentment.
There is no need to make major changes or to focus on it unduly.

Your money house is pretty much empty this year. It is only later in
year, from August 20 onwards, that a planet energizes this house.
Mars will spend an unusual amount of time in your money house.
Generally, he stays in a sign and house for a month and a half, but this
year he will be in your 2nd house for over four months. So this is when
the focus sharpens.

Mars camping out in your money house indicates many things. It
shows activism. It can make you more risk taking (generally Taurus is
not a risk taker). It can lead to quick financial decisions – also very
un-Taurus-like. When your intuition is on, these decisions and risks
will work out. But if your intuition is off, there can be setbacks because
of this. The good news is that your intuition is likely to be on target.
Mars is the ruler of your 12th house of spirituality, so you will be relying more on intuition. In fact, your intuition will be trained in financial
matters. You will be more charitable during this period. And your
involvement in charities and causes – altruistic activities – will enhance
the bottom line.

Fast-moving Mercury is your financial planet. During the course of
the year he will move through your entire Horoscope – all the signs and
houses. Thus, there are many short-term trends in finance that are
best discussed in the monthly reports.

Career is the real headline this year. You seem very successful. Your
status and position will be very much enhanced. But – and this is a big
but – you will earn every bit of it. Saturn in your career 10th house
shows this. You succeed because you are the best at what you do.
Perhaps bosses are over-demanding. But the proper strategy this year
is to give them more than they ask for. There seems to be a lot of
career-related travel too this year.

Your career planet, Uranus, has been in your 1st house for many
years now and will be there for some more to come. This is a happy
career signal. It shows the favour of bosses (even though they are
demanding), parents and authority figures. Happy career opportunities
come to you: you don't need to run after them. You look and feel

successful. You dress the part. People look up to you. They see you as successful.

Love and Social Life

Your 7th house of love is not prominent this year and is not a house of power. Also, almost all of the long-term planets are in the independent Eastern sector of your chart, the sector of self. So, this is not a very active romantic year. The focus is more on yourself and your personal interests.

With Uranus in your own house you are even more independent than usual. The spouse, partner or current love can see you as rebellious and self-willed – unwilling to cooperate. This can test existing relationships. Those involved with Taurus romantically need to give them a lot of space – as much as possible, so long as it isn't destructive.

Uranus is not the only thing that is testing relationships this year. The four eclipses that happen this year all fall along your 1st and 7th house axis. Two of them – the lunar eclipse of May 16 and the solar eclipse of October 25 – occur in your 7th house of love. The other two eclipses – the solar eclipse of April 30 and the lunar eclipse of November 8 – occur in your partner's 7th house of love. So love is being tested on both sides. This doesn't necessarily mean a break-up. It only means that more work will be needed to hold things together.

Singles should probably not marry this year. They can date and have relationships, but marriage is not advisable. The love life seems too unstable.

This is another life lesson for you, Taurus. Generally, you don't like change. You love your routines and the status quo. Learning to handle change – to even embrace it – is very important these days.

While romance is challenging, the area of friendships seems very happy. (The Cosmos always compensates. When one area is weak, another becomes strong. When it takes from one place it gives in another.) You are meeting new and significant people – spiritual people. Perhaps you're involved with spiritual-type groups.

Parents and parent figures are also having their relationships tested this year. Siblings and sibling figures have had their relationships tested from 2018 to 2020. Things are easier now. Children and children figures in your life have serious love in their lives and, if they are of appropriate age, marriage could happen. Grandchildren, if you have them, are having a stable love and social year.

Self-improvement

The year ahead is going to be deeply spiritual, as we mentioned. Those already on a spiritual path will deepen it and make good progress. Those not yet on a path are likely to embark on one. Jupiter will move into your 12th house of spirituality on May 11 and spend approximately half the year here. The spiritual practice becomes enjoyable, and there is no jaw-clenching, tight-lipped sense of discipline. You look forward to your practice and this makes all the difference in the world.

This is a year where spirit will lead you to detox, and not just a physical detox, but mental and emotional detoxing as well. Jupiter is the ruler of your 8th house which governs these things. The main blockage to spiritual progress (and to the operation of the spiritual laws) is negative mental and emotional habits – negative thinking. These need to be rooted out. Sometimes these things have been indulged in for many, many years (even lifetimes), and often there is much support for such thinking from the world – the mass consciousness. So, rooting these things out is a big job. It doesn't happen overnight. But if you do your bit day by day, you will see improvements day by day. Never mind that the ultimate goal is not yet attained. Never mind that it seems far away. Every day you get closer to it and that is what's important. There are many methods of psychological detoxing. In my book *A Technique for Meditation* we give two workable ways. There is also much information on this on my website, www.spiritual-stories.com.

This is a year where you learn that all the challenges in your life – the social, romantic and career challenges – are all necessary for your evolution. The same is true for all the sudden and dramatic personal changes and instability. They are guideposts on the path, orchestrated from above.

We mentioned earlier that your spiritual planet, Mars, will spend an unusual amount of time in your money house this year. This would be a good time to go deeper into the spiritual laws of affluence. Taurus as a rule tends to depend on material things that they can see and touch. They rely on their bank balances and investments. But spirit is not at all concerned with how much you have. It is about how much spirit has – and it has it all. When you operate the spiritual laws of affluence – of Divine Supply – you are working with the resources of the universe, not just your own. Spirit will enlarge and activate the 'human capital' – the ideas and skill sets, the insights – that create wealth. It will be a good idea to read as much as you can on the subject of Divine Supply (the works of Emmet Fox and Ernest Holmes are good places to start, but there is much other literature on the subject).

Month-by-month Forecasts

January

Best Days Overall: 2, 3, 11, 12, 21, 22, 29, 30
Most Stressful Days Overall: 4, 5, 18, 19, 25, 26, 31
Best Days for Love: 2, 3, 11, 12, 21, 22, 25, 26, 29, 30
Best Days for Money: 2, 3, 6, 11, 12, 13, 14, 16, 23, 25
Best Days for Career: 2, 3, 4, 5, 11, 12, 21, 22, 29, 30, 31

A good month, Taurus. First comes happiness, then comes success. Until the 20th your 9th house of travel and intellectual life is full of planets. An optimistic and expansive period. Health is good during that period too. Many of you will travel. College-level students should do well in their studies. If you are involved in legal issues they go well. There is a strong interest in religion, philosophy and theology this month. When the 9th house is this strong, people prefer a good theological discussion to a night out on the town.

Then comes success. On the 20th the Sun moves into your 10th house and you begin a yearly career peak. Usually when the career focus is this strong, one must balance family needs with the career. But this month there seems no problem with this. Family is supportive of the career – and actively involved. The family as a whole is elevated in status this month.

Health is good until the 20th and then needs more watching. The two planets involved in health – Mercury, the generic health planet, and Venus, your actual health planet – are both retrograde (Mercury is retrograde from the 14th; Venus from the 1st to the 29th), so this is not a good time for doing medical tests or procedures. The probabilities of error greatly increase. Reschedule these things for another time if you can (next month will be much better for this). In the meantime, enhance the health through back and knee massage. A visit to the chiropractor or osteopath might also be a good idea. Most importantly, make sure to get enough rest from the 20th onwards.

Marriage is not in the cards these days, but love seems happy. Your love planet Pluto is getting much positive stimulation.

Mercury's retrograde from the 14th onwards complicates finances, but it doesn't stop them. Try to make important purchases or investments before this date. After then, study the lie of the land more.

Mercury will be in your career house from the 2nd to the 27th. So earnings can come from pay rises and/or your good career reputation. Bosses and authority figures seem supportive of your financial goals.

February

Best Days Overall: 7, 8, 17, 18, 26, 27
Most Stressful Days Overall: 1, 14, 15, 16, 21, 22, 23, 28
Best Days for Love: 7, 8, 17, 18, 21, 22, 23, 27
Best Days for Money: 2, 3, 8, 9, 10, 11, 12, 13, 19, 20, 21, 22, 28
Best Days for Career: 1, 7, 8, 17, 18, 26, 27, 28

Mercury, your financial planet, moves forward again on the 4th, clearing up much financial doubt and improving the finances. He hovers between two signs this month – Capricorn and Aquarius. Your financial planet in Capricorn (until the 15th) brings sound financial judgement and an eye for what things will be worth many years from now. You take the long-term perspective on wealth. This transit favours slow, steady wealth building. On the 15th Mercury enters Aquarius (again), which is his strongest position. He is exalted in this sign. He is strongly positioned as well – at the top of the chart. This spells increased earning power. It shows more experimentation in financial matters and favours the go-go-go high-tech world. A good time to buy high-tech equipment or upgrade existing software. Seems like a good investment. Pay rises – official or unofficial – are likely.

Health still needs watching this month, but the planets involved with your health are now moving forward, so it is safer to have those tests or procedures done. Continue to rest and relax more. Back and knee massage, like last month, will enhance the health. You might be more experimental in financial matters, but in health matters you seem very conservative. You're likely to gravitate to orthodox medicine.

Mars, your spiritual planet, has been 'out of bounds' since January 12. He is still 'out of bounds' until the 10th, indicating that in spiritual matters you are outside your usual orbit. When Venus travels with Mars on the 15th and 16th you benefit from spiritual-healing techniques.

You are still in a yearly career peak until the 18th so it is right and proper to continue to focus here. Like last month, family seems very involved and supportive. The family as a whole seems elevated.

Your 11th house of friends has been powerful for some months, and this month it becomes even more powerful as the Sun joins Jupiter and Neptune in this house. So, while romance seems stable this year, the area of friendships and group activities seems very active. You are meeting new and significant people; they seem spiritual, refined, creative types. With the 11th house so strong your interest in astrology is heightened. Many people have their Horoscopes done under this kind of transit.

March

Best Days Overall: 6, 7, 8, 16, 17, 25, 26
Most Stressful Days Overall: 1, 14, 15, 21, 22, 27, 28
Best Days for Love: 8, 9, 18, 19, 21, 22, 26, 27, 28
Best Days for Money: 1, 2, 3, 9, 10, 11, 12, 21, 22, 30, 31
Best Days for Career: 1, 6, 7, 8, 16, 17, 25, 26, 27, 28

The month ahead is still very successful, but the health needs watching. The demands of career are strong and probably unavoidable. So work steadily. Focus on the essentials of your life and let lesser things go. Do your best to maximize energy.

Your health planet, Venus, moves into Aquarius, your 10th house, on the 6th. On the same day Mars also moves into your 10th house – so the career is active. You're working hard. But you're successful. You're successful not only because of your professional skills and strong work ethic, but also because of who you are. Your personal appearance and overall demeanour play a big role in your success.

Venus in Aquarius shows that health is enhanced through calf and ankle massage. Plain old fresh air is a natural health tonic too.

Mars in your career house from the 6th shows that being involved in charities and altruistic activities enhances the career. You are probably known as much for this as for your professional skills. We see this in other ways too. Mars, your spiritual planet, travels with Venus, the ruler of your Horoscope, from the 1st to the 12th. So you are in an altruistic frame of mind. This transit also shows that spiritual-healing methods are powerful until the 12th.

Your 11th house of friends, groups and group activities is still very strong this month. So the social life is active, but not necessarily romantic. It's more about being involved with friends.

The month ahead should be financially good too. Mercury moves speedily this month, through three signs and houses of your chart. This indicates confidence – someone who makes rapid progress. Mercury will travel with Jupiter on the 20th and 21st: a nice financial period. Then Mercury will travel with Neptune (on the 22nd and 23rd). This can bring financial opportunity from friends, social media or online activities. In addition, it brings enhanced financial intuition.

Take note of the dream life on the 22nd and 23rd – financial guidance and advice can be given.

April

Best Days Overall: 3, 4, 13, 14, 21, 22, 30
Most Stressful Days Overall: 10, 11, 17, 18, 23, 24
Best Days for Love: 4, 8, 14, 17, 18, 22, 25, 26, 27
Best Days for Money: 1, 2, 5, 6, 8, 9, 12, 13, 17, 18, 21, 22, 26, 27
Best Days for Career: 3, 4, 13, 14, 21, 22, 23, 24, 30

Basically, it is a happy month ahead – and even the solar eclipse of the 30th will do little to dampen it. (The eclipse does, however, strongly affect you, so take it easy then.)

Health and energy are vastly improved, as the short-term planets are moving away from their stressful aspect. And, on the 20th the Sun will move into your own sign, bringing extra energy, personal charisma and star quality. Self-confidence and self-esteem will be strong. You begin a yearly personal pleasure peak.

The solar eclipse of the 30th occurs in your sign, making its effects powerful. It indicates a need to redefine yourself, your image and self-concept. The events of the eclipse will show why this is necessary. People probably have the wrong idea about you – and you have the wrong idea about yourself. You will change this in the coming months. The spouse, partner or current love experiences social dramas – either with you or friends. Because the Sun is your home and family planet, every solar eclipse impacts the family. There are dramas in their lives (especially a parent or parent figure). Passions at home can be volatile so be more patient. (In fact, when tempers flare it is a cosmic signal that you are in the eclipse period and need to start taking it easy.) Hidden flaws in the home tend to be discovered during this kind of eclipse, so you are able to make corrections. The dream life can be erratic – and often scary – but pay it no mind; this is just the psychic flotsam and jetsam stirred up by the eclipse.

Though the eclipse tends to shake things up, it seems profitable for you. Venus and Jupiter are conjunct on the 30th, so it will be a good financial day. Indeed, you will have financial increase even before the

30th. Mercury, your financial planet, will enter your sign on the 11th. This brings windfalls and happy financial opportunities. The money people in your life are devoted to you. It's as if money chases you rather than the other way around.

All the planets are moving forward this month. Your birthday begins a yearly waxing solar cycle. The cosmic solar cycle is waxing as well. So, from your birthday onwards you're in a great period for starting new projects or launching new ventures.

May

Best Days Overall: 1, 10, 11, 19, 25, 26
Most Stressful Days Overall: 7, 8, 9, 14, 15, 21
Best Days for Love: 1, 7, 8, 11, 14, 15, 16, 17, 20, 28
Best Days for Money: 2, 3, 4, 6, 12, 13, 16, 18, 19, 25, 28, 30, 31
Best Days for Career: 1, 10, 11, 19, 21, 27, 28

A very eventful month ahead, Taurus. Much change is happening. First, Jupiter makes an important move from your 11th house to your 12th house of spirituality, on the 11th. Three planets are having their solstices this month – Venus, Mars and Jupiter. This is highly unusual. These planets pause in their latitudinal motion and then change direction. This shows a pause and change of direction in these departments of life. Finally, we have a strong lunar eclipse on the 16th which occurs in your 7th house of love. This will test a current relationship. The tests can vary. Sometimes it's the relationship itself that is amiss. Sometimes the testing happens because of dramas in the life of the spouse, partner or current love. Good relationships tend to survive, but shaky ones can go down the tubes.

Since the Moon, the eclipsed planet, rules your 3rd house of communication and intellectual interests, every lunar eclipse affects this area. Students have disruptions at school. Perhaps they change schools or educational plans. There are dramas in the lives of siblings and sibling figures. They need to redefine themselves – their image and self-concept. There can be disruptions in your neighbourhood and with neighbours. Cars and communication equipment get tested – it will be a good idea to drive more carefully over this period. Good for both you and your spouse, partner or current love to reduce your schedules too. This eclipse impacts on Saturn, so college-level students are also changing educational plans or schools. Legal issues can take a dramatic turn one way or another. There are disruptions in your place of worship and dramas in the lives of worship leaders.

Venus's solstice happens from the 4th to the 8th. This suggests a personal pause in your affairs and then a change of direction. This is so in health matters as well.

Mars's solstice occurs from the 27th to June 2. This shows a pause in your spiritual life and then a change of direction. (This is not a surprise as, with Jupiter now in your 12th house, you are expanding your spiritual life.)

Jupiter's solstice is very prolonged – he is a slow-moving planet. It occurs from the 12th onwards (and well into next month). There is a pause in the spouse, partner or current love's financial affairs. This is a good pause. When it is finished next month, there will be more energy and a change of financial direction.

June

Best Days Overall: 6, 7, 15, 16, 23, 24, 25
Most Stressful Days Overall: 4, 5, 11, 12, 17, 18
Best Days for Love: 6, 7, 11, 12, 16, 25, 26
Best Days for Money: 4, 6, 7, 13, 17, 21, 26, 27
Best Days for Career: 6, 7, 15, 16, 17, 18, 23, 24

Mars and Jupiter are still in their solstices this month. Mars is solstitial until the 2nd and Jupiter until the 12th. Review our discussion of this last month.

The month ahead is prosperous. You've been in a yearly financial peak since May 21 and this continues until the 21st. Your financial planet, Mercury, starts moving forward on the 3rd, bringing financial clarity and confidence. Your financial planet in your own sign (until the 14th) is a classic signal for prosperity. Money and opportunity chase you, not the other way around. Just go about your daily routine and money will find you. Your financial planet will enter the money house on the 14th, where he is strong (Mercury is in his own sign and house).

This indicates increased earnings. More importantly, Venus, the ruler of your Horoscope, will enter the money house on the 23rd. This is always favourable as the ruler of your Horoscope is perhaps your greatest beneficent planet. So you are very focused on finance. You adopt the image of wealth. You spend on yourself. You earn from work, trading, retailing and family connections. With so many planets in your money house money can come from many sources and in many ways.

Health and energy are good this month too. Though you still have two long-term planets in stressful alignment with you (you will have this all year), the short-term planets are either in good aspect or leaving you alone. Until the 23rd you can enhance the health further through neck massage and craniosacral therapy. Good health also means 'looking good' – the vanity component in health is very strong. After the 23rd enhance the health through arm and shoulder massage and plain old fresh air. If you feel under the weather get out in the fresh air and just breathe deeply.

Venus in your own sign adds beauty and grace to the image. You dress fashionably. You have excellent, artistic taste: it will be good to buy clothing and accessories this month.

Venus will travel with Uranus on the 10th and 11th. This brings a sudden, unexpected career opportunity to you. You are close – in harmony with – bosses, elders and authority figures. A sudden job opportunity can also happen.

July

Best Days Overall: 4, 5, 12, 13, 21, 22, 31
Most Stressful Days Overall: 1, 2, 8, 9, 14, 15, 28, 29
Best Days for Love: 5, 6, 7, 8, 9, 13, 15, 22, 26
Best Days for Money: 1, 2, 8, 10, 11, 16, 17, 18, 19, 23, 24, 28, 29
Best Days for Career: 4, 5, 12, 13, 14, 15, 21, 22, 31

Retrograde activity increases this month. By the end of the month 40 per cent of the planets are moving backwards. Though this is a substantial percentage we are still not at the maximum for the year.

(This will happen in September.) The problem here is that Mars will move into your sign on the 5th and stay there for the rest of the month. This has many good points – it increases your energy and 'can do' spirit – but it can also make you impetuous and in a rush; not a good thing with so many retrogrades. Make haste by all means, but mindfully.

Health will be good this month – especially until the 23rd. Afterwards you need to rest and relax more. Enhance the health with arm and shoulder massage until the 18th and with abdominal massage afterwards. Diet becomes important healthwise after the 18th as well. Good emotional health is also important. Getting into emotional wellness is not only important this month but for the next two months as well.

Taurus is always interested in finance, but the interest is waning this month. Mercury leaves the money house on the 5th and Venus on the 18th. I read this as a good signal. Financial objectives (the short-term ones at least) have been attained and you can start focusing on other things.

Your 3rd house is powerful this month – a great transit for students below the college level. They should be successful in their studies. There is focus here. But this transit also enhances the mind and communication abilities. So, it is a good time to read more and take courses in subjects that interest you. Some of you will perhaps teach others in your area of expertise. It is also a good month for those of you involved in sales, marketing, advertising and retailing. Trading seems lucrative from the 5th to the 19th.

Mars squares your love planet on the 1st and 2nd. This can create conflict with the spouse, partner or current love. Be more patient with them.

Mars will travel with Uranus on the 30th and 31st, which is a dynamic aspect. Be more mindful on the physical plane – this holds true for parents, parent figures and bosses as well.

August

Best Days Overall: 1, 9, 10, 17, 18, 27, 28
Most Stressful Days Overall: 4, 5, 11, 12, 25, 26
Best Days for Love: 1, 4, 5, 10, 15, 18, 25, 26, 28
Best Days for Money: 7, 9, 15, 17, 18, 20, 21, 25, 29
Best Days for Career: 1, 9, 10, 11, 12, 17, 18, 27, 28

Mars is still travelling with Uranus on the 1st and 2nd, so review our discussion of this last month.

Career is important all year, but this month you can devote more energy to your home and family, and – more importantly – to your emotional wellness. Your career planet, Uranus, starts to retrograde on the 24th and your 4th house of home and family is now strong (this began last month). Also, the night side of the Horoscope is dominant this month. So, this is a time for setting up the structures – the emotional and domestic foundations – for future career success, for your future career push.

When the 4th house is powerful, there is a strong nostalgia energy. The past is with us and we are interested in it. We remember distant events that are seemingly insignificant from the rational perspective but very significant emotionally. This is nature's healing process. We cannot deal with our entire past all in one month – this is the work of years (and some say lifetimes) – but we can work on the issues at hand, the things that need re-evaluation from the present state of consciousness. Things that are devastating to a four-year-old bring smiles to the adult. Looking at these past experiences will take much of the trauma out of them. This work will not only help your emotional health but your physical health as well.

Retrograde activity increases even further this month. By the end of the month, half the planets will be travelling backwards. Babies born during this time will be late bloomers – regardless of their actual Horoscope. It is good to understand these things.

Happily your financial planet, Mercury, is not retrograde. In fact, he is moving speedily this month. Thus, while there are many delays in many areas of life, finance is progressing forward. Until the 4th family and family connections are important. Family support seems good. From the

4th to the 26th you're in a period for 'happy money' – you earn it in fun ways and spend on fun things. From the 26th onwards you earn the old-fashioned way – through your work and practical service to others.

September

Best Days Overall: 5, 6, 13, 14, 15, 23, 24
Most Stressful Days Overall: 1, 2, 7, 8, 21, 22, 28, 29
Best Days for Love: 1, 2, 4, 5, 6, 13, 14, 15, 24, 28, 29
Best Days for Money: 3, 7, 8, 11, 16, 17, 21, 24, 30
Best Days for Career: 5, 6, 7, 8, 14, 15, 23, 24

Retrograde activity spikes to a yearly high this month: 60 per cent of the planets are moving backwards, from the 10th onwards. This includes Mercury, your financial planet. So events are moving slowly this month. And, with your 5th house of fun and creativity strong since August 23 you might as well enjoy things – go on vacation, or involve yourself in leisure activities. You're not going to miss very much.

Mercury's retrograde will have a far stronger effect than the previous ones you've experienced this year. This is because so many other planets are also retrograde. The effect is cumulative. Finances will happen but much slower than usual and with more glitches and delays. With so many planets retrograde, the Cosmos is calling us to slow down and be perfect in all that we do. This is especially so in finance. Being perfect, handling the details of life perfectly, will not eliminate delays but will minimize them.

The good news is that health is excellent this month. Plus, you're enjoying life. The rare Grand Trine in Earth which began last month is still in effect. This enhances your already good management skills and gives a down-to-earth practical approach to life.

In addition to the Grand Trine in Earth we also have a Grand Trine in Air. Two Grand Trines in one month! This is great for teachers, students, writers, sales and marketing people. The mental faculties are very much enhanced. You will find that people in general are more communicative.

Your health planet, Venus, spends most of the month in your 5th house. This indicates various things. You could be more concerned with the health of children and children figures than with your own health. A creative hobby is unusually therapeutic. Joy itself is a powerful healing force – so stay happy. Massage of the lower abdomen will also be therapeutic.

Your spiritual planet Mars is in your money house all month. This shows a need to explore the spiritual dimensions of wealth. We have discussed this in the yearly report. Intuition will solve many problems.

Love seems happy until the 23rd. But your love planet, Pluto, is retrograde, so there's no need to rush into anything. Enjoy love for what it is without trying to project too much on to it.

October

Best Days Overall: 2, 3, 11, 12, 21, 22, 30
Most Stressful Days Overall: 4, 5, 18, 19, 25, 26
Best Days for Love: 3, 4, 5, 12, 13, 14, 22, 25, 26
Best Days for Money: 2, 3, 8, 9, 13, 14, 18, 23, 24, 26, 27
Best Days for Career: 2, 3, 4, 5, 11, 12, 21, 22, 30

Retrograde activity is still extensive, but much less so than last month. By the end of the month retrograde activity will be cut in half, down to only 30 per cent of the planets. So life is starting to move forward.

It is good that you're focusing on health until the 23rd, as after that health seems stressed. This early-month focus will stand you in good stead for later. It's as if you're banking health credits.

The main headline for October is the solar eclipse of the 25th. As eclipses go this one is rather weak as it is a partial one. However, if this hits planets in your Natal chart (cast for your exact date, time and place of birth) it can have a powerful effect, so it won't hurt to reduce your schedule that period. (You should be taking it easy from the 23rd onwards anyway, but especially around the eclipse period.)

This eclipse occurs in your 7th house and will test the current relationship and friendships. Dirty laundry, long suppressed, comes up to be dealt with. Good relationships don't usually dissolve over this, but flawed ones can. With Uranus planted in own your sign for some years now, relationships have been getting tested in general. This eclipse only adds to it. Since the Sun rules your 4th house of home and family, every solar eclipse brings family dramas and dramas in the lives of family members (as we've said before). Passions will run high at home. More patience (and understanding) is needed over this period. If there are hidden flaws in the home, now is the time that you find out about them. Often repairs are necessary.

The good news here is that you will be in a yearly love and social peak from the 23rd onwards. You will be focused on your relationship and friendships. This focus will help you get through the trials of the eclipse.

You can enhance the health from the 23rd onwards through detox regimes. Good health for you means more than just 'no physical symptoms' – it means good social health, a healthy love life. So, if health problems arise, work to restore harmony in love as quickly as you can.

November

Best Days Overall: 7, 8, 17, 18, 26, 27
Most Stressful Days Overall: 1, 2, 15, 16, 22, 23, 28, 29
Best Days for Love: 3, 4, 8, 9, 13, 18, 22, 23, 24, 27
Best Days for Money: 3, 4, 10, 11, 13, 14, 23, 24, 25
Best Days for Career: 1, 2, 7, 8, 17, 18, 26, 27, 28, 29

The lunar eclipse of the 8th is arguably more powerful than last month's solar eclipse. (Generally solar eclipses are considered more powerful than lunar ones.) For a start, it is a total eclipse – the Native Americans call it a 'blood Moon'. Even more importantly, it impacts three other planets – Mercury, Uranus and Venus. (And if it hits important planets in your Natal Horoscope, it becomes even more powerful.) So let's take it easy over this period. You need to take it easy until the 22nd anyway, but especially during the eclipse period.

This eclipse occurs in your own sign, forcing you to redefine yourself, your image and how you want to be perceived by others. Generally, this kind of redefinition is a good thing. We are changing, evolving beings, and making periodic adjustments to our opinion of ourselves is healthy. But here it happens 'by force' – you must do it. So it is less pleasant. If you haven't been careful in dietary matters this eclipse can bring a detox of the body. It can seem like sickness, but it isn't. It is just the body getting rid of things that don't belong there. Because Mercury is impacted, there are financial changes and course corrections. The events of the eclipse will show you where your financial plans and strategy were unrealistic. The impact on Venus and Uranus shows job and career changes. The conditions of the workplace change and there can be disruptions at work and with co-workers. If you employ others there can be a degree of staff turnover. There are dramas in the lives of parents, parent figures, bosses and elders – life-changing dramas. In coming months there can be important changes to the health regime too. The spouse, partner or current love has social upheavals.

Health and energy will improve after the 22nd. In the meantime, enhance health through detox regimes and through massage of the colon and bladder reflexes. After the 16th enhance health with thigh massage and massage of the liver reflex (the reflex points are shown in the yearly report).

Mars remains in your money house all month, but he is retrograde. Intuition is important in finance, but make sure you verify your hunches.

December

Best Days Overall: 4, 5, 6, 14, 15, 16, 23, 24
Most Stressful Days Overall: 12, 13, 19, 20, 25, 26
Best Days for Love: 2, 3, 6, 14, 15, 16, 19, 20, 23, 24
Best Days for Money: 1, 2, 3, 7, 8, 11, 14, 15, 20, 21, 23, 24, 29
Best Days for Career: 4, 5, 14, 15, 23, 24, 25, 26

A happy and eventful month ahead. Jupiter moves back into your 12th house of spirituality on the 21st. Next year he will move into your sign. You're being prepared spiritually for success and prosperity. Health is much improved over last month, and gets really good after the 21st. Retrograde activity is much reduced this month: 80 per cent of the planets are moving forward until the 24th (and after that the figure is still 70 per cent). Things are moving in the world and in your life.

Your 8th house of regeneration is very strong until the 22nd. Thus you are in a more sexually active kind of period. Regardless of your age or stage in life, libido is stronger than usual. More importantly, this is a month for getting rid of the effete and useless in your life. It is very good for losing weight and for detox regimes. Good for financial detoxing, tax and insurance planning – and for those of you of an appropriate age, for estate planning too.

On the 22nd your 9th house becomes powerful. (Venus, the ruler of your Horoscope will be there even before then – from the 10th onwards.) Thus there is foreign travel or the opportunity for it. College-bound students hear good news, and college students succeed in their studies. It is a period for theological and philosophical breakthroughs.

Three planets are outside their usual orbits this month, which is unusual. Mars, your spiritual planet, has been 'out of bounds' since last month. This indicates that in spiritual matters you are outside your normal sphere, probably exploring spiritual paths that you weren't brought up in. Venus 'out of bounds' from the 2nd to the 24th shows that you are outside your orbit in your personal life, in the way you dress and present yourself. Also that you are exploring health regimes and therapies that are outside the mainstream. Mercury, your financial planet, is 'out of bounds' from the 1st to the 22nd, so this phenomenon is happening in your finances too. This is a month where you think and act 'outside the box'.

Mercury goes retrograde on the 24th. This retrograde should be milder in its impact than the last one in September. But still it has an effect. Try to wrap up important purchases and investments before then.

Love improves after the 22nd, but marriage is still not in the cards. Enjoy love for what it is without projecting too far into the future.

Gemini

∏

THE TWINS

Birthdays from
21st May to
20th June

Personality Profile

GEMINI AT A GLANCE

Element – Air

Ruling Planet – Mercury
  Career Planet – Neptune
  Love Planet – Jupiter
  Money Planet – Moon
  Planet of Health and Work – Pluto
  Planet of Home and Family Life – Mercury

Colours – blue, yellow, yellow-orange

Colour that promotes love, romance and social harmony – sky blue

Colours that promote earning power – grey, silver

Gems – agate, aquamarine

Metal – quicksilver

Scents – lavender, lilac, lily of the valley, storax

Quality – mutable (= flexibility)

Quality most needed for balance – thought that is deep rather than superficial

Strongest virtues – great communication skills, quickness and agility of thought, ability to learn quickly

Deepest need – communication

Characteristics to avoid – gossiping, hurting others with harsh speech, superficiality, using words to mislead or misinform

Signs of greatest overall compatibility – Libra, Aquarius

Signs of greatest overall incompatibility – Virgo, Sagittarius, Pisces

Sign most helpful to career – Pisces

Sign most helpful for emotional support – Virgo

Sign most helpful financially – Cancer

Sign best for marriage and/or partnerships – Sagittarius

Sign most helpful for creative projects – Libra

Best Sign to have fun with – Libra

Signs most helpful in spiritual matters – Taurus, Aquarius

Best day of the week – Wednesday

Understanding a Gemini

Gemini is to society what the nervous system is to the body. It does not introduce any new information but is a vital transmitter of impulses from the senses to the brain and vice versa. The nervous system does not judge or weigh these impulses – it only conveys information. And it does so perfectly.

This analogy should give you an indication of a Gemini's role in society. Geminis are the communicators and conveyors of information. To Geminis the truth or falsehood of information is irrelevant, they only transmit what they see, hear or read about. Thus they are capable of spreading the most outrageous rumours as well as conveying truth and light. Geminis sometimes tend to be unscrupulous in their communications and can do both great good and great evil with their power. This is why the sign of Gemini is symbolized by twins: Geminis have a dual nature.

Their ability to convey a message – to communicate with such ease – makes Geminis ideal teachers, writers and media and marketing people. This is helped by the fact that Mercury, the ruling planet of Gemini, also rules these activities.

Geminis have the gift of the gab. And what a gift this is! They can make conversation about anything, anywhere, at any time. There is almost nothing that is more fun to Geminis than a good conversation – especially if they can learn something new as well. They love to learn and they love to teach. To deprive a Gemini of conversation, or of books and magazines, is cruel and unusual punishment.

Geminis are almost always excellent students and take well to education. Their minds are generally stocked with all kinds of information, trivia, anecdotes, stories, news items, rarities, facts and statistics. Thus they can support any intellectual position that they care to take. They are awesome debaters and, if involved in politics, make good orators. Geminis are so verbally smooth that even if they do not know what they are talking about, they can make you think that they do. They will always dazzle you with their brilliance.

Finance

Geminis tend to be more concerned with the wealth of learning and ideas than with actual material wealth. As mentioned, they excel in professions that involve writing, teaching, sales and journalism – and not all of these professions pay very well. But to sacrifice intellectual needs merely for money is unthinkable to a Gemini. Geminis strive to combine the two. Cancer is on Gemini's solar 2nd house of money cusp, which indicates that Geminis can earn extra income (in a harmonious and natural way) from investments in residential property, restaurants and hotels. Given their verbal skills, Geminis love to bargain and negotiate in any situation, and especially when it has to do with money.

The Moon rules Gemini's 2nd solar house. The Moon is not only the fastest-moving planet in the zodiac but actually moves through every sign and house every 28 days. No other heavenly body matches the Moon for swiftness or the ability to change quickly. An analysis of the Moon – and lunar phenomena in general – describes Gemini's financial attitudes very well. Geminis are financially versatile and flexible; they can earn money in many different ways. Their financial attitudes and needs seem to change daily. Their feelings about money change also: sometimes they are very enthusiastic about it, at other times they could not care less.

For a Gemini, financial goals and money are often seen only as means of supporting a family; these things have little meaning otherwise.

The Moon, as Gemini's money planet, has another important message for Gemini financially: in order for Geminis to realize their financial potential they need to develop more of an understanding of the emotional side of life. They need to combine their awesome powers of logic with an understanding of human psychology. Feelings have their own logic; Geminis need to learn this and apply it to financial matters.

Career and Public Image

Geminis know that they have been given the gift of communication for a reason, that it is a power that can achieve great good or cause unthinkable distress. They long to put this power at the service of the highest and most transcendental truths. This is their primary goal, to communicate the eternal verities and prove them logically. They look up to people who can transcend the intellect – to poets, artists, musicians and mystics. They may be awed by stories of religious saints and martyrs. A Gemini's highest achievement is to teach the truth, whether it is scientific, inspirational or historical. Those who can transcend the intellect are Gemini's natural superiors – and a Gemini realizes this.

The sign of Pisces is in Gemini's solar 10th house of career. Neptune, the planet of spirituality and altruism, is Gemini's career planet. If Geminis are to realize their highest career potential they need to develop their transcendental – their spiritual and altruistic – side. They need to understand the larger cosmic picture, the vast flow of human evolution – where it came from and where it is heading. Only then can a Gemini's intellectual powers take their true position and he or she can become the 'messenger of the gods'. Geminis need to cultivate a facility for 'inspiration', which is something that does not originate in the intellect but which comes through the intellect. This will further enrich and empower a Gemini's mind.

Love and Relationships

Geminis bring their natural garrulousness and brilliance into their love life and social life as well. A good talk or a verbal joust is an interesting prelude to romance. Their only problem in love is that their intellect is too cool and passionless to incite ardour in others. Emotions sometimes disturb them, and their partners tend to complain about this. If you are in love with a Gemini you must understand why this is so. Geminis avoid deep passions because these would interfere with their ability to think and communicate. If they are cool towards you, understand that this is their nature.

Nevertheless, Geminis must understand that it is one thing to talk about love and another actually to love – to feel it and radiate it. Talking about love glibly will get them nowhere. They need to feel it and act on it. Love is not of the intellect but of the heart. If you want to know how a Gemini feels about love you should not listen to what he or she says, but rather, observe what he or she does. Geminis can be quite generous to those they love.

Geminis like their partners to be refined, well educated and well travelled. If their partners are more wealthy than they, that is all the better. If you are in love with a Gemini you had better be a good listener as well.

The ideal relationship for the Gemini is a relationship of the mind. They enjoy the physical and emotional aspects, of course, but if the intellectual communion is not there they will suffer.

Home and Domestic Life

At home the Gemini can be uncharacteristically neat and meticulous. They tend to want their children and partner to live up to their idealistic standards. When these standards are not met they moan and criticize. However, Geminis are good family people and like to serve their families in practical and useful ways.

The Gemini home is comfortable and pleasant. They like to invite people over and they make great hosts. Geminis are also good at repairs and improvements around the house – all fuelled by their need to stay active and occupied with something they like to do. Geminis have many hobbies and interests that keep them busy when they are home alone.

Geminis understand and get along well with their children, mainly because they are very youthful people themselves. As great communicators, Geminis know how to explain things to children; in this way they gain their children's love and respect. Geminis also encourage children to be creative and talkative, just like they are.

Horoscope for 2022

Major Trends

Although 2021 was successful, 2022 will be even more successful, Gemini. Your career is expanding by leaps and bounds. Your professional status likewise. If you are in business, the business will be elevated in its standing too. Jupiter is moving through your 10th career house this year and will be there until May 11. (It will return briefly later, from October 29 to December 21 – just in case there is some unfinished career business to redeem.) More on this later.

Health is good, but will get even better after May 11 when Jupiter moves away from his stressful aspect. After May 11 there will be only one long-term planet in stressful alignment with you – Neptune. All the others are either making harmonious aspects or leaving you alone. More details later.

Finances don't seem a big deal this year; your money house is not prominent. However, generally, when the career is going well, finances tend to follow. More on this later.

Pluto has been in your 8th house of regeneration for many, many years and will still be there in the year ahead. (He is about to move on next year, and by 2024 he will be completely out.) So you have been dealing with death and death issues for a while. Perhaps there were surgeries or near-death kinds of experiences in the lives of uncles, aunts and in-laws. This is still a concern in the year ahead.

Saturn has been in your 9th house since 2021 (he made a brief visit in 2020). Thus your religious, philosophical and metaphysical beliefs are getting re-ordered. Travel has been restricted. College students have had to work harder in their studies. This trend continues in the year ahead.

Uranus has been in your 12th house of spirituality for some years now, indicating much experimentation and change in your spiritual life. You change teachings and teachers quite rapidly. You gravitate to new paths and new systems. More on this later.

Your most important interests this year will be sex, personal transformation and occult studies; higher education, religion, philosophy, theology and foreign travel; career; friends, groups, group activities and science (from May 11 to October 29 and from December 21 onwards); spirituality; and the body, image and personal appearance (from August 20 onwards).

Your paths of greatest fulfilment will be career (until May 11 and from October 29 to December 21); friends, groups, group activities and science (from May 11 to October 29 and from December 21 onwards); and spirituality.

Health

(Please note that this is an astrological perspective on health and not a medical one. In days of yore there was no difference, both these perspectives were identical. But these days there could be quite a difference. For a medical perspective, please consult your doctor or health practitioner.)

Health as we mentioned earlier looks good this year. Until May 11 there are only two long-term planets in stressful alignment with you, and after then there is only one. (From October 29 to December 21, when Jupiter retrogrades back into Pisces, there are again two – but this is temporary).

Your 6th house of health is empty this year, which I read as a positive. You have no need to overly focus on health as there's nothing wrong. People who have pre-existing conditions should see them more in abeyance this year.

Keep in mind that there will be periods in the year where health is less easy than usual. These periods come from the transits of the short-term planets and are temporary and not trends for the year. When they pass your normally good health and energy return.

Good though your health is you can make it better. Give more attention to the following – the vulnerable areas of your Horoscope this year (the reflex points are shown in the chart opposite):

- The heart is important until May 11 and from October 29 to December 21, and the reflex point is shown above. Chest massage – especially of the breastbone and upper rib cage – will be good as well. The important thing with the heart is to avoid worry and anxiety – the two emotions that stress it out. Cultivate faith rather than worry.

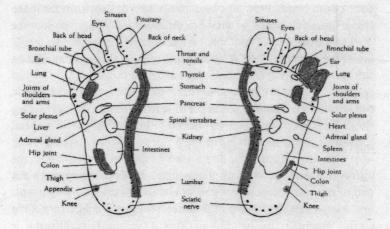

Important foot reflexology points for the year ahead

Try to massage all of the foot on a regular basis – the top of the foot as well as the bottom – but pay extra attention to the points highlighted on the chart. When you massage, be aware of 'sore spots' as these need special attention. It's also a good idea to massage the ankles – and especially below them.

- The arms, shoulders, lungs and respiratory system. These are always important for Gemini. Arms and shoulders should be regularly massaged, as tension tends to collect in the shoulders and needs to be released. Hand reflexology would be a wonderful therapy. Make sure to get enough fresh air and to breathe deeply and rhythmically.
- The colon, bladder and sexual organs. These are always important for Gemini as Pluto (the ruler of these areas) is your health planet. Safe sex and sexual moderation are always important.
- The spine, knees, bones, skeletal alignment, teeth and skin. These areas have been important for the past twenty or so years, and remain so in the year ahead, although by 2024 they will become less prominent. Regular back and knee massage would be beneficial, as would regular visits to a chiropractor or osteopath: the vertebrae need to be kept in right alignment. If you're out in the sun use a good sunscreen. Good dental hygiene is also important.

Your health planet Pluto has been in the sign of Capricorn for many years. Thus you would gravitate to orthodox medicine. You like the tried and true. Even if you opted for alternative therapies you would prefer the ones that have stood the test of time. (In spiritual matters you are very experimental, but not so in health.)

With your health planet in an Earth sign you would have a good connection to the healing powers of the earth element. Crystal therapy would be interesting and potent. If you feel under the weather spend some time in the mountains or old forests – places where the earth energy is very strong. You don't need to do much, just absorb the energy (these are good places to meditate). Mud packs applied to any part of the body that bothers you would also be useful. Some people like to soak in waters with a high mineral content (minerals are of the earth element) – this would work nicely for you. Natural water is always best, but if this isn't practical you can buy minerals and add them to your bath.

Home and Family

This is not an especially important area this year, Gemini. There are various reasons for this. First, your 4th house is basically empty; only short-term planets move through there and their impact is temporary. In addition, your 10th house of career is very powerful – especially until May 11. And perhaps most importantly, *all* the long-term planets are in the day side of your chart – the hemisphere of outer activity and achievement. So this is a year where you serve your family best by being successful – by being the good provider. It's nice to be there for the kids and attend all the plays and soccer games, but being success-ful will serve them better.

This is the kind of year where outer success will produce emotional harmony.

Family is always important to you, Gemini – Mercury, the ruler of your Horoscope, is also your family planet. This shows a strong bond and connection. But this year less so than usual.

Mercury is a fast-moving planet and during the course of the year he will move through your entire horoscope. So, there are many short-term family trends that depend on where Mercury is and the kinds of aspects that he receives. These are best dealt with in the monthly reports.

Mercury will go retrograde three times this year (which is usual). These periods are from January 14 to February 3, from May 10 to June 2, and from September 10 to October 1. This last retrograde will probably have the strongest effect as many other planets are also retrograde, amplifying the impact. So, during these times avoid making important home or family decisions. Work for clarity. Get more facts. Resolve all doubts. The truth may not be what you think.

Mars will not move through your 4th house this year, so if you're planning major renovations or construction work, it is probably better to wait until next year. However, if you're redecorating in a cosmetic kind of way or buying art objects for the home, September 5 to September 10 would be a good period for this – also October 29 to November 16.

The parents or parent figures in your life are having a very good year. One is having a great social year, the other a great financial year – he or she is living the high life. If the parent figure is of child-bearing age, there is heightened fertility. A move for them is not likely. (They might be renovating the existing home, however.)

Siblings and sibling figures are more likely to move in 2024 than now. Children and children figures may also be renovating the home, but a move is not likely. However, grandchildren, if you have them (or those who play that role in your life), are likely to move this year or next.

Finance and Career

The career – your life work and mission – is much more important than mere money this year. Your money house is basically empty. Only short-term planets will move through there and the effects will also be short term. This can be read as a good thing. It shows contentment with things as they are, and no special need to make important changes. It tends to the status quo. Earnings will be more or less like last year.

We will have two lunar eclipses this year, and since the Moon is your financial planet these will bring course corrections and dramas in the financial life. This is not a big deal, as you go through this twice (sometimes three times) a year, and by now you know how to handle these things. The lunar eclipses are on May 16 and November 8, and we will discuss them more fully in the monthly reports.

The Moon is the fastest moving of all the planets. Where Mercury, Venus and the Sun need a year to move through your chart (although this year Mercury and Venus will do this in eleven months), the Moon will move through the entire chart every month. So, there are many short-term financial trends that are best dealt with in the monthly reports. In general, your earning power will be strongest when the Moon is waxing and growing in size.

As a Gemini you are strong in all areas that involve communication – journalism, writing, telecommunications, advertising, teaching and lecturing. It would also favour transportation, retailing and trading – buying and selling.

With the Moon as your financial planet you can also earn through residential real estate, the food business, restaurants, hotels and motels and all industries that cater to the homeowner. The field of psychology is also interesting.

As we mentioned, career is the main headline this year. Jupiter will move through your 10th house until May 11 (and then move back in from October 29 to December 21). This is a classic signal of career success and expansion. New horizons and opportunities are revealed. Previous limitations fall by the wayside.

Jupiter is your love planet. This gives many messages. The spouse, partner or current love seems very active and helpful in your career. Friends too. Your social contacts are playing a huge role here. In general, your social grace brings you to the heights and opens doors for you. Your spouse, partner or current love – and friends too – are very successful. You are able to meet high and mighty people – on a social level – who can help you careerwise. (There are other meanings to this too which we will discuss later on.) It will be very important this year to attend or host the right gatherings and parties.

Another way to read this transit is that your social life, your marriage and love life, is the real career this year – just being there for the spouse, partner and friends.

Love and Social Life

The love and social life seem very happy this year. Though your 7th house of love is basically empty – only short-term planets will move through there – your love planet, Jupiter, is very strongly positioned right at the top of the chart – his most powerful position. Jupiter is also in his own sign until May 11, which further strengthens him. So there is strong social grace and strong attractive power this year. The social life will expand. Singles could marry this year. And those involved in relationships will tend to have more romance within the relationship.

With your love planet in the 10th house you are attracted to people of power and prominence. Power is a strong aphrodisiac these days. But status and power are not enough. You also are attracted to spiritual, creative and idealistic kinds of people: Jupiter is in Pisces and travelling close to Neptune. So your ideal mate (for those of you who are single) is someone of high status but who is also involved in charity and good works. Someone who is perhaps the CEO of a corporation but who likes to write poetry or music on the side. A practical person who perhaps spends his or her vacation on spiritual retreat or in an ashram. These are the kinds of people you gravitate to. And you will be meeting these kinds of people as well.

The love planet in the 10th house indicates that a lot of your socializing is career related. However, one of the problems with this transit is a tendency to opt for relationships of convenience rather than real love. You will have to question yourself about this. Romantic and social opportunities happen as you pursue your career goals and perhaps with people involved in your career.

On May 11 Jupiter will move into your 11th house of groups and friends and stays there until October 29. He will then move back into your 11th house on December 21. With Jupiter in the 11th house, the love attitudes shift a bit. Now you tend to gravitate to relationships of peers – of equals – rather than hierarchical ones. You want to be friends with the beloved as well as his or her lover.

The love planet in Aries from May 11th signals someone who falls in love at first sight. You become more aggressive in love. You're not playing games. You're direct. If you like someone, that person will

know it. There is a tendency to jump into relationships very quickly –
perhaps too quickly.

The love planet in the 11th house indicates that romantic opportunities can happen online, through social media and online dating sites.
It often shows that someone who was 'just a friend' can become more
than that. Often friends like to play Cupid.

The love planet in the 11th house tends to be fortunate. It shows a
period where 'fondest hopes and wishes' in love come true.

Self-improvement

Uranus has been in your spiritual 12th house for some years now and
he will be there for some more years to come. Our regular readers
know that the transit of a slow-moving planet is not really an event, but
a 'process'. And this is the case in your spiritual life. Spiritually you're
throwing out all the old rule books – the old traditions, the old do's and
don'ts – and learning what works for you. The traditional paths are
guidelines to the spirit, but ultimately 'I am the way': each person
achieves their path in their own way. So there is much change and
ferment happening here. You study the different paths, you study
under different teachers and teachings, you seek out the new and the
untried. You're learning what works for you through trial and error.

Uranus rules your 9th house of religion. Thus the Horoscope is
indicating that it is time to explore the mystical paths of your own
native religion. You've always had the keys to enlightenment, but you
didn't know it. Travelling to sacred places would also assist the
spiritual path.

Uranus also favours a scientific approach to the Divine. There is a
science behind all the apparent 'mumbo jumbo'. This is a good year to
explore this. The transit also favours esoteric astrology – the spiritual
and philosophical side of astrology. This is a valid path. (Some of you
might enjoy my book *A Spiritual View of the 12 Signs*, which deals with
esoteric astrology.)

Venus is your spiritual planet. So when you are in love – in a state of
harmony – you easily make contact with the Divine. Love itself is a
viable path.

Venus also rules your 5th house of creativity. Thus the path of creativity is also very valid. By learning and applying the laws of creation one can understand the workings of the Great Creator.

Month-by-month Forecasts

January

Best Days Overall: 4, 5, 13, 14, 23, 24, 31
Most Stressful Days Overall: 1, 6, 7, 21, 22, 27, 28
Best Days for Love: 1, 2, 3, 6, 11, 12, 16, 21, 22, 27, 21, 25, 28, 29, 30
Best Days for Money: 2, 3, 6, 11, 12, 16, 17, 23, 25
Best Days for Career: 6, 7, 17, 26

All the planets, with the exception of the Moon (and that only temporarily) are in the day side of your chart. Your 10th house of career is very strong, while your 4th house of home and family is basically empty. (Only the Moon moves through here this month, on the 21st and 22nd.) So we have a very clear message. Focus on the career and let family matters go for a while.

The month ahead is very successful, and future months will bring even more success. You're just getting started in your success track. You are elevated in your career and social status.

Jupiter, your love planet, is right at the top of your chart in your 10th house. This is wonderful for both the career and the romantic life. It shows focus. Love is high on your agenda, high on your list of priorities. Romantic opportunities happen as you pursue your career goals or with people involved in your career. Status and power are strong aphrodisiacs. A lot of your socializing involves the career. You are meeting important, influential people socially. Your social contacts boost the career.

Health is basically good this month. Pluto, your health planet, is receiving positive aspects. The 1st, 2nd, 27th and 28th seem especially good for health – and good for jobseekers as well. You can enhance the health further in the ways mentioned in the yearly report.

Finance is not a big deal this month. Your money house is empty. (Only the Moon will move through there, on the 16th and 17th.) This tends to the status quo. Career is more exciting and important than mere money. (Generally, if the career is going well, finances tend to go well too – but not always.) A prestigious position that pays less is more attractive to you than a non-prestigious position that pays more. In general, you will have more financial energy and enthusiasm from the 2nd to the 17th as the Moon waxes. This period is good for increasing earnings and making investments. After the 17th is a good period to use spare cash to reduce debt.

Mercury, the ruler of your Horoscope, makes a dynamic aspect with Uranus from the 12th to the 17th. Try to avoid long trips during that period. Be more careful driving and be more mindful on the physical level. You will have a tendency to test the limits of the body over this period. This is OK, but do it mindfully and not recklessly.

February

Best Days Overall: 1, 9, 10, 11, 19, 20, 28
Most Stressful Days Overall: 2, 3, 17, 18, 24, 25
Best Days for Love: 2, 3, 7, 8, 12, 13, 17, 18, 21, 22, 24, 25, 27
Best Days for Money: 1, 2, 3, 9, 10, 12, 13, 21, 22, 23
Best Days for Career: 2, 3, 12, 13, 22, 23

A happy and successful month ahead, Gemini, enjoy. Your 9th house – a very beneficent house – remains powerful until the 18th. Like last month this favours higher studies – it is a wonderful period for college-level students and for those looking to enter college – foreign travel and religious and theological studies.

On the 18th the Sun will cross your Mid-heaven and enter your 10th house. You begin a yearly (and for many of you a lifetime) career peak. Much success is happening. There is success in the career and success in love as well.

Health will need more attention from the 18th onwards. There is nothing serious afoot, just short-term stress caused by the short-term planets. As always, make sure to get enough rest. Career demands are hard, but you can work on them steadily. Let go of the inessential in your life and focus on priorities. Enhance the health in the ways mentioned in the yearly report.

Mercury moves forward on the 4th and from then on *all* the planets are moving forward. So events are happening quickly. You have confidence and clarity.

Most of the planets are in the Western, social sector of your chart and your love planet, Jupiter, is still very prominent. So, self-assertion and self-will are not called for now. This is a time for developing your social skills and for getting things done by consensus rather than personal will. Allow your good to come to you rather than forcing it to happen.

The communication skills of Gemini are legendary. This month superiors take notice: they boosts the career. Social contacts continue to boost the career as well.

Finance is still not a big deal – the tendency will be to the status quo. Your money house remains empty, with only the Moon moving through there, on the 12th and 13th. Focus on the career and money will follow eventually. You are strongest financially from the 1st to the 16th as the Moon, your money planet, waxes. This is when you should save, invest and work to increase your income. After the 16th it will be good to use spare cash to reduce debt (something you want to get rid of).

March

Best Days Overall: 1, 9, 10, 18, 19, 27, 28
Most Stressful Days Overall: 2, 3, 16, 17, 23, 24, 30, 31
Best Days for Love: 2, 3, 9, 11, 12, 18, 19, 21, 22, 23, 24, 27, 28, 30, 31
Best Days for Money: 2, 3, 11, 12, 13, 21, 22, 23, 30, 31
Best Days for Career: 2, 3, 11, 12, 21, 22, 30, 31

Continue to watch your health and energy until the 20th. As always, make sure to get enough rest and listen to the messages your body sends you. Enhance the health in the ways mentioned in the yearly report.

Mars will travel with Pluto from the 2nd to the 4th – a very dynamic aspect. Be more mindful on the material plane. Surgery can be suggested to friends or to you. There can be some disturbance at the workplace. Later this month, Mars will make dynamic aspects with Uranus, from the 20th to the 22nd. Again, be more mindful on the physical plane. Drive more carefully and watch the temper. This applies to your friends as well.

You are still in a strong success track this month. Mercury, the ruler of your Horoscope, will enter your 10th house on the 10th. This shows personal success. You are recognized for who you are as much as for your professional abilities. You seem on top – above everyone in your world. (Sometimes this indicates someone who aspires to be above everyone in their world.) Career is good all month but something really wonderful happens on the 27th or 28th. Mercury travels with Neptune, your career planet.

Love is also happy this month. The Sun travels with your love planet Jupiter from the 4th to the 6th. This brings happy romantic and social opportunities. Mercury will travel with your love planet on the 20th and 21st, which signals a happy romantic meeting for singles. Your social grace has seldom been stronger.

On the 29th and 30th, Mercury (a very important planet in your chart, as you know) has his solstice. He pauses in the heavens – in his latitudinal motion – and then changes direction. So it is with you. There is a pause in your personal affairs and then a change of direction. It is a good pause – a natural pause – not something enforced. You emerge from it refreshed and energetic.

Finances continue to be stable, with the career much more important than mere money. Your money house is still empty, with only the Moon moving through there on the 11th, 12th and 13th. Your financial power is strongest from the 2nd to the 18th as your financial planet waxes. This is a time to increase earning power, make deposits into your savings or investment accounts, and so on – to do things that increase your income. After the 18th use spare cash to pay down debt.

April

Best Days Overall: 5, 6, 15, 16, 23, 24
Most Stressful Days Overall: 13, 14, 19, 20, 25, 26
Best Days for Love: 8, 9, 17, 18, 19, 20, 25, 26, 27
Best Days for Money: 1, 2, 8, 9, 10, 11, 17, 18, 20, 21, 26, 27, 30
Best Days for Career: 9, 18, 25, 26, 27

Health still needs watching this month – especially from the 15th onwards. Give the heart more attention. Massage the reflex points (see p. 83) and also the chest. Enhance the health in the ways discussed in the yearly report.

The demands of the career are still very strong. Mars will cross the Mid-heaven and enter your 10th house on the 15th. This signals a need for aggressiveness in the career. You seem very combative. You're dealing with competition. On the other hand, friends seem successful and are helping your career.

Jupiter travels with your career planet Neptune from the 1st to the 17th. This brings more career expansion and opportunity – very positive developments are happening here. It is also a good sign for love. Singles have love opportunities with bosses or high-status people now. The problem is that you need to be sure that it is love and not just a relationship of convenience.

The month ahead is socially active – both romantically and with friends. You seem very devoted to friends and they to you.

On the 20th the Sun enters your 12th house and you begin a strong spiritual period. This can be complicated as your career focus is strong and so is your spiritual focus. You need to integrate both. (This has been a life-long challenge, and especially so nowadays.)

A solar eclipse on the 30th occurs in your spiritual 12th house. Thus there are spiritual changes going on with you – changes of teachers, teachings and practice. There can be upheavals and shake-ups in spiritual or charitable organizations that you're involved with and dramas in the lives of teachers or guru figures. This eclipse is relatively mild, but it's probably a good idea to drive more carefully over the period. Cars and communication equipment can behave erratically. The good news is that your 12th house is very strong after the 20th, and spiritual activity and focus is the best way to deal with an eclipse.

Finance is stable this month. Earning power is strongest from the 1st to the 16th. Work to increase income during that period as the Moon is waxing. After the 16th use any spare cash to pay down debt.

May

Best Days Overall: 2, 3, 4, 12, 13, 21, 30, 31
Most Stressful Days Overall: 10, 11, 16, 17, 23, 24
Best Days for Love: 6, 7, 8, 15, 16, 17, 24
Best Days for Money: 5, 6, 10, 11, 16, 20, 25, 30
Best Days for Career: 6, 15, 23, 24

The month ahead is eventful – with some challenges – but basically happy. Jupiter, your love planet, makes a major move from Pisces to Aries on the 11th. The planetary power is now overwhelmingly in the Eastern sector of self: at least 70 per cent (and sometimes 80 per cent) of the planets are in the East this month. Your 1st house becomes very strong from the 21st onwards. Add to this a lunar eclipse on the 16th and you have a recipe for dramatic change.

You are now – this month and the next – in a period of maximum personal independence. So this is a time to exercise personal initiative and take responsibility for your own happiness. Make the changes that need to be made in your life. You don't need to consult with others or have their approval – especially if the changes are non-destructive. (Even your love planet, Jupiter, is in the East, so others will more or less assent to your independence.)

The move of the love planet from Pisces to Aries, from your 10th house to the 11th, shows a major shift in love attitudes and needs. Now you seem a 'love at first sight' kind of person. You seem fearless in love. If you like someone, that person knows it. You go after what you want. You are proactive in love. And you're attracted to people who are also like that. Where love was more spiritual over the past few months, now it is more physical. Love and social opportunities happen as you get involved with groups, organizations and group activities – also with social media and the online world.

The lunar eclipse of the 16th occurs in your 6th house of health and work, indicating job changes or changes in the conditions of work. Sometimes there is a health scare, but with health good this month it is probably no more than that – a scare. You will, however, be making important changes to the health regime in the coming months. If you employ others there can be staff turnover. This eclipse impacts on Saturn, and so there can be psychological encounters with death – or near-death kinds of experiences. Every lunar eclipse affects finances, of course. Such eclipses show you the need for a course correction – usually through some upheaval or disturbance. They happen twice a year and the end result is good (although not so pleasant while they're in progress).

June

Best Days Overall: 9, 10, 17, 18, 26, 27
Most Stressful Days Overall: 6, 7, 13, 14, 19, 20
Best Days for Love: 4, 6, 7, 13, 14, 16, 21, 26
Best Days for Money: 1, 2, 3, 4, 9, 10, 13, 18, 21, 28, 29, 30
Best Days for Career: 2, 3, 12, 19, 20, 29, 30

A happy month ahead Gemini, enjoy.

Last month on the 21st the Sun entered your own sign and you began one of your yearly personal pleasure peaks. This remains the case until the 21st of this month, so this is a time for enjoying all the pleasures of the senses, for pampering the body and for getting it into the shape that you want. Self-esteem and self-confidence are good – especially from the 14th onwards as Mercury also enters your sign. You look good too. The personal appearance shines. The opposite sex takes notice.

You are still in the maximum period of personal independence this month – perhaps even more than last month. So make those changes that need to be made. Later on, when the planets shift to the West, it will be more difficult.

The month ahead seems very prosperous as well. On the 21st the Sun enters the money house and you begin a yearly financial peak. In addition, your financial planet, the Moon, moves through the money house for a much longer period than usual. She visits the money house twice (usually only once) and her stay is extended to boot. Instead of being in the 2nd house for two days during the month she will be there for six. This a plus for earnings. It shows focus.

The Sun in the money house from the 21st indicates earnings arising from your core strengths – communication, sales, marketing, writing, teaching, advertising, PR and trading. Your communication skills are the avenue to profits.

Health is good this month; if you want to enhance it further do so according to the ways mentioned in the yearly report.

Someone you considered a friend might want to be more than that. Children and children figures in your life are having a very strong social period. If they are of the appropriate age serious romance is happening.

July

Best Days Overall: 6, 7, 14, 15, 23, 24
Most Stressful Days Overall: 4, 5, 10, 11, 16, 17, 31
Best Days for Love: 1, 2, 6, 7, 10, 11, 15, 18, 19, 26, 28, 29
Best Days for Money: 1, 2, 8, 9, 10, 11, 17, 18, 19, 26, 27, 28, 29
Best Days for Career: 9, 16, 17, 27

Health and energy are excellent this month. Your challenge is to use the extra energy, which is like money in the bank, in positive ways.

Finance is the main headline this month. Your money house is the strongest in the Horoscope: 30 per cent (sometimes 40 per cent) of the planets are moving through there this month. You are still in the midst of your yearly financial peak, and you should be richer at the end of the month than you were at the beginning.

This month we see an interesting reversal. Early in the year – until May 11 – career was more important than money. You wanted prestige and status more than money. Now it is the reverse. Money is more important than career now. You would take a position of lesser status if it paid more. (Perhaps you have all the status you need and now want to enhance your bottom line.)

Love becomes more complicated as your love planet, Jupiter, starts to retrograde on the 28th. If you're making important love decisions do so before the 28th. Venus in your sign until the 18th signals much social grace and physical beauty. This is a good time to buy clothing and accessories as your taste is excellent. Personal appearance is important financially – especially from the 5th to the 19th. You are dressing the part – expensively – projecting wealth.

Venus's move into your 2nd money house on the 18th indicates good financial intuition. In addition, it shows happy money – money that is earned in enjoyable ways and which is spent on enjoyable things. Children and children figures in your life are supportive financially. If they are young, they inspire you to earn more and perhaps have profitable ideas. If they are older, they are supportive in more practical ways.

Mercury makes nice aspects to Neptune (your career planet) on the 16th and 17th – so there is something wonderful happening career-wise. Then on the 22nd and 23rd Mercury makes nice aspects to your love planet, Jupiter – this brings romantic opportunity for singles.

August

Best Days Overall: 2, 3, 11, 12, 20, 21, 29, 30
Most Stressful Days Overall: 1, 7, 8, 13, 14, 27, 28
Best Days for Love: 4, 5, 7, 8, 15, 25, 26
Best Days for Money: 7, 8, 15, 16, 22, 23, 25
Best Days for Career: 5, 13, 14, 23

Though this month the night side of your Horoscope is as strong as it will ever be this year, it is still not dominant. However, it is a good time to shift your energy from the career to the home, family and your emotional wellness. Career is still very important, and you can't ignore it, but you can shift some energy to the family. Indeed, with your career planet retrograde you might as well focus on the family. Career issues will need time to resolve and there's not much you can do to hasten things.

Though retrograde activity is strong this month (with up to 50 per cent of the planets travelling backwards) the important planets in your chart – Mercury, the ruler of your Horoscope and the Moon, your financial planet – are moving forward. So you're making personal and financial progress.

The month ahead seems happy. Health and energy are good until the 23rd – and even after the 23rd the stresses are coming from short-term planets and are temporary. After the 23rd make sure to get enough rest, and enhance the health in the ways mentioned in the yearly report.

The month ahead is happy in that your 3rd house – your favourite house – is ultra-powerful. The Cosmos impels you to do the things that you most love to do – read, write, study, teach and communicate. The mental faculties, always good, are even better this month. Students excel in their studies.

Venus remains in the money house until the 11th. This shows good financial intuition and a speculative kind of streak. You spend on the family and children and can earn from them as well. By the 12th, however, your short-term financial goals have been achieved and you can focus on what you love – communication and the pursuit of intellectual interests. (Even more than at the beginning of the month.)

Mercury, a very important planet in your chart, has his solstice from the 22nd to the 24th. He pauses in the heavens (in his latitudinal motion) and then changes direction (in latitude). So this brings a pause and change of direction in your personal life.

September

Best Days Overall: 7, 8, 16, 17, 26, 27
Most Stressful Days Overall: 3, 4, 9, 10, 23, 24, 30
Best Days for Love: 3, 4, 5, 11, 13, 14, 15, 21, 30
Best Days for Money: 3, 5, 6, 11, 14, 15, 18, 19, 20, 21, 25, 26, 30
Best Days for Career: 2, 9, 10, 19, 20, 29

Mars moved into your sign on August 20 and will spend the rest of the year here. There are good points and bad points to this. The good points are more personal courage, a can-do spirit, an ability to get things done quickly. You will excel in sports and exercise regimes –

achieving your personal best. The bad points are impatience (not a good thing when retrograde activity is hitting its maximum extent for the year this month), a combative spirit and temper. You do not suffer fools gladly these days. Rush and impatience can lead to accidents and injury. So make haste, but in a mindful way.

Health needs a little attention this month but this is a temporary thing caused by short-term planetary transits. There is nothing serious afoot. Those of you with pre-existing conditions can feel them more – but this will pass. Enhance the health with more rest and in the ways mentioned in the yearly report.

The planetary power this month is in your 4th house of home and family. Life is slowing down with all the retrograde activity going on so you might as well focus on the family and your emotional wellness. Those of you involved in formal psychological therapies will make much progress. You have greater insight into your moods, feelings and emotions these days. And even if you're not involved in formal thera-peutics, nature will therapize you. Old memories will surface for you to look at and re-interpret from your present state of consciousness. Many of you will enjoy researching your family history and lineage these days.

Heath and energy (and overall wellness) return on the 23rd. The Sun moves into your 5th house of creativity and you begin another of your personal pleasure peaks. Many Geminis are writers, and this is an excellent month for creative writing. Your taste in books will be more of the entertainment kind rather than educational ones. A good period to curl up with a good novel or romance and lose yourself in it.

Love is more complicated after the 23rd. Your love planet Jupiter is still retrograde and receiving stressful aspects. So love is bumpy. This might not be your fault; it is possible that the beloved is having a rough time and this is the cause of the problem. Also, you seem more distant with the beloved. You see things in opposite ways. The challenge will be to bridge your differences and find middle ground.

October

Best Days Overall: 4, 5, 13, 14, 23, 24
Most Stressful Days Overall: 1, 7, 21, 22, 27, 28
Best Days for Love: 1, 4, 5, 8, 9, 13, 14, 18, 25, 26, 27, 28
Best Days for Money: 4, 5, 8, 9, 13, 14, 16, 17, 18, 25, 26, 27
Best Days for Career: 7, 8, 17, 26

Health is good this month but a solar eclipse on the 25th can compli-cate things. It occurs in your 6th house of health and work and will bring changes to the health regime in the coming months. Sometimes there is a health scare. There can be job changes or changes in the conditions of work. If you employ others there can be employee turn-over and dramas in the lives of employees. Every solar eclipse affects siblings and sibling figures in your life. It brings drama and crises into their lives. Often these are life-changing. It will also test cars and communication equipment – they can behave erratically and often repair or replacement is needed. Students experience disruptions at school and are changing educational plans. Sometimes they change schools.

Jupiter is still retrograde, but after the 23rd he receives better aspects. Love should improve after the 23rd. Jupiter will have his solstice from the 1st to the 16th. He pauses in the heavens (in latitude) and then changes direction (in latitude). So there is a pause in your love life and then a change of direction. (We see this change of direction in other ways too: Jupiter is changing signs again at the end of the month – moving out of Aries and back into Pisces.)

We will have a Grand Trine in the Air element all month. This is wonderful for you. Air is your native element. Your communication and intellectual faculties are very much enhanced. The problem can come from too much of a good thing – too much speech, too much thinking, too much intellectual activity. The mind gets overstimulated and consumes energy that the body needs for other things – cell repair, immunity, etc. Use your mind but don't let it use you.

Mercury has another solstice from the 13th to the 16th. Don't be alarmed if your personal life seems paused. It's actually a good thing. The prelude to a change of direction.

Finance tends to the status quo this month. Your money house is mostly empty, with only the Moon moving through there on the 16th and 17th. From the 1st to the 9th and from the 25th onwards it is good to do things that build wealth. From the 9th to the 25th use spare cash to pay down debt and reduce expenses.

November

Best Days Overall: 1, 2, 10, 11, 19, 20, 28, 29
Most Stressful Days Overall: 3, 4, 17, 18, 24, 25, 30
Best Days for Love: 3, 4, 13, 14, 23, 24, 25
Best Days for Money: 3, 4, 12, 13, 14, 23, 24, 25
Best Days for Career: 3, 4, 13, 14, 23, 30

The main headline this month is the lunar eclipse of the 8th. Though it doesn't hit you directly it impacts many important planets in your chart – Mercury, Uranus and Venus. Also it is a total eclipse, which adds more strength to it. So relax and take it nice and easy over that period.

The eclipse occurs in your 12th house of spirituality and brings disruptions in a spiritual or charitable organization that you're involved with. There are dramas in the lives of guru figures. There are likely to be changes in your spiritual practice, teachings and teachers. Since the Moon is your financial planet there are likely to be financial disturbances and shake-ups. These can be severe. You have to make changes. Your financial planning was not realistic. The impact on Mercury shows that you need to redefine yourself and your self-concept – how you think of yourself and how you want others to think about you. This will lead to the creation of a new look – a new image – in the coming months. If you haven't been careful in dietary matters this eclipse can bring a detox of the body. This is not sickness, it's just the body getting rid of things that don't belong there. Since Mercury is also your family planet, there can be dramas at home and in the lives of family members. Often repairs are needed in the home. The impact on Uranus suggests shake-ups in the educational plans of college students or those looking to enter college. Plans change. Courses can change. Sometimes there is a change of school. It is not a good time for a foreign trip over this period. If you must travel, try to schedule it around the eclipse. There are disruptions in your place of worship and in the lives of worship leaders.

All in all, a pretty eventful eclipse.

Health is basically good until the 22nd. You seem focused on it as well. Jobseekers have many opportunities to find positions. After the 22nd you need to rest and relax more. Enhance the health in the ways mentioned in the yearly report.

On the 22nd the Sun enters your 7th house of love and you begin a yearly love and social peak. There are plenty of love opportunities for singles, but Jupiter, your love planet, is still retrograde so don't march down the aisle just yet.

Mercury will be in your 7th house from the 17th onwards. This shows personal popularity. You are there for your friends. You're supportive and on their side. You put their interests ahead of your own, and this makes for popularity. (In addition, the planetary power is in the Western, social sector of your chart – so this is the right attitude. Put others first.)

Finance doesn't seem a major focus this month. Your money house is basically empty – only the Moon will move through there on the 12th and 13th. This tends to the status quo. Earning power will be strongest from the 1st to the 8th and from 28th onwards – as the Moon waxes. As always, it is good to do things that expand income while the Moon waxes (make investments or save) and good to pay down debt when the Moon wanes from the 8th to the 28th.

December

Best Days Overall: 7, 8, 17, 18, 25, 26
Most Stressful Days Overall: 1, 14, 15, 16, 21, 22, 27, 28
Best Days for Love: 1, 2, 3, 11, 14, 20, 21, 22, 23, 24, 29
Best Days for Money: 1, 2, 3, 9, 10, 11, 13, 20, 21, 22, 23, 29
Best Days for Career: 1, 10, 11, 20, 27, 28

The planetary power is still mostly in the Western social sector of your chart. Even Mercury, the ruler of your Horoscope, is in the West. So, like last month, the focus is on others and their needs. Personal independence is weaker than usual, but on the other hand it isn't necessary now. Your job is to cultivate your social skills and attain objectives through consensus. Good comes to you through others and not so much by your own efforts.

You're still in the midst of a yearly love and social cycle until the 22nd. Moreover, your love planet is moving forward again and changes signs on the 21st. Love should be much improved – it goes much more smoothly. Your love planet will be in your 11th house of friends well into next year. This shows romantic opportunities through friends – perhaps they play Cupid – through online activities and social media, and often through someone you consider a friend who becomes more than that.

Your 8th house of regeneration is powerful this month as well. Thus it is a more sexually active kind of month. Whatever your age or stage in life, libido is stronger than usual. But power in the 8th house shows other things too. Though your personal finances are stable, the spouse, partner or current love is having a banner financial month. He or she will be more generous with you. This is also a good month for tax and insurance planning. For those of you of an appropriate age it is good for estate planning.

With the 8th house powerful from the 7th onwards, this is a month for 'getting rid' of unneeded or unnecessary things from your life. It is a month for giving birth (or making progress) to the ideal 'you' – the 'you' that you want to be. But before this can happen a lot of effete material needs to go. This would include needless possessions, as well as thoughts and emotional patterns that are no longer useful. The Cosmos will show you how to do this.

Health improves dramatically after the 22nd.

Cancer

⑨

THE CRAB

Birthdays from
21st June to
20th July

Personality Profile

CANCER AT A GLANCE

Element – Water

Ruling Planet – Moon
  Career Planet – Mars
  Love Planet – Saturn
  Money Planet – Sun
  Planet of Fun and Games – Pluto
  Planet of Good Fortune – Neptune
  Planet of Health and Work – Jupiter
  Planet of Home and Family Life – Venus
  Planet of Spirituality – Mercury

Colours – blue, puce, silver

Colours that promote love, romance and social harmony – black, indigo

Colours that promote earning power – gold, orange

Gems – moonstone, pearl

Metal – silver

Scents – jasmine, sandalwood

Quality – cardinal (= activity)

Quality most needed for balance – mood control

Strongest virtues – emotional sensitivity, tenacity, the urge to nurture

Deepest need – a harmonious home and family life

Characteristics to avoid – over-sensitivity, negative moods

Signs of greatest overall compatibility – Scorpio, Pisces

Signs of greatest overall incompatibility – Aries, Libra, Capricorn

Sign most helpful to career – Aries

Sign most helpful for emotional support – Libra

Sign most helpful financially – Leo

Sign best for marriage and/or partnerships – Capricorn

Sign most helpful for creative projects – Scorpio

Best Sign to have fun with – Scorpio

Signs most helpful in spiritual matters – Gemini, Pisces

Best day of the week – Monday

Understanding a Cancer

In the sign of Cancer the heavens are developing the feeling side of things. This is what a true Cancerian is all about – feelings. Where Aries will tend to err on the side of action, Taurus on the side of inaction and Gemini on the side of thought, Cancer will tend to err on the side of feeling.

Cancerians tend to mistrust logic. Perhaps rightfully so. For them it is not enough for an argument or a project to be logical – it must feel right as well. If it does not feel right a Cancerian will reject it or chafe against it. The phrase 'follow your heart' could have been coined by a Cancerian, because it describes exactly the Cancerian attitude to life.

The power to feel is a more direct – more immediate – method of knowing than thinking is. Thinking is indirect. Thinking about a thing never touches the thing itself. Feeling is a faculty that touches directly the thing or issue in question. We actually experience it. Emotional feeling is almost like another sense which humans possess – a psychic sense. Since the realities that we come in contact with during our lifetime are often painful and even destructive, it is not surprising that the Cancerian chooses to erect barriers – a shell – to protect his or her vulnerable, sensitive nature. To a Cancerian this is only common sense.

If Cancerians are in the presence of people they do not know, or find themselves in a hostile environment, up goes the shell and they feel protected. Other people often complain about this, but one must question these people's motives. Why does this shell disturb them? Is it perhaps because they would like to sting, and feel frustrated that they cannot? If your intentions are honourable and you are patient, have no fear. The shell will open up and you will be accepted as part of the Cancerian's circle of family and friends.

Thought-processes are generally analytic and dissociating. In order to think clearly we must make distinctions, comparisons and the like. But feeling is unifying and integrative.

To think clearly about something you have to distance yourself from it. To feel something you must get close to it. Once a Cancerian has accepted you as a friend he or she will hang on to you. You have to be really bad to lose the friendship of a Cancerian. If you are related to Cancerians they will never let you go no matter what you do. They will always try to maintain some kind of connection even in the most extreme circumstances.

Finance

The Cancer-born has a deep sense of what other people feel about things and why they feel as they do. This faculty is a great asset in the workplace and in the business world. Of course it is also indispensable in raising a family and building a home, but it has its uses in business. Cancerians often attain great wealth in a family business. Even if the business is not a family operation, they will treat it as one. If the Cancerian works for somebody else, then the boss is the parental figure and the co-workers are brothers and sisters. If a Cancerian is the boss, then all the workers are his or her children. Cancerians like the feeling of being providers for others. They enjoy knowing that others derive their sustenance because of what they do. It is another form of nurturing.

With Leo on their solar 2nd money house cusp, Cancerians are often lucky speculators, especially with residential property or hotels and restaurants. Resort hotels and nightclubs are also profitable for the Cancerian. Waterside properties attract them. Though they are basically conventional people, they sometimes like to earn their livelihood in glamorous ways.

The Sun, Cancer's money planet, represents an important financial message: in financial matters Cancerians need to be less moody, more stable and fixed. They cannot allow their moods – which are here today and gone tomorrow – to get in the way of their business lives. They need to develop their self-esteem and feelings of self-worth if they are to realize their greatest financial potential.

Career and Public Image

Aries rules the 10th solar career house cusp of Cancer, which indicates that Cancerians long to start their own business, to be more active publicly and politically and to be more independent. Family responsibilities and a fear of hurting other people's feelings – or getting hurt themselves – often inhibit them from attaining these goals. However, this is what they want and long to do.

Cancerians like their bosses and leaders to act freely and to be a bit self-willed. They can deal with that in a superior. They expect their leaders to be fierce on their behalf. When the Cancerian is in the position of boss or superior he or she behaves very much like a 'warlord'. Of course the wars they wage are not egocentric but in defence of those under their care. If they lack some of this fighting instinct – independence and pioneering spirit – Cancerians will have extreme difficulty in attaining their highest career goals. They will be hampered in their attempts to lead others.

Since they are so parental, Cancerians like to work with children and make great educators and teachers.

Love and Relationships

Like Taurus, Cancer likes committed relationships. Cancerians function best when the relationship is clearly defined and everyone knows his or her role. When they marry it is usually for life. They are extremely loyal to their beloved. But there is a deep little secret that most Cancerians will never admit to: commitment or partnership is really a chore and a duty to them. They enter into it because they know of no other way to create the family that they desire. Union is just a way – a means to an end – rather than an end in itself. The family is the ultimate end for them.

If you are in love with a Cancerian you must tread lightly on his or her feelings. It will take you a good deal of time to realize how deep and sensitive Cancerians can be. The smallest negativity upsets them. Your tone of voice, your irritation, a look in your eye or an expression on your face can cause great distress for the Cancerian. Your slightest gesture is registered by them and reacted to. This can be hard to get used to, but stick by your love – Cancerians make great partners once you learn how to deal with them. Your Cancerian lover will react not so much to what you say but to the way you are actually feeling at the moment.

Home and Domestic Life

This is where Cancerians really excel. The home environment and the family are their personal works of art. They strive to make things of beauty that will outlast them. Very often they succeed.

Cancerians feel very close to their family, their relatives and especially their mothers. These bonds last throughout their lives and mature as they grow older. They are very fond of those members of their family who become successful, and they are also quite attached to family heirlooms and mementos. Cancerians also love children and like to provide them with all the things they need and want. With their nurturing, feeling nature, Cancerians make very good parents – especially the Cancerian woman, who is the mother *par excellence* of the zodiac.

As a parent the Cancerian's attitude is 'my children right or wrong'. Unconditional devotion is the order of the day. No matter what a family member does, the Cancerian will eventually forgive him or her, because 'you are, after all, family'. The preservation of the institution – the tradition – of the family is one of the Cancerian's main reasons for living. They have many lessons to teach others about this.

Being so family-orientated, the Cancerian's home is always clean, orderly and comfortable. They like old-fashioned furnishings but they also like to have all the modern comforts. Cancerians love to have family and friends over, to organize parties and to entertain at home – they make great hosts.

Horoscope for 2022

Major Trends

Now that Saturn has moved away from his adverse aspect (and this move began at the end of 2020) health and energy are vastly improved. With more energy, more can be accomplished. More on this later.

Saturn, your love planet, has been in your 8th house since December 2020 and he will remain there for the year ahead. This would tend to limit (though not eliminate) the sexual urges. You are urged to focus on quality rather than quantity. In love, sexual magnetism seems the most important thing, but there's no need to overdo things. More on this later.

Neptune has been in your 9th house of religion, philosophy and theology for many years now and will be there for a few more years yet. Thus your religious beliefs are becoming spiritualized and more refined. This transit would also impact on your travel preferences. You would prefer travelling by water – cruises – rather than by air or land. With Jupiter also in your 9th house until May 11, and from October 29 to December 21, there is more travel in the year ahead in general. You will travel in various ways, but sea travel seems the most alluring. This is a year to take that cruise.

The year ahead is very successful, as will next year. On May 11 Jupiter will move into your 10th house of career and this is a classic signal of success. You have a good work ethic and superiors make a note of this.

Uranus has been in your 11th house of friends for some years now. So the social circle is changing. You meet new friends suddenly and unexpectedly, and you are drawn to unconventional types of people. Existing friends are making many, many personal changes.

Mars will spend an unusual amount of time in your spiritual 12th house. Normally he spends about a month and a half in any house, but this year he will spend over four months here. So the spiritual life will become more active, from August 20 onwards. These activities help the career. More details later.

Your areas of greatest interest this year are love and romance; sex, personal transformation and occult studies; higher education, religion, philosophy, theology and foreign travel; career (from May 11 to October 29 and from December 21st onwards); and spirituality (from August 20 onwards).

Your paths of greatest fulfilment this year are religion, philosophy, theology and foreign travel (until May 11 and from October 29 to December 21); career (from May 11 to October 29 and from December 21 onwards); and friends, groups, groups activities and science.

Health

(Please note that this is an astrological perspective on health and not a medical one. In days of yore there was no difference, both these perspectives were identical. But these days there could be quite a difference. For a medical perspective, please consult your doctor or health practitioner.)

Health is very much improved since 2021, as we mentioned. Pluto is still in a stressful alignment, but only those of you born late in the sign of Cancer (July 18 to 22) are feeling it. Most of you are not. Jupiter, your health planet, will make stressful aspects from May 11 to October 29 and from December 21 onwards. But his stresses are mild, and can still bring good and expansiveness with them. Whenever health dramatically improves, the tendency is to credit a doctor, a therapist, or a new drug or treatment – and these could very well have been the means for the improvements – but the reality is that the planetary power shifted in your favour.

Good though your health is you can make it even better. Give more attention to the following – the vulnerable areas of your Horoscope this year (the reflex points are shown in the chart opposite):

- The heart has been important for you for the last twenty or so years, ever since Pluto moved into Capricorn. Over the coming years, as Pluto moves out of Capricorn, it will become less important. The reflex to the heart is shown above. In addition, chest massage – especially of the breastbone and upper rib cage – will energize the heart and restore balance. The important thing with the heart is to avoid worry and anxiety, the two emotions that stress it out. Replace worry with faith.
- The stomach and breasts are always important for the Cancerian. Diet is very important to you – more so than for most signs. (Perhaps this is why Cancerians are such great cooks.) *What* you eat is important and should be checked with a professional. But *how* you eat is perhaps just as important. The act of eating should be elevated above mere satisfaction of appetite to an act of worship. The energy vibrations of the act should be elevated. Meals should be taken in a calm and relaxed way. Food should be blessed (in your own words) and thanks for it (in your own words) should

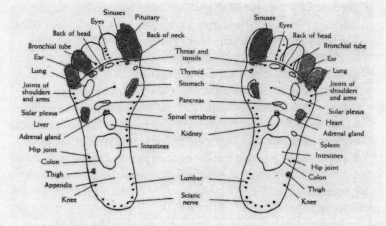

Important foot reflexology points for the year ahead

*Try to massage your feet on a regular basis – the top of the feet as well as the
bottom – but pay extra attention to the points highlighted on the chart.
When you massage, be aware of 'sore spots' as these need special attention.
It's also a good idea to massage the ankles and below them.*

be said before and after meals. This will not only elevate the
vibrations of the food – you will only get the highest and best from
it – but also the vibrations of the digestive system. Food will digest
better. It will be more nutritious. For women regular breast
examinations would be a good idea.

- The liver and thighs are areas that are also always important for
  you, Cancer. Regular thigh massage will not only strengthen the
  thighs, but the liver and lower back as well.

- The feet are important this year until May 11, and from October 29
  to December 21. Regular foot massage (see the chart above) will be
  wonderful.

- The head and face. These areas become important from May 11 to
  October 29 and from December 21 onwards – and well into next
  year, when your health planet Jupiter moves into Aries. Regular
  scalp and face massage will be beneficial. You will not only
  strengthen the scalp and face but the entire body as well.
  Craniosacral therapy is excellent for the scalp.

- The adrenals. Like the head and face these become important from May 11 to October 29 and from December 21 onwards, into 2023. The reflex point are shown above. The important thing with the adrenals is to avoid anger and fear, the two emotions that stress them out. Meditation will be a big help here.
- The musculature also gains in importance from May 11 to October 29 and from December 21 onwards. You don't need to be a body builder. You only need good muscle tone. Vigorous physical exercise is important – according to your age and stage in life. Weak or flabby muscles can knock the spine and skeleton out of alignment and this can cause all kinds of other problems.

Your health planet, Jupiter, will spend approximately half the year in the sign of Pisces. Not only that, he will travelling with Neptune, the most spiritual of all the planets. So this is a year where you will benefit from – and respond to – spiritual-healing techniques. If you feel under the weather, see a spiritual healer.

Home and Family

Home and family are always important to you, Cancer, but everything in life is relative. This year – and we have seen this for the past few years – the home and family are less important than usual. Your 4th house is basically empty, while your 10th house of career becomes very powerful after May 11. Only short-term planets will move through your 4th house this year, and their impact is temporary. Not only that but the day side of your Horoscope – the area of outer achievement – will always dominate the night side. *All* the long-term planets will be in the upper half of your Horoscope. The night side, which emphasizes home, family and emotional wellness, will get stronger as the year progresses, but will never be dominant.

I read this as you making choices to serve your family by being successful in your outer affairs and career. Making that new deal or sale, or getting that promotion, might be better long term than attending school plays or soccer games. You won't ignore your family, only serve them in a different way.

This lack of focus can be read as a good thing. It shows contentment – acceptance – there is no need to make dramatic changes at home as all is basically well. It tends to the status quo. Moves are not likely.

Venus is your family planet and, as regular readers know, she is a fast-moving planet. During the course of a year she will move through your entire Horoscope. Thus there are many short-term home and family trends that depend on where she is and the kinds of aspects she receives. These are best dealt with in the monthly reports.

Venus as your family planet shows that you work for a loving and harmonious family and family life. You like a beautiful home. There will be objects of beauty in the home and constant redecorating.

If you're planning major renovations or construction work in the home, it's probably better to wait until next year, as this year Mars will never move through your 4th house. (There will be periods this year where Mars and Venus are travelling together or making nice aspects to each other, which would be good times if you *have* to undertake renovations: March 1–9 and October 1–20 are two such periods.) Still, if such work is not urgent it would be better to wait till next year.

If you're planning to repaint or to redecorate in a cosmetic kind of way, September 29 to October 23 would be a good time. This period would also be good for buying objects of beauty for the home.

A parent or parent figure is making home renovations this year. He or she is also having a very strong love and social year. If he or she is single, serious romance and even marriage can happen. The other parent or parent figure is having a strong financial year. He or she is living the high life – travelling and enjoying all the pleasures of the senses. But moves are not likely.

Siblings and sibling figures in your life are also having strong romantic years. Marriage, or relationships that are 'like' marriage, can happen. A move can happen after May 11 and even next year.

Children and children figures probably shouldn't move this year. They should use the space they have more efficiently. A little reorganizing would do the trick.

Grandchildren, if you have them, are having a good year – there is prosperity – but things at home tend to the status quo.

Finance and Career

Your money house is not strong this year; it is not a house of power. Only short-term planets will move through there and their effects are short term. So money doesn't seem a big issue this year. Career is much more important. You have the kind of chart where a job with more status but less money would be preferable to a lower-status job that paid better.

This lack of focus on money can be read as a good thing. You seem content with finances as they are and have no need to make major changes (these will happen anyway). Earnings should be on a par with last year.

We have two solar eclipses this year, which will impact on finances (the Sun is your financial planet). There is a solar eclipse on April 30 and another one on October 25. These create financial shake-ups and force you to make course corrections in your financial life. Usually the events brought on by these eclipses show where your financial assumptions and strategies are unrealistic. This is not a big deal. You go through this twice a year and by now you know how to handle them.

The Sun is a fast-moving planet, travelling through every sign and house of your Horoscope in the course of a year. Thus there are many short-term financial trends that depend on where the Sun is and the kinds of aspects he receives. We will cover these short-term trends in the monthly reports.

Career is the main headline this year. You are going to be very successful. Jupiter, as we mentioned earlier, will move through your 10th house of career from May 11 to October 29 and from December 21 onwards. This transit brings prestigious job opportunities and a general expansion of your career horizons. Jupiter is also your health and work planet. So, one way to read this is that staying healthy is your real mission. It can also indicate career opportunities in the health field. Also, as was mentioned, you have a good work ethic and this brings success.

Your career planet, Mars, will spend an unusual amount of time this year in your 12th house of spirituality. This will be from August 20 onwards. This signals a desire for a more spiritual type of career –

something more meaningful to the soul. But it also tends to show that involvement in charities or altruistic activities would foster the career. These things are good in themselves, but they would also boost the career as a side effect (perhaps by allowing you to make important connections or by burnishing your professional profile).

Love and Social Life

Your 7th house of love has been strong for many years, and especially so from 2018 to 2020. This year it is a bit less prominent, but it is still an important focus.

With Saturn as your love planet you tend to be conservative in love. Traditional. But since last year, when Saturn moved into Aquarius, you seem more experimental in love. You like the good provider and the ambitious person, but you also like them to be more unconventional – more exciting. You would find scientists, astronomers, astrologers, programmers and inventors alluring. You like romantic partners who are a bit off the beaten path.

Your love planet rules from your 8th house of regeneration. This would signal an attraction to wealth. Those of you already in a relationship are seeing the current love prospering – they are very money focused. This is perhaps good, because it offsets your own lack of financial focus this year.

Your love planet in the 8th house indicates the importance of sexual magnetism. The person can be a genius, rich and successful, but if the sexual magnetism is not there it is unlikely to work between you. On the other hand, a good sexual magnetism alone cannot hold a relationship together. Yes, good sex will cover many sins in a relationship, but only for so long. Other things are needed.

Pluto, the generic ruler of sex, has been in your 7th house for around twenty years now. This reinforces the importance of sexual magnetism.

Singles are unlikely to marry this year. They are better off with serial relationships – where they can explore and experiment with love. The ruler of your 5th house of fun and creativity in your house of love also works against marriage. You want fun in love these days (and perhaps are meeting these kinds of people). You're not interested in dealing with the rough spots and tough times.

There are romantic opportunities through online dating sites and social media. Also, by getting involved in groups and organizations. Romantic opportunities can arise at funerals, wakes, or as you comfort a bereaved person.

The area of friendships is also very active this year. There is much ferment happening. Many friendships are being tested. Often this is not because of the relationship itself, but because of the personal dramas and changes happening in the lives of friends. Many of them are having life-changing experiences – in some cases surgery or near-death kinds of experiences. Friendships can end this year, but new ones will come into the picture as well. New friends can manifest at any time in any place. Often when you least expect it.

By the time Uranus is finished with you – in the next few years – you will be in a new social circle.

Self-improvement

The year ahead will be a strong spiritual period – especially from August 20 onwards. Mars, your career planet, will spend many months in your 12th house.

There are many messages here. If you are in a worldly career, you can enhance it with your spiritual practice and understanding. Also, as we mentioned, your involvement with charities, spiritual organizations and altruistic causes will enhance the career.

But another way to read this is that your spiritual practice, your spiritual growth, *is* the actual career at this time. Your true mission.

Mars in your 12th house favours an active kind of spirituality. There is a desire to express your spiritual ideals and understanding through constructive actions. It's not just about meditating and contemplating. It's not just about 'contacting the silence'. It's about bringing spiritual values into activity. Thus, it favours paths such as Hatha yoga (the yoga of the physical body) and Karma yoga (the yoga of action). You should read up on these things as much as possible.

Mars in the 12th house is a picture of the spiritual warrior. There is a wonderful book called *The Way of the Peaceful Warrior* by Dan Millman. War is waged but in a peaceful kind of way. Many of the problems happening in the world today (perhaps *all* the problems we see) are not flesh-and-blood conflicts. This is only where things play out. They are spiritual conflicts – conflicts between invisible spiritual forces. The way to overcome these problems is by spiritual means. Many of you will be called to join the conflict.

Mercury is your spiritual planet. This shows that though you are a natural 'Bhakti' person – naturally drawn to the path of love and devotion – you need some logic and rationality to back it up. You need a more rational approach to the spirit. Relying on feelings alone is highly unstable. In a good mood you see God and the heavenly choirs. But in a bad mood you can become atheistic. Rationality will keep you stable. You will maintain your faith regardless of the mood.

Mercury is a fast-moving planet, moving through all the signs and houses of your Horoscope in any given year. So there are many short-term spiritual trends that are best dealt with in the monthly reports.

Mercury normally goes retrograde three times a year. This year this will happen from January 14 to February 3, May 10 to June 2, and from September 10 to October 1. These are times to carefully verify your intuition and dreams. You might be misinterpreting them. Take time to resolve your doubts.

Month-by-month Forecasts

January

Best Days Overall: 6, 7, 16, 17, 25, 26
Most Stressful Days Overall: 2, 3, 8, 9, 23, 24, 29, 30
Best Days for Love: 2, 3, 4, 5, 11, 12, 13, 14, 21, 22, 23, 24, 29, 30, 31
Best Days for Money: 2, 3, 6, 11, 12, 16, 18, 19, 23, 25
Best Days for Career: 1, 8, 9, 19, 29

Though health has been much improved recently, and certainly over what it was in 2019 and 2020, this month, because of short-term planets, it needs watching. So, as always, make sure to get enough rest. Foot massage and spiritual healing methods will be beneficial. This month give more attention to the heart. Chest massage and massage of the heart reflex will be very helpful. Since Mars is in your

6th house of health until the 25th, head and face massage, vigorous physical exercise and massage of the adrenal reflex will be beneficial. These are all temporary measures. By the 20th you should see a dramatic improvement in health and energy.

The planetary power is overwhelmingly in the West this month – at least 80 per cent, sometimes 90 per cent, of the planets are in the Western social sector. Your 7th house of love and social activities is very powerful, while your 1st house of self is basically empty (only the Moon will move through there on the 16th and 17th). So this is not a time for personal independence or self-assertion. It's about getting on with others and attaining your goals by consensus. Put others first and your good will come to you naturally and normally.

You are in a yearly love and social peak until the 20th. But love will be good even after that too. Singles seem to be dating more than usual and have many romantic options. Those already in a relationship are mixing with all kinds of different people.

Your financial planet, the Sun, will be in the 7th house until the 20th. This would show the importance of social contacts in finance. Friends are rich and provide good investment opportunities. Your social grace (which you are cultivating this month) plays a big role in finance. The financial planet in Capricorn is good in that it indicates sound financial judgement – a realistic perspective on finances. This is a very good transit for setting up long-term savings and investment plans. After the 20th your financial planet moves into Aquarius and this favours more experimentation. It favours start-ups and the tech and online world. You prosper this month by prospering others. As you do this, your own supply will come naturally and normally by the karmic law.

February

Best Days Overall: 2, 3, 12, 13, 21, 22, 23
Most Stressful Days Overall: 5, 6, 19, 20, 26, 27
Best Days for Love: 1, 7, 8, 9, 10, 11, 17, 18, 19, 20, 26, 27, 28
Best Days for Money: 1, 2, 3, 9, 10, 12, 13, 14, 15, 16, 21, 22, 23
Best Days for Career: 5, 6, 7, 8, 17, 18, 26, 27

Health is much improved over last month. You can enhance it further with foot massage and spiritual-healing techniques.

Mars, your career planet, moved into your 7th house on January 25 and will spend the rest of this month there. This gives many messages. First off, avoid power struggles in love. If you can manage this, the transit is a good signal for love. It shows that it is high on your priorities. Your mission this month is your marriage and friends – to be there for them. There are romantic opportunities with important, powerful people – people above you in status. Your career is boosted through social means – by attending or hosting the right parties and gatherings. Much of your socializing this month is career related.

Your financial planet is in your 8th house of regeneration until the 18th. This is a wonderful financial signal for the spouse, partner or current love. He or she is having a strong financial month – and you are probably involved in this. The Sun in the 8th house favours tax and insurance planning. For those of you of an appropriate age it favours estate planning. It is good to go through your possessions and get rid of things that you don't need or use. Sell them or give them to charity. Clear the decks for the new and better that wants to come in. If you have good business ideas, this is a time to attract outside investors to your projects. It is also a good time for paying off debt, or for taking on loans, depending on your need.

Your 9th house has been powerful all this year so far, and it becomes even more powerful after the 18th. Many of you will travel. Many will have religious or philosophical breakthroughs. College-level students are successful in their studies and those seeking to enter college have good fortune.

There is a brief financial crisis on the 3rd and 4th, but it passes quickly. The financial planet in your 9th house from the 18th is positive for earnings.

Career is starting to become more important, as from January 25 *all* the planets (with the exception of the Moon) are in the upper half, the day side of your chart. So it is time to start focusing on your outer goals.

March

Best Days Overall: 2, 3, 11, 12, 13, 21, 22, 30, 31
Most Stressful Days Overall: 4, 5, 18, 19, 25, 26
Best Days for Love: 1, 9, 10, 18, 19, 25, 26, 27, 28
Best Days for Money: 2, 3, 11, 12, 14, 15, 21, 22, 23, 30, 31
Best Days for Career: 4, 5, 9, 18, 19, 27, 28

Until the 20th health is excellent. It is good even after that date, but it does need more watching. The problem is short-term stress caused by short-term planets. Enhance the health by maintaining high energy levels and through foot massage and spiritual-healing techniques. After the 20th, chest massage and massage of the heart reflex will be good. Swimming and water sports are excellent exercises these days.

Though your money house is basically empty, and finance doesn't seem a big deal, the month ahead is prosperous. Your financial planet, the Sun, is in the expansive 9th house – a beneficent house – until the 20th. Then he crosses the Mid-heaven and enters your 10th house, which is also good for finances. From the 4th to the 6th the Sun will travel with Jupiter, bringing a nice payday. On the 11th and 12th he travels with Neptune, the ruler of your 9th house and a beneficent planet in your chart: more financial increase. Foreigners or foreign companies can be important in finance this month. When the Sun enters your 10th house on the 20th there can be pay rises – official or unofficial – happening. Bosses, elders, parents and parent figures are supportive of your financial goals. Your good career reputation brings financial opportunity.

The Sun's move into your 10th house initiates a yearly career peak. Career should be very good. You seem very focused. All the planets are still in the day side of the chart. This is the kind of period where success and outer achievement leads to emotional and family harmony.

There are some short-term home and family dramas from the 18th to the 20th. But these will pass quickly – keep your focus on the career.

Your career planet Mars moves into your 8th house on the 6th and spends the rest of the month there. Thus there can be dramas with parents, parent figures and bosses. Perhaps there is some surgery on the cards, or near-death kinds of experiences. Your career planet in the

8th house shows that you are working to create the career of your dreams – to completely transform things. You should make progress here this month.

April

Best Days Overall: 8, 9, 17, 18, 25, 26
Most Stressful Days Overall: 1, 2, 15, 16, 21, 22, 28, 29
Best Days for Love: 5, 6, 8, 15, 16, 17, 18, 21, 22, 23, 24, 25, 26, 27
Best Days for Money: 1, 2, 8, 9, 10, 11, 17, 18, 20, 21, 26, 27, 30
Best Days for Career: 1, 2, 5, 6, 17, 25, 26, 28, 29

You are still in a very successful period this month, Cancer, still in a yearly career peak. So focus on the career and let home and family issues go for a while. You can serve your family best by being successful in the outer world. There are many ways to serve your family and this is a legitimate way.

Finances are still good. Your financial planet remains in your career house until the 20th. This shows, like last month, the financial favour of bosses, elders, parents and parent figures. It also indicates pay rises – official or unofficial. A solar eclipse on the 30th will cause some financial shake-ups but these will work out well. The changes need to be made. Your financial thinking hasn't been realistic.

This eclipse occurs in your 11th house and brings dramas in the lives of friends; perhaps friendships are being tested. There are shake-ups in trade or professional organizations that you're involved with. High-tech equipment and gadgetry can behave erratically, and often repairs or replacement is necessary. Keep your anti-virus, anti-hacking software up to date, and don't open suspicious-looking e-mails. Have all your important files backed up. There can be dramas in the lives of the money people in your life as well. A parent or parent figure is also making important financial changes. The spouse, partner or current love can experience job changes. He or she will be making important changes to the health regime too. Children and children figures in your life are having career changes. Siblings and sibling figures are going through spiritual changes.

Jupiter, your health planet, is travelling with Neptune from the 1st to the 17th. Spiritual healing has been powerful all year, but especially so right now. If you feel under the weather, see a spiritual healer. Health will improve after the 20th. In the meantime, continue to massage the chest and heart reflex point.

The Sun's entry into your 11th house on the 20th is good for finance. The 11th house is a beneficent house. But the eclipse is shaking things up.

May

Best Days Overall: 5, 6, 14, 15, 23, 24
Most Stressful Days Overall: 12, 13, 19, 25, 26
Best Days for Love: 3, 4, 7, 8, 13, 16, 17, 19, 21, 22, 31
Best Days for Money: 6, 7, 8, 9, 10, 11, 16, 20, 25, 30
Best Days for Career: 7, 8, 9, 17, 18, 25, 26

Last month was successful and this month will be even more so. Jupiter makes a major move into your 10th house of career on the 11th. Venus will be in the 10th house from the 3rd to the 28th and Mars will enter there on the 25th. So there is career expansion and elevation. Your horizons are expanded. Things that didn't seem possible before are now very possible. Your family seems very supportive of the career as well. Perhaps they see it as a 'family project'. The family as a whole also seems elevated and successful this month.

Health will need some attention this month. Your health planet, Jupiter, changing signs signals a change in health needs and attitudes. Until the 11th enhance the health with foot massage and spiritual-healing techniques. But after that, scalp, face and head massage will be beneficial. Massage of the adrenal reflex will be good too, as will vigorous physical exercise. As always, the most important thing is to maintain high energy levels – this is always the first defence against disease.

We have a lunar eclipse this month, on the 16th. It occurs in your 5th house and so impacts children and children figures in your life. They (and you) will need to redefine themselves – the image and self-concept – the way that they think of themselves and the way that they want others to think of them. For you, this is pretty normal. You go through this twice a year. For the children it could be more traumatic. All of you should reduce your schedules over that period. There can be detoxes of the body for you and the children. This is not sickness, though the symptoms can seem that way. It is only the body getting rid of what doesn't belong there. A parent or parent figure is forced to make important financial changes. Siblings and sibling figures should drive more carefully. If they are students, there could be changes to educational plans and sometimes even changes of schools.

Finances should be good this month. The Sun is moving through the 11th house until the 21st. The Sun in Taurus signals sound financial judgement. The Sun will travel with Uranus on the 4th and 5th and this can bring some financial change. You and the spouse, partner or current love need to cooperate financially. On the 21st the financial planet moves into your spiritual 12th house and stays there for the rest of the month. Thus your financial intuition becomes important. Financial guidance will come in dreams or through psychics, tarot readers, astrologers or spiritual channels. Spirit is active in your financial life. Concerned about it.

June

Best Days Overall: 1, 2, 3, 11, 12, 19, 20, 28, 29, 30
Most Stressful Days Overall: 3, 9, 10, 15, 16, 21, 22
Best Days for Love: 2, 3, 6, 7, 10, 15, 16, 18, 26, 29, 30
Best Days for Money: 4, 5, 9, 10, 13, 18, 21, 28, 29
Best Days for Career: 4, 13, 14, 21, 22

Career is still very successful this month, but a pause and change of direction on the 1st and 2nd might be good. This is what your career planet is doing in the heavens.

The month ahead is very spiritual. This can pose some challenges as the career house is very strong too. Often worldly goals and spiritual goals are at odds. Your job is to integrate them. One can be spiritual and still have worldly success. They need not conflict.

The month ahead is prosperous. The Sun, your financial planet, remains in your 12th house until the 21st. So, like the latter part of last month, follow intuition – the short cut to wealth. True intuition – even for a millisecond – is worth many years of hard labour. It will be a good period to go deeper into the spiritual laws of affluence. You will probably be more charitable too. Involvement with charities and altruistic causes can also enhance the bottom line. Important contacts can be made. On the 21st the Sun crosses your Ascendant and enters your own sign, which brings prosperity. Financial windfalls happen. Financial opportunity seeks you out. There's nothing special that you need to do, just go about your daily business. The money people in your life seem devoted to you – on your side and favourably disposed. Expensive personal items are likely to come. You spend on yourself. You adopt the image of wealth. People see you as prosperous.

The Sun's move into your sign is good for both the health and your personal appearance. It gives charisma and star quality. The opposite sex takes notice. The Moon, your ruling planet, will be in your sign for triple the normal time this month. Usually she stays in a sign for two days. This month she is in your sign for six. This too enhances the personal appearance, self-esteem and self-confidence.

Love seems happy until the 21st. Saturn, your love planet, is receiving positive aspects. However, Saturn goes retrograde on the 4th, so there can be delays in love and uncertainties. Still, you can enjoy things for what they are without projecting too much into the future.

July

Best Days Overall: 8, 9, 16, 17, 26, 27
Most Stressful Days Overall: 6, 7, 12, 13, 18, 19, 20
Best Days for Love: 6, 7, 12, 13, 15, 24, 26
Best Days for Money: 1, 2, 8, 9, 10, 11, 17, 18, 19, 28, 29
Best Days for Career: 2, 3, 12, 13, 18, 19, 20, 21, 22

A happy and prosperous month ahead, Cancer, enjoy. Your 1st house is even more powerful than last month. And you are in a period of maximum personal independence. Since last month the Eastern sector of self dominates the Western sector of others. It is time to have things your own way. Time to focus on number one. Time to take personal responsibility for your happiness. It's really up to you. Now is the time to make the changes that need to be made for your happiness. Later on, when the planets shift Westward again, it will be more difficult. Personal initiative matters.

Prosperity increases this month. Your financial planet is still in your sign until the 22nd. So financial windfalls and opportunities are still happening, and wealth is pursuing you. You look and feel rich and people are still seeing you that way – a prosperous person. On the 23rd the Sun will enter your money house – his own sign and house. He is very powerful here, so earning power will be very strong. Also, you begin a yearly financial peak. The new Moon of the 28th is an excellent financial day. More importantly, it will bring financial clarity. All the information that you need to make good financial decisions will come to you in natural ways.

The personal appearance also shines this month. The Sun in your sign, like last month, brings charisma and star quality. Mercury will be in your sign from the 5th to the 19th. He will bring glamour to the image – a spiritual quality – an unearthly kind of beauty. On the 18th Venus also moves into your sign. She also brings beauty, charm and social grace. She brings a sense of style and elegance to the image. This will help the love life, but Saturn, your love planet, is still retrograde, so take things slowly in romantic matters.

Career is starting to ease up this month. Jupiter is still in your 10th house but he is retrograde, signalling that many career issues need time to resolve. Mars, your actual career planet, moves into your 11th house on the 5th. This shows that social connections, high-tech expertise and online activities boost the career. Friends seem successful and helpful. You can boost the career through involvement with trade and professional organizations.

Health is good, but if you want to enhance it further, get into exercise and head, face and scalp massage. Avoid anger and fear to boost your adrenal glands. Heat-oriented therapies are good as well.

August

Best Days Overall: 4, 5, 13, 14, 22, 23
Most Stressful Days Overall: 2, 3, 9, 10, 15, 16, 29, 30
Best Days for Love: 3, 4, 5, 9, 10, 12, 15, 21, 25, 26, 30
Best Days for Money: 7, 8, 15, 16, 25, 26
Best Days for Career: 1, 9, 10, 15, 16, 18, 19, 29

Though the night side of your Horoscope is not dominant, it's about as strong as it ever will be this year. Career and outer objectives are still the priority, but you can shift some attention – not a lot – to the home, family and your emotional wellness. In your 10th house of career Jupiter is still retrograde, so many career issues – though positive – will need more time to develop.

Health is good this month. You can enhance it further with exercise, scalp, face and head massage, craniosacral therapy and massage of the adrenal reflexes.

Retrograde activity increases this month. Until the 24th 40 per cent of the planets are travelling backwards; after the 24th half will be retrograde. So events are slowing down. There is much indecision in the world. Patience is the keyword these days.

Two very important planets in your chart never go retrograde – the Sun, your financial planet, and the Moon, the ruler of your Horoscope. So finances don't seem affected this month. In fact the month ahead is prosperous. You're still very much in a yearly financial peak until the 23rd. You spend on the children and children figures in your life, but they can also be a catalyst for earnings. When they are younger they can inspire you to earn more, and when they are older they can contribute in more material ways. Your family planet Venus will enter your money house on the 12th. This brings good family support and the help of friends in finance.

The Moon's forward motion shows that personal goals are moving forward.

On the 23rd, the financial planet moves into Virgo, your 3rd house of communications. This favours writing, teaching, sales, marketing, advertising and PR. Retailing and trading are also favourable. Whatever it is you do, it's important to get the word out about your product.

Love is stressful this month but should improve after the 23rd. Saturn, your love planet, is not only retrograde but receives stressful aspects. Love needs patience these days.

Children and children figures have wonderful job opportunities these days, but some research is needed: these jobs might not be all that they appear.

September

Best Days Overall: 1, 2, 9, 10, 18, 19, 20, 28, 29
Most Stressful Days Overall: 5, 6, 11, 12, 26, 27
Best Days for Love: 4, 5, 6, 7, 8, 13, 14, 15, 16, 17, 26, 27
Best Days for Money: 3, 5, 6, 7, 8, 11, 14, 15, 21, 23, 24, 30
Best Days for Career: 7, 8, 11, 12, 16, 17, 26, 27

A lot of positive things are happening in the world this month, and since you too are part of the world it is good for you as well. We have two Grand Trines this month. Even one is rare, now we have two. One is in the element of Earth (and we had this last month too); the other is in Air. This shows an ease of energy flow in material and intellectual matters. Organizing skills, communication skills and intellectual faculties are much enhanced – in the world and in yourself.

Though the night side of your Horoscope is far from dominant, it is now at its maximum power for the year. You are in the magical midnight hour of your year. Good to refresh and regroup your energies and plans. Good to shift some energy from the career, which is still very positive, to the home and family and to the activities of night. Pursue career goals through 'interior' actions, through visualization and meditation and constructive dreaming – dreaming that is under the will. Overt actions will follow as surely as night follows day. But perhaps not immediately.

Health needs more attention after the 23rd. There is nothing serious amiss, only temporary stresses caused by short-term planets. As always, make sure to maintain high energy levels and enhance the health with exercise, head, face and scalp massage and massage of the adrenal reflexes. More attention to the heart would also be good. Chest massage and massage of the heart reflex will be a big help.

Finances should be good this month. Until the 23rd sales, marketing, advertising and PR are favoured. Good use of the media is important. Writers, teachers and sales people should do well. The financial judgement is sound. After the 23rd, as your financial planet moves into your 4th house, earning money from home and through the family and family connections is favoured. You spend more on the home and family but will earn from there too. For investors this transit favours residential real estate, hotels, motels, restaurants and the food business in general. On the 10th and 11th the Sun makes nice aspects to Uranus. This favours technology, computers and the online world. It is a good period to attract outside investors to projects. Also good for taking on loans or paying down debt.

October

Best Days Overall: 7, 16, 17, 25, 26
Most Stressful Days Overall: 2, 3, 9, 10, 23, 24, 30
Best Days for Love: 2, 3, 4, 5, 13, 14, 23, 24, 25, 30
Best Days for Money: 4, 5, 8, 9, 13, 14, 18, 19, 25, 26, 27
Best Days for Career: 5, 9, 10, 14, 15, 24

Last month saw the maximum amount of retrograde activity for the year. This month retrograde activity is still strong but is getting less and less. By the end of the month, it will be half what it was last month. So there are still delays, but movement is happening.

The two planets that are involved in your career – Mars and Jupiter – are both retrograde this month. So, you can focus on the home and family (your true love) without missing out. Home, family and emotional wellness are the foundations upon which successful careers stand; it is time to work on these foundations.

This is a month for psychological breakthroughs and insights. The past always lives with us, but it need not deter us from our goals. They can be redefined and reinterpreted in a healthier way. Even historical events – things that affected the whole world – can be redefined and reinterpreted.

Health still needs attention until the 23rd. Review our discussion of this last month. You will see dramatic improvement after that date. It will be as if some 'cosmic switch' was thrown and energy returns.

The month ahead is happy. On the 23rd, as the Sun enters your 5th house of fun and creativity, you begin one of your yearly personal pleasure peaks. It is time to enjoy life. Time to enjoy your children and children figures in your life. Time to become a bit more childlike yourself. It is the children (and the inner child) that know how to be happy.

We have a solar eclipse on the 25th that occurs in your 5th house. Its effect is relatively mild on you personally but it does impact your children and children figures in your life and they should reduce their schedules over this time. Some of the crises they face are the normal ones that happen growing up – puberty, first love, going to school, etc. But for them it is an upheaval. A parent or parent figure is forced to make financial changes and adjustments. And this is so for you as well. Though you are in a speculative mood these days – especially after the 23rd – better to avoid this during the eclipse period.

November

Best Days Overall: 3, 4, 12, 13, 22, 23, 30
Most Stressful Days Overall: 5, 6, 19, 20, 26, 27
Best Days for Love: 1, 2, 3, 4, 10, 11, 13, 19, 20, 23, 24, 26, 27, 28, 29
Best Days for Money: 3, 4, 13, 14, 15, 16, 23
Best Days for Career: 1, 2, 5, 6, 10, 11, 19, 20, 28, 29

The lunar eclipse of the 8th is probably the main headline of the month. It is very powerful. Not only is it a total eclipse, but it impacts on many other planets – Mercury, Uranus and Venus. So its effects are strong personally and for the world at large.

Now every lunar eclipse affects you strongly. The Moon is the ruler of your Horoscope. So every lunar eclipse brings challenges, Cancer, forcing you to redefine yourself, your image and self-concept. It forces you to change the way you think of yourself and the way you want others to think of you. So a reduced schedule is definitely called for. Things that must be done should be done, but non-essentials (especially if they are stressful) should be rescheduled. The spouse, partner or current love has social dramas. Friendships get tested (this eclipse happens in your 11th house). There are dramas in the lives of friends. High-tech gadgetry can behave erratically and often repairs are necessary. The impact on Mercury brings spiritual changes and upheavals in a spiritual or charitable organization that you're involved with. There are dramas in the lives of gurus and guru figures. Cars and communication equipment get tested. There are dramas in the family and in the lives of family members. Repairs could be needed in the home. Financial changes are happening for you and siblings and sibling figures. The dream life is apt to be disturbing as well, but such dreams have no real significance during this period: they merely reflect the turmoil on the astral plane.

In spite of the eclipse you seem happy this month. You're still in a yearly personal pleasure peak until the 22nd. A parent or parent figure is having a strong financial month and health is good.

Speculations, though you are in the mood for it, are not advisable this period – especially around the period of the lunar eclipse. However, finance should be good and the changes you make should also be good. Until the 22nd you spend on the children and children figures in your life. You earn and spend in happy ways. On the 22nd, as the financial planet enters Sagittarius, earnings should increase.

December

Best Days Overall: 1, 9, 10, 11, 19, 20, 27, 28
Most Stressful Days Overall: 2, 3, 17, 18, 23, 24, 29, 30
Best Days for Love: 2, 3, 7, 8, 14, 17, 18, 23, 24, 25, 26
Best Days for Money: 1, 2, 3, 11, 12, 13, 20, 21, 22, 23, 29
Best Days for Career: 2, 3, 7, 8, 17, 18, 25, 26, 29, 30

The planetary power is mostly in the Western, social sector this month – it's been this way for a few months, but now it is at its maximum extent. This is a time to focus on your social skills and put others and their needs ahead of your own. Your way might not be the best way these days. (The planetary energy is supporting others over you.) This is a month to make progress through the practice of social grace and gaining consensus. It is not a time for personal assertion or initiative.

Take care of others and your own good will come to you naturally and normally.

Health is good this month, but after the 22nd it will need watching. Health is further complicated by the fact that your health planet, Jupiter, hovers between two signs – Pisces and Aries. So, until the 21st (while your health planet is in Pisces) enhance the health with foot massage (which strengthens the whole body) and spiritual-healing techniques. After the 21st scalp, face, head massage, massage of the adrenal reflexes and exercise will be powerful. (In fact, you should do a little of both this month.)

Love will be active and happy this month. Your love planet, Saturn, is moving forward and your 7th house of love becomes very powerful from the 22nd onwards. Also, as we mentioned, the Western, social sector of your chart is very strong all month. So singles have many, many opportunities to meet new people. The social judgement is good. (Next month will also be positive for love.)

Jupiter moves into your 10th house of career again on the 21st and will be there well into next year. So career ends the year successfully (and it will be even more successful next year). Your career planet, Mars, is not only retrograde – creating some delays and glitches – but also 'out of bounds'. In career matters you seem outside your normal orbit.

This is also the case in other areas of life – it seems to be the fad on a world level. Two other planets are also 'out of bounds' – Venus and Mercury. So family members are going outside their normal orbit. You are this way in spiritual matters and in your intellectual interests. Thinking outside the box – living outside the body – seems helpful to you.

Leo

♌

THE LION

Birthdays from
21st July to
21st August

Personality Profile

LEO AT A GLANCE

Element – Fire

Ruling Planet – Sun
 Career Planet – Venus
 Love Planet – Uranus
 Money Planet – Mercury
 Planet of Health and Work – Saturn
 Planet of Home and Family Life – Pluto

Colours – gold, orange, red

Colours that promote love, romance and social harmony – black, indigo, ultramarine blue

Colours that promote earning power – yellow, yellow-orange

Gems – amber, chrysolite, yellow diamond

Metal – gold

Scents – bergamot, frankincense, musk, neroli

Quality – fixed (= stability)

Quality most needed for balance – humility

Strongest virtues – leadership ability, self-esteem and confidence, generosity, creativity, love of joy

Deepest needs – fun, elation, the need to shine

Characteristics to avoid – arrogance, vanity, bossiness

Signs of greatest overall compatibility – Aries, Sagittarius

Signs of greatest overall incompatibility – Taurus, Scorpio, Aquarius

Sign most helpful to career – Taurus

Sign most helpful for emotional support – Scorpio

Sign most helpful financially – Virgo

Sign best for marriage and/or partnerships – Aquarius

Sign most helpful for creative projects – Sagittarius

Best Sign to have fun with – Sagittarius

Signs most helpful in spiritual matters – Aries, Cancer

Best day of the week – Sunday

Understanding a Leo

When you think of Leo, think of royalty – then you'll get the idea of what the Leo character is all about and why Leos are the way they are. It is true that, for various reasons, some Leo-born do not always express this quality – but even if not they should like to do so.

A monarch rules not by example (as does Aries) nor by consensus (as do Capricorn and Aquarius) but by personal will. Will is law. Personal taste becomes the style that is imitated by all subjects. A monarch is somehow larger than life. This is how a Leo desires to be.

When you dispute the personal will of a Leo it is serious business. He or she takes it as a personal affront, an insult. Leos will let you know that their will carries authority and that to disobey is demeaning and disrespectful.

A Leo is king (or queen) of his or her personal domain. Subordinates, friends and family are the loyal and trusted subjects. Leos rule with benevolent grace and in the best interests of others. They have a powerful presence; indeed, they are powerful people. They seem to attract attention in any social gathering. They stand out because they are stars in their domain. Leos feel that, like the Sun, they are made to shine and rule. Leos feel that they were born to special privilege and royal prerogatives – and most of them attain this status, at least to some degree.

The Sun is the ruler of this sign, and when you think of sunshine it is very difficult to feel unhealthy or depressed. Somehow the light of the Sun is the very antithesis of illness and apathy. Leos love life. They also love to have fun; they love drama, music, the theatre and amusements of all sorts. These are the things that give joy to life. If – even in their best interests – you try to deprive Leos of their pleasures, good food, drink and entertainment, you run the serious risk of depriving them of the will to live. To them life without joy is no life at all.

Leos epitomize humanity's will to power. But power in and of itself – regardless of what some people say – is neither good nor evil. Only when power is abused does it become evil. Without power even good things cannot come to pass. Leos realize this and are uniquely qualified to wield power. Of all the signs, they do it most naturally. Capricorn,

the other power sign of the zodiac, is a better manager and administrator than Leo – much better. But Leo outshines Capricorn in personal
grace and presence. Leo loves power, whereas Capricorn assumes
power out of a sense of duty.

Finance

Leos are great leaders but not necessarily good managers. They are
better at handling the overall picture than the nitty-gritty details of
business. If they have good managers working for them they can
become exceptional executives. They have vision and a lot of
creativity.

Leos love wealth for the pleasures it can bring. They love an opulent
lifestyle, pomp and glamour. Even when they are not wealthy they live
as if they are. This is why many fall into debt, from which it is sometimes difficult to emerge.

Leos, like Pisceans, are generous to a fault. Very often they want to
acquire wealth solely so that they can help others economically. Wealth
to Leo buys services and managerial ability. It creates jobs for others
and improves the general well-being of those around them. Therefore
– to a Leo – wealth is good. Wealth is to be enjoyed to the fullest.
Money is not to be left to gather dust in a mouldy bank vault but to be
enjoyed, spread around, used. So Leos can be quite reckless in their
spending.

With the sign of Virgo on Leo's 2nd money house cusp, Leo needs
to develop some of Virgo's traits of analysis, discrimination and purity
when it comes to money matters. They must learn to be more careful
with the details of finance (or to hire people to do this for them). They
have to be more cost-conscious in their spending habits. Generally,
they need to manage their money better. Leos tend to chafe under
financial constraints, yet these constraints can help Leos to reach their
highest financial potential.

Leos like it when their friends and family know that they can depend
on them for financial support. They do not mind – and even enjoy –
lending money, but they are careful that they are not taken advantage
of. From their 'regal throne' Leos like to bestow gifts upon their family
and friends and then enjoy the good feelings these gifts bring to every-

body. Leos love financial speculations and – when the celestial influences are right – are often lucky.

Career and Public Image

Leos like to be perceived as wealthy, for in today's world wealth often equals power. When they attain wealth they love having a large house with lots of land and animals.

At their jobs Leos excel in positions of authority and power. They are good at making decisions – on a grand level – but they prefer to leave the details to others. Leos are well respected by their colleagues and subordinates, mainly because they have a knack for understanding and relating to those around them. Leos usually strive for the top positions even if they have to start at the bottom and work hard to get there. As might be expected of such a charismatic sign, Leos are always trying to improve their work situation. They do so in order to have a better chance of advancing to the top.

On the other hand, Leos do not like to be bossed around or told what to do. Perhaps this is why they aspire so for the top – where they can be the decision-makers and need not take orders from others.

Leos never doubt their success and focus all their attention and efforts on achieving it. Another great Leo characteristic is that – just like good monarchs – they do not attempt to abuse the power or success they achieve. If they do so this is not wilful or intentional. Usually they like to share their wealth and try to make everyone around them join in their success.

Leos are – and like to be perceived as – hard-working, well-established individuals. It is definitely true that they are capable of hard work and often manage great things. But do not forget that, deep down inside, Leos really are fun-lovers.

Love and Relationships

Generally, Leos are not the marrying kind. To them relationships are good while they are pleasurable. When the relationship ceases to be pleasurable a true Leo will want out. They always want to have the freedom to leave. That is why Leos excel at love affairs rather than commitment. Once married, however, Leo is faithful – even if some Leos have a tendency to marry more than once in their lifetime. If you are in love with a Leo, just show him or her a good time – travel, go to casinos and clubs, the theatre and discos. Wine and dine your Leo love – it is expensive but worth it and you will have fun.

Leos generally have an active love life and are demonstrative in their affections. They love to be with other optimistic and fun-loving types like themselves, but wind up settling with someone more serious, intellectual and unconventional. The partner of a Leo tends to be more political and socially conscious than he or she is, and more libertarian. When you marry a Leo, mastering the freedom-loving tendencies of your partner will definitely become a life-long challenge – and be careful that Leo does not master you.

Aquarius sits on Leo's 7th house of love cusp. Thus if Leos want to realize their highest love and social potential they need to develop a more egalitarian, Aquarian perspective on others. This is not easy for Leo, for 'the king' finds his equals only among other 'kings'. But perhaps this is the solution to Leo's social challenge – to be 'a king among kings'. It is all right to be regal, but recognize the nobility in others.

Home and Domestic Life

Although Leos are great entertainers and love having people over, sometimes this is all show. Only very few close friends will get to see the real side of a Leo's day-to-day life. To a Leo the home is a place of comfort, recreation and transformation; a secret, private retreat – a castle. Leos like to spend money, show off a bit, entertain and have fun. They enjoy the latest furnishings, clothes and gadgets – all things fit for kings.

Leos are fiercely loyal to their family and, of course, expect the same from them. They love their children almost to a fault; they have to be careful not to spoil them too much. They also must try to avoid attempting to make individual family members over in their own image. Leos should keep in mind that others also have the need to be their own people. That is why Leos have to be extra careful about being over-bossy or over-domineering in the home.

Horoscope for 2022

Major Trends

Health and energy need attention this year, Leo, as two long-term – and powerful – planets are in stressful alignment with you. Make sure you get enough rest. More on this later.

Love was better last year than it will be this year. Love needs more work and effort, but with your love planet in your 10th house you do seem likely to put in the effort. Singles will probably not marry this year. More on this later.

Your 8th house is very strong all year – but especially until May 11. So the year ahead is a sexually active kind of year. Regardless of your age and stage in life, libido will be stronger than usual. With Neptune's presence in your 8th house for many years now, your sexual expression is becoming more refined and spiritualized, and this is still the trend in the year ahead.

Finances don't seem like a big deal this year as your money house is basically empty. But the spouse, partner or current love is having a banner financial year and will pick up the slack. More details later.

Jupiter will move into your 9th house on May 11 and stay there until October 29, only to return there again from December 21 onwards. This shows foreign travel during that period. It is a wonderful transit for college students or students who are applying to university. It shows good fortune.

Uranus, your love planet, has been in your 10th house of career for some years now. (He will be there for some more years to come, too.) This shows that love is high on your agenda and you are focused on it. It also shows many career changes. Your likeability and social grace bring career success. More on this later.

Your most important areas of interest this year are health and work; love and romance; sex, personal transformation and occult studies; higher education, foreign travel, religion, philosophy and theology; career; and friends, groups and group activities (from August 20 onwards).

Your paths of greatest fulfilment this year will be sex, personal transformation and occult studies (until May 11 and from October 29 to December 21); foreign travel, higher education, religion, theology and philosophy (from May 11 to October 29 and from December 21 onwards); and career.

Health

(Please note that this is an astrological perspective on health and not a medical one. In days of yore there was no difference, both these perspectives were identical. But these days there could be quite a difference. For a medical perspective, please consult your doctor or health practitioner.)

Health, as we mentioned, needs more attention and focus this year as two powerful planets – Saturn and Uranus – make stressful aspects to you. But if you make sure to get enough rest you should come through with flying colours.

It will be very wise to give more attention to the following – the vulnerable areas of your Horoscope this year (the reflex points are shown in the chart below). This is where problems are most likely to

Important foot reflexology points for the year ahead

Try to massage all of the foot on a regular basis – the top of the foot as well as the bottom – but pay extra attention to the points highlighted on the chart. When you massage, be aware of 'sore spots' as these need special attention. It's also a good idea to massage the ankles especially, and below them.

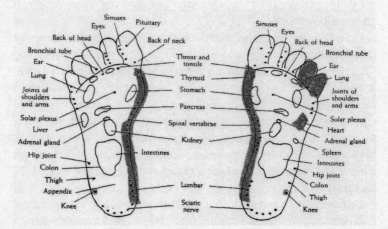

happen. By keeping them healthy and fit much of this can be avoided, and even if problems can't be totally avoided they can be softened to a great extent.

- The heart, which is always important for Leo, has been especially so in the past few years. Chest massage – especially of the breastbone and upper rib cage – will do wonders for you. As always, cultivate faith rather than worry and anxiety and heart function will improve. Meditation will be a big help.
- The spine, knees, teeth, bones and overall skeletal alignment. These areas are always important for you, as Saturn is your health planet. Regular back and knee massage should be part of your overall health regime. Regular visits to a chiropractor or osteopath would be beneficial; the vertebrae need to be kept in right alignment. If you're out in the sun use a good sunscreen. Yoga and Pilates are excellent therapies for the spine. Regular visits to the dental hygienist are also recommended.
- The ankles and calves only became important last year, but they will still need focusing on in the year ahead. Ankles and calves should be regularly massaged. A weak ankle can knock the spine out of alignment, and this will cause all kinds of other problems.

Your health planet Saturn spends the year in your 7th house of love. So, there is a strong love connection to overall health. Good health for you means a healthy love life. Problems here can impact on physical health. So if, God forbid, problems arise, restore harmony here as quickly as possible.

Over the past few years you have been very conservative in health matters. But this changed last year. You are still fairly conservative but are a bit more experimental now. You seem willing to try new things and new health regimes. With Saturn as your health planet you normally would tend to orthodox medicine. But this year you seem more open to alternative therapies. However, even here you are likely to choose the more recognized therapies – the ones that have stood the test of time. I read this as someone who is 'cautiously experimental' in health matters.

Home and Family

Your 4th house of home and family is not a house of power this year – not prominent. Only short-term planets move through there this year and their effect is short lived. This tends to the status quo. Many of you moved in 2020 and there is no need for that this year. There is a sense of contentment with things as they are.

Your family planet, Pluto, has been in your 6th house of health for about twenty years now. Thus you have been making the home as much a health spa as a home. You've been buying all kinds of health and exercise equipment for the home. You've been making the home healthier in other ways too – clearing out mould, mildew or toxic kinds of paints.

You are probably more concerned with the health of family members than with your own health.

If you're planning a major renovation to the home or a construction project, it is probably better to wait until next year. However, if it must be done, February 26 to March 6 and August 13–16 would be good times. If you're merely redecorating or otherwise beautifying the home, October 23 to November 16 would be a good time. This is also a good period for buying objects of beauty for the home.

Though home and family life seem stable this year, there will be a few shake-ups and dramas. Two eclipses occur in your 4th house – a lunar eclipse on May 16 and a solar eclipse on October 25. These will bring dramas in the lives of family members and perhaps home repairs. We will discuss them more fully in the monthly reports.

One of the parents or parent figures in your life has been undergoing many personal changes of late, and this continues in the year ahead. He or she seems restless – antsy – perhaps he or she lives in different places for long periods of time. A move would be more likely in 2023–24 than now. This parent seems difficult to deal with as you don't know where you stand from one moment to the next. He or she seems temperamental. The other parent or parent figure is having a good time this year. If this parent is a mother figure, she seems more fertile this year. After May 11, this parent or parent figure has wonderful job opportunities. A move could have happened last year. This year things tend to the status quo.

The marriage of the parents or parent figures is being tested this year – more so than in previous years. All four eclipses this year will impact their marriage and test it even further.

Siblings or sibling figures could have moved last year. This year is more or less status quo for them. If your siblings are single and of the appropriate age, there is love this year and perhaps even a marriage. This would happen after May 11 – but it could also happen next year.

Children or children figures in your life could move this year and it seems happy. They are having a fun kind of year and, if they are female, seem very fertile. Grandchildren, if you have them, are having a stable, quiet home and family year.

Finance and Career

Your money house is not prominent this year and is not a house of power. Only short-term planets move through this house and their effects are short lived. This has been the case for many years now. Thus finance is not a big concern. This tends to the status quo. It tends to show contentment with things as they are, with no need to make dramatic changes.

If financial problems do arise it could be that you're not paying enough attention – so you will have to focus more.

Mercury, a fast-moving planet, is your financial planet. During the year he will move through your entire horoscope, all the signs and houses. And so there are many short-term financial trends that depend on where Mercury is and the kinds of aspects that he receives. These are best dealt with in the monthly reports.

Mercury rules both your finances and friendships. Thus there is a strong social connection with finance. Your friends tend to be rich and tend to be helpful. As ruler of the 11th house, Mercury favours the electronic media, the online world and technology. These are all interesting as jobs, investments or businesses.

Career seems more important than mere money. Your 10th house of career is strong this year while your money house is empty. Thus, status and prestige are more important than simple cash. The prestigious position that pays less is preferable to the less prestigious job that pays more.

Uranus has been in your 10th house for some years now and will be there for some more to come – this is a long-term transit. This also favours careers involving technology, science and the online world. Even if you are in a different field, your technological expertise is very important.

Uranus is your love planet. This signals many things. You need a career that offers social opportunities. You like to socialize with important and prestigious people. Your social contacts (and especially the spouse, partner or current love) seem very involved in the career and in a helpful way. A lot of your socializing is career related. Your likeability is important in the career. It is not enough that you have good professional skills, you need to get on with others.

Uranus in the 10th house would also favour the arts, the beauty industry and companies that are about beautifying people and the world.

As we mentioned earlier, you need change and excitement in your career, and the freedom to innovate. You seem more content in a freelance type of career than in a mundane 9 to 5 kind.

Love and Social Life

Love is a mixed picture this year. There is great focus here – a good thing. Your 7th house of love is powerful and prominent. But perhaps even more important than that is your love planet in your 10th house – a powerful and prominent position. This will tend to success, but you will certainly earn it. There is much work and challenge involved in love.

The two planets involved in love – Saturn (who occupies your 7th house) and Uranus, your actual love planet – are not especially great for marriage. Marriage is probably not advisable for singles. Existing relationships are getting stress-tested this year. In some ways it is good – though not usually pleasant. Manufacturers will often subject their products to severe stresses, more than would happen from ordinary use of their product. This enables them to see the weaknesses and to correct them. Something similar is happening in your relationship. If your relationship can survive this testing it can probably survive anything.

Normally Leo is a love-at-first-sight kind of person, but this is very much toned down this year. You are definitely more cautious in love. You take more time.

Romantic opportunities happen as you pursue your career and health goals this year. People involved in your career or your health are very alluring. Co-workers are also more alluring, though these days this can be complicated.

The workplace is as much a social centre as a workplace. Jobseekers will look at the social dimension of any job opportunity as much as at other concerns.

A visit to the doctor's surgery or to a therapist can become much more than that. In general, health professionals are alluring.

Power and status have been important in love for some years now. 'Power,' as Henry Kissinger said, 'is the ultimate aphrodisiac.' This might not be so for everyone, but for you it is. You are meeting power-ful people in the year ahead. You are mixing socially with these kinds of people. And this is helpful to your career. As we mentioned, much of your socializing is career-related this year.

One of the challenges these days is getting involved in relationships of convenience rather than real love. This is a strong temptation.

Self-improvement

Uranus has been in your 10th house for some years now and will remain there for a while yet. The main life lesson here is to become comfortable with seeming career instability and change. Things can change in the career path and in the rules of the game in a trice. Suddenly and unexpectedly. A cultivation of faith would be very useful now. There is no stability in the three-dimensional world. Anything can happen at any time. But knowing that the changes are good and for your ultimate benefit will be a big help. In many cases these changes are freeing you up to find a better career path. Celebrate the change as it leads to ultimate good.

Neptune has been in your 8th house of regeneration for many years now. (We have written of this in previous years' reports.) The sex life is becoming more spiritualized, more refined, deeper. It is being raised from mere animal lust to an act of worship. This year the trend is even stronger than in previous years. Jupiter joins Neptune in your 8th house for approximately half the year. Leo is sexually active by nature, and now even more so. There is nothing wrong with this as this is your nature. However, if sex is mere lust, there can be physical and health dangers. So, as we have written in past reports, this is a time to explore the spiritual dimensions of sex. Read all you can about Kundalini and Tantra yoga. The hermetic sciences also deal with this (they give a Western approach). Performing the sex act in a spiritual way will not only bring you closer to the Divine but will shield you from health dangers as well.

The Moon, the fastest-moving of all the planets, is your spiritual planet. This favours the Bhakti path. The emotions and feelings need to be elevated. It favours singing, chanting and drumming. These elevate the emotions and harmonize them. Your moods are important in your prayer and emotional life. Before you meditate work to get into a harmonious mood. Then begin your prayers or meditation.

The Moon as your spiritual planet shows that you have many ways to connect to the Divine within. There is no one way for you. At different times different things work, and because the Moon moves so quickly, techniques that worked yesterday might not work today. You have to shift your approach constantly. If you practise only one way, you'll note that some days are easier to make the inner connection and some days more difficult. This is due to the Moon's position and the aspects she receives. When the aspects are harmonious, your meditations will go better. When they are discordant, difficulties arise. Don't be discouraged. Keep at it. The problem is not you.

Month-by-month Forecasts

January

Best Days Overall: 1, 8, 9, 18, 19, 27, 28
Most Stressful Days Overall: 4, 5, 11, 12, 25, 26, 31
Best Days for Love: 2, 3, 4, 5, 11, 12, 21, 22, 29, 30, 31
Best Days for Money: 4, 5, 6, 13, 14, 16, 21, 22, 23, 25
Best Days for Career: 2, 3, 11, 12, 21, 22, 29, 30

You begin your year with your 6th house of health and work very powerful: 50 per cent, sometimes 60 per cent of the planets are either there or moving through there. This is a great month for jobseekers. There are many opportunities. You are in demand. Even those already employed will have opportunities for overtime or second jobs. There is also a strong focus on health. Though health is good until the 20th this focus will stand you in good stead after then, when health needs more attention.

As we mentioned in the yearly report, you have two long-term planets – powerful ones – in stressful aspect with you. On the 20th short-term planets join the party, increasing the stress. So make sure to get enough rest at this time, and enhance the health in the ways mentioned in the yearly report.

Though health and energy could be better after the 20th nice things are happening. The Sun enters your 7th house of love and you begin a yearly love and social peak. You are more popular this month as you are putting others first and go out of your way for others. You take a proactive attitude to love. You make things happen. If you like someone that person knows it. You're not playing games. But love is complicated – perhaps you like it that way. Leo loves drama. If there is none, they will create some. So, if you are in a relationship you'll need to work harder to keep things together. You and the beloved don't seem in agreement. You might think that you're acting in his or her best interest, but the beloved might not agree. Still, you should be successful in love. It is important to you and you give it much focus, and you're willing to overcome all the challenges that arise.

Your financial planet, Mercury, goes retrograde from the 14th onwards. Try to wrap up important purchases or investments before then. After the 14th work to get clarity in your finances. Mercury's retrograde won't stop earnings, but only slow things down a bit. Make sure to handle all the details of financial transactions perfectly. This will minimize delays.

February

Best Days Overall: 5, 6, 14, 15, 24, 25
Most Stressful Days Overall: 1, 7, 8, 16, 21, 22, 23, 28
Best Days for Love: 1, 7, 8, 17, 18, 26, 27, 28
Best Days for Money: 2, 3, 8, 12, 13, 17, 18, 19, 20, 21, 22, 28
Best Days for Career: 7, 8, 17, 18, 27

Your financial planet Mercury goes forward on the 4th and thus finances improve. Until the 15th he will be in Capricorn, your 6th house. This has many good points. The financial judgement will be sound – conservative (perhaps too conservative for your taste). It favours long-term savings and investment plans. Money comes through work – the old-fashioned way.

On the 15th Mercury enters Aquarius and you become more experimental in financial matters. This transit favours partnerships, start-ups, and the high-tech and online worlds. Investors will have a good feeling for these sectors. You probably spend more on technology, but can earn from this as well. Mercury travels with Pluto on the 10th and 11th. This can bring a job opportunity (or a second job). Mercury will be in adverse aspect with Uranus on the 23rd and 24th and there can be some financial disagreements with the spouse, partner or current love. You may need to make some financial adjustments.

Love is still happy this month – and still full of drama. You're still in a yearly love and social peak until the 18th, so the social life is active. Your social grace will help the bottom line as well. A partnership or joint venture opportunity can occur. The Sun travels with Saturn on the 3rd and 4th. For singles this can bring a romantic opportunity with a co-worker or someone involved in your health.

On the 18th the Sun enters your 8th house. Jupiter has been there since the beginning of the year, so the spouse, partner or current love is enjoying even greater prosperity than last month. You seem very involved in this. With the 8th house so strong – and full of beneficent planets – there is more than usual sexual activity. It is a wonderful time for personal transformation: giving birth to the you that you want to be. But before this can happen, old, effete material – whether they be possessions or mental and emotional patterns – need to go. It is a month for growing by eliminating the unnecessary. It's not about adding things to yourself. That will come later on. So it is good to explore your thinking and feeling and see what is destructive, and get rid of it. There are many spiritual techniques that can help you. (Some of you might want to visit my blog www.spiritual-stories.com for more information on this.)

March

Best Days Overall: 4, 5, 14, 15, 23, 24
Most Stressful Days Overall: 1, 6, 7, 8, 21, 22, 27, 28
Best Days for Love: 1, 6, 7, 9, 16, 17, 18, 19, 25, 26, 27, 28
Best Days for Money: 1, 2, 3, 11, 12, 16, 17, 21, 22, 30, 31
Best Days for Career: 6, 7, 8, 9, 18, 19, 27, 28

Both Mars and Venus move into your 7th house of love on the 6th, making the 7th house very strong. So, although it is not a yearly love and social peak, the social life is active. These transits bring opportunities for love affairs but not necessarily serious committed love. Mars rules your 5th house of fun, so it is more about having fun with people. Love is an amusement, like going to the movies or theatre. Still it is fun for what it is.

The month ahead looks prosperous. Mercury moves speedily this month, signalling fast financial progress and confidence. The Sun will travel with Jupiter from the 4th to the 6th, which should bring a nice payday. It is also good for speculations, though you should never do these things automatically – only by using intuition. Still, you are more risk-taking than usual. Mercury, your financial planet, will also travel with Jupiter on the 20th and 21st. This too brings financial expansion.

Health needs watching this month – though you will see major improvement from the 20th onwards. In the meantime, four – sometimes five – planets are in stressful alignment with you. As always, make sure to maintain high energy levels, and enhance the health in the ways mentioned in the yearly report.

Your 8th house is strong until the 20th, so keep in mind our discussion of this last month. A new birth tends to be a messy business. But the end result is good. With the Sun in the 8th house until the 20th many of you are confronting death on a psychological level. It probably won't touch you physically – though you can have close calls – but it is going to force you to become more serious about life. That's the point.

On the 20th the Sun enters your 9th house and stays there for the rest of the month. All the planets are moving forward and the Sun is in dynamic Aries. Events move quickly. The pace of life is faster than usual. Many of you will travel to foreign countries. College-level students will do well in their studies. There are religious and philosophical breakthroughs happening.

April

Best Days Overall: 1, 2, 10, 11, 19, 20, 28, 29
Most Stressful Days Overall: 3, 4, 17, 18, 23, 24, 30
Best Days for Love: 3, 4, 8, 13, 14, 17, 18, 21, 22, 23, 24, 25, 26, 27, 30
Best Days for Money: 1, 2, 8, 9, 12, 13, 14, 17, 18, 21, 22, 26, 27
Best Days for Career: 3, 4, 8, 17, 18, 25, 26, 27, 30

Though health still needs keeping an eye on, the month ahead is successful. The Sun in your 9th house is a happy transit. There is optimism and expansion of your horizons. Foreign travel could have happened last month, but, if not, it can still happen in the month ahead.

The action this month is in the career. Uranus has been in your 10th house for some years now. On the 20th the Sun will enter here and you will begin a yearly career peak. You seem very successful. You seem above everyone in your world. Even younger Leos who don't yet have careers will aspire – and perhaps behave – as if they were top dog, in charge.

When the ruler of your Horoscope is at the top of the chart, people feel that 'I'm born to rule – born to be in charge – I belong here at the top'. Many celebrities and politicians have this aspect in their birth charts.

A solar eclipse on the 30th occurs in your 10th house, bringing career shake-ups – shake-ups in your corporate hierarchy or in your industry. Often it brings changes in the rules and regulations that impact your industry or company. Thus the rules of the game change. Often such an eclipse brings life-changing events to bosses, elders, parents or parent figures. All these shake-ups seems to open up opportunities for you. They create uncertainty, but they open doors.

Every solar eclipse has a strong effect on you because the eclipsed planet is your ruling planet. Thus there will be a need to redefine yourself, to upgrade your image, self-concept and personal appearance. This is basically a healthy thing. We are growing, evolving beings and our thinking should reflect this growth. So, you will be changing the way that you think about yourself and the way that you want others to think about you. This will lead to wardrobe changes, changes of hairstyle and overall look in the coming months.

Reduce your schedule during the eclipse period. Parents, bosses and elders should also take it easy.

Health, as we mentioned, needs watching. Enhance the health in the ways mentioned in the yearly report. The problem is that your 6th house is empty, and you could be tempted to ignore things.

May

Best Days Overall: 7, 8, 9, 16, 17, 25, 26
Most Stressful Days Overall: 1, 14, 15, 21, 27, 28
Best Days for Love: 1, 7, 8, 10, 11, 16, 17, 19, 21, 27, 28
Best Days for Money: 2, 3, 4, 6, 10, 11, 12, 13, 16, 18, 19, 25, 28
Best Days for Career: 1, 7, 8, 16, 17, 27, 28

The career is going very well this month – very active and successful. The demands are hard, but the rewards are good. However, a lunar eclipse on the 16th, which occurs in your 4th house of home and family, will force you to pay more attention to this area.

The Moon is the generic ruler of home and family, and the lunar eclipse in the 4th house merely emphasizes things. There are dramas among the family and especially with a parent or parent figure. Passions will run high at home. There can be repairs needed in the home as hidden flaws come to light. Siblings and sibling figures have financial dramas. The Moon is the spiritual planet in your chart, so every lunar eclipse brings spiritual changes – changes of teachings, teachers and practice. Usually this is a good thing. These changes tend to come from inner growth – it is a sign of progress. There can be shake-ups and disruptions in spiritual or charitable organizations that you're involved with, and dramas in the lives of guru figures. The dream life will tend to be hyperactive this period, but shouldn't be given too much weight. The images you see – and they'll probably be disturbing – are merely psychic flotsam and jetsam caused by the eclipse. Friends experience financial shake-ups and will need to make changes.

This eclipse impacts Saturn, your health planet, and there could be health scares – but always get a second opinion on these matters. In the coming months there will be important changes to the health regime. Such an impact on Saturn often signals job changes and dramas and shake-ups in the workplace. If you employ others there can be employee turnover now (and in the coming months).

Health needs watching this month and you should take it as easy as possible. This is so until the 20th but especially around the eclipse period. Enhance the health in the ways mentioned in the yearly report.

Finances are good but complicated. Your financial planet, Mercury, goes retrograde on the 10th. Try to wrap up important purchases or investments before then. After the 10th take a wait-and-see attitude on important financial decisions.

June

Best Days Overall: 4, 5, 13, 14, 21, 22
Most Stressful Days Overall: 11, 12, 17, 18, 23, 24, 25
Best Days for Love: 6, 7, 15, 16, 17, 18, 23, 24, 26
Best Days for Money: 4, 6, 7, 13, 17, 21, 26, 27
Best Days for Career: 6, 7, 16, 23, 24, 25, 26

The two planets involved with your 9th house had their solstice last month, continuing into the month ahead. Mars, the ruler of the 9th house, began his solstice on May 27 and this goes on until the 2nd.

Jupiter, the occupant of your 9th house (and its generic ruler) began his solstice on May 12 and this goes on until the 11th. They pause in the heavens (in latitudinal motion) and then change direction (in latitude). So college-level students have a pause in their affairs and then change direction. The same holds true with legal issues (if you're involved with those things).

Health and energy are much improved over last month. If there were problems in May you see a remarkable turnaround now. Perhaps some pill, potion or therapy will get the credit, but working behind it is the change in planetary energy.

Most of your career goals (the short-term ones at least) have been achieved and you can now get involved in the fruits of career success – being involved with friends and group activities that befit your status. The power this month is in your 11th house of friends. Many fondest hopes and wishes will come to pass and, as night follows day, you will form new 'fondest hopes and wishes'. There will be a greater interest in science and technology. Your understanding of these things will expand. Many people have their Horoscopes done when the 11th house is strong: the 11th house rules astrology. It is a good time to buy high-tech equipment this month too, especially after the 14th. Your purchases will be sound.

Finances are improved this month. Your financial planet starts to move forward on the 4th and will be strongly positioned. Until the 14th Mercury will be in your 10th house of career. This often signals pay rises, official or unofficial. Mercury is strong when he is at the top of the chart and thus earning power is stronger. On the 14th Mercury moves into Gemini, his own sign and house, and he's very strong there too. Very comfortable. All of this signals enhanced earning power.

Mars and Jupiter are travelling together these days. This indicates positive achievement – positive actions. Foreign travel is likely.

July

Best Days Overall: 1, 2, 10, 11, 18, 19, 20, 28, 29
Most Stressful Days Overall: 8, 9, 14, 15, 21, 22
Best Days for Love: 4, 5, 6, 7, 12, 13, 14, 15, 21, 22, 26, 31
Best Days for Money: 1, 2, 4, 5, 8, 10, 11, 16, 17, 18, 19, 28, 29, 31
Best Days for Career: 6, 7, 15, 21, 22, 26

Mars will cross your Mid-heaven and enter your 10th house on the 5th. Normally this would indicate a degree of aggressiveness and combativeness in the career. Perhaps this will happen, but in your chart Mars is a beneficent planet; he is the ruler of your 9th house, so perhaps you are combative, but the results are good. There is career-related travel this month.

Mars will square Pluto on the 1st and 2nd so family members and especially a parent or parent figure should be more mindful on the physical plane. Perhaps surgery is recommended to them. (It doesn't mean that it *has* to happen – but it can be recommended.) Towards the end of the month – on the 30th and 31st – Mars travels with Uranus. This too is a dynamic aspect. Be more mindful on the physical plane – this applies to the spouse, partner or current love as well. This transit can bring a foreign trip with the beloved.

The month ahead is spiritual. The action is in your 12th house of spirituality. It is normal to want solitude – aloneness – under this kind of transit, and there is nothing wrong with you if you do. There is a need to feel your own aura and get comfortable with yourself – to be comfortable in your own skin. You will be more involved with charities and charitable giving. Your financial planet will be in your 12th house from the 5th to the 19th, signalling that financial intuition will be good. Financial guidance will come in dreams or through astrologers, psychics, tarot readers and/or spiritual channels. You will learn that the Divine is very concerned about your financial well-being. (Only, you have to do things its way.)

On the 23rd the Sun will move into your sign and your 1st house, and you begin one of your yearly personal pleasure peaks. Time to enjoy the pleasures of the body and senses. Time to get the body into the shape that you want. Time to do things that enhance your physical appearance.

Finances are good this month. Your financial planet will move into your own sign on the 19th, which brings windfalls and financial opportunities. You spend on yourself and you have the image of a prosperous person. People see you this way. The money people in your life are devoted to you.

Health improves after the 23rd but needs attention before that. Enhance the health in the ways mentioned in the yearly report.

August

Best Days Overall: 7, 8, 15, 16, 25, 26
Most Stressful Days Overall: 4, 5, 11, 12, 17, 18
Best Days for Love: 1, 4, 5, 9, 10, 11, 12, 15, 17, 18, 25, 26, 27, 28
Best Days for Money: 1, 7, 9, 15, 17, 18, 25, 27, 28, 29
Best Days for Career: 4, 5, 15, 17, 18, 25, 26

A happy and prosperous month ahead Leo, enjoy.

You're still very much in a yearly personal pleasure peak until the 23rd. You look good. The personal appearance shines. The Sun in your sign brings charisma and star quality (it enhances your innate star quality and makes it stronger). Venus in your sign brings beauty and grace to the image and a sense of style. Mercury (which will be there until the 4th) brings financial windfalls and opportunity. You have abundant self-confidence and self-esteem. You are more of a Leo now than ever.

Health is much improved this month – especially from the 20th onwards when Mars leaves his stressful aspect with you. Those who are for you (planetary-wise) are stronger than those who are against you.

Retrograde activity among the planets increases this month, and by the end of the month 50 per cent of the planets will be moving backwards. Next month the percentage will increase even further. So, the pace of life is slower these days, which is not the way you like things. It is a time for learning and practising patience, and for being more perfect in all that you do. This will minimize – though not eliminate – the many delays and glitches going on.

Prosperity increases this month too. It was good last month but gets even better now. On the 4th your financial planet, Mercury, moves into the money house – his own sign and house. He is strong there and acts with more power on your behalf. This signals increased earning power. On the 23rd the Sun, the ruler of your Horoscope, also enters the money house and you begin a yearly financial peak. The ruler of the Horoscope in the 2nd house is considered very fortunate.

When Mercury enters Virgo on the 4th we will have a Grand Trine in the Earth signs – a very fortunate configuration. This will bring a down-to-earth attitude to life and an ability to create ease on the material plane. Your organizational and management skills will be enhanced. Financial judgement will be better as well.

Love will improve after the 23rd. The 10th and 11th seem stressful for love, but such stress is short term.

September

Best Days Overall: 3, 4, 11, 12, 21, 22, 30
Most Stressful Days Overall: 1, 2, 7, 8, 13, 14, 15, 28, 29
Best Days for Love: 4, 5, 6, 7, 8, 13, 14, 15, 23, 24
Best Days for Money: 3, 7, 8, 11, 16, 21, 23, 24, 30
Best Days for Career: 4, 5, 13, 14, 15

Retrograde activity hits its maximum extent for the year. From the 10th onwards 60 per cent of the planets will be moving backwards. So, like last month – in fact, even more so than last month – patience, patience, patience. Retrogrades can be used to your advantage, providing good times to get clear on your goals and plans in various departments of your life. Once clarity is attained you can move forward with confidence when the planets start to move forward.

In spite of all the retrogrades, many nice things are happening. The Grand Trine in Earth that began last month continues all this month. In addition, we will have another Grand Trine – and it's highly unusual to have two at the same time – in the Air signs. Together they will enhance both your practical abilities (Earth) and your intellectual and communication skills (Air).

You're still in the midst of a yearly financial peak until the 23rd. The only problem with finance is Mercury's retrograde, which begins on the 10th. This retrograde will have a stronger effect than the previous ones in the past year. Because it happens when many other planets are retrograde there is a cumulative effect. So, try to finalize important purchases and investments before the 10th. After the 10th take a wait-and-see attitude to finance. Mercury's retrograde won't stop earnings – they should still be strong – but it will delay things and bring glitches.

Though your love planet, Uranus, is now retrograde and important love decisions shouldn't be made, love seems happy this month. Your love planet is receiving nice aspects. So singles will date and have good romantic opportunities. But there's no need to rush down the aisle just yet. Let love take its course. The 10th and 11th seem especially good for love.

Health is good this month. With your health planet Saturn retrograde for many months now, avoid making major changes to the health regime. There are job opportunities coming this month, but they should be examined carefully. Things might not be as they are being presented.

On the 23rd, as the Sun enters your 3rd house the focus shifts to communication and intellectual interests. Students below college level will do well. They seem focused on their studies. This is an excellent time to read, study, write and pursue your intellectual interests. Siblings and sibling figures are having a good month.

October

Best Days Overall: 1, 9, 10, 18, 19, 27, 28
Most Stressful Days Overall: 4, 5, 11, 12, 25, 26
Best Days for Love: 2, 3, 4, 5, 11, 12, 13, 14, 21, 22, 25, 30
Best Days for Money: 2, 3, 8, 9, 13, 18, 21, 22, 23, 24, 26, 27
Best Days for Career: 4, 5, 11, 12, 13, 14, 25

Health is good this month, but it needs watching from the 23rd onwards. A solar eclipse on the 25th also seems stressful, so make sure you relax and reduce your schedule from the 23rd onwards – and especially around the eclipse period. Enhance the health in the ways mentioned in the yearly report.

This eclipse occurs in your 4th house of home and family, bringing personal dramas in the lives of family members – and especially to a parent or parent figure. People who are 'like' family to you can also be affected. Family members should also reduce their schedules during this time. The eclipse can impact on the family's reputation and status. There are shake-ups here. Siblings and sibling figures in your life are forced to make important financial changes. There can be repairs needed in the home as hidden flaws come to light. The dream life will be hyperactive but shouldn't be taken too seriously. Disturbing images can be cleared and discharged with 'touch and let go' (see my *A Technique for Meditation*) or by writing them through.

This eclipse can have some positive therapeutic effects. It will unearth long-buried memories and perhaps traumas that ordinarily wouldn't surface. They will arise spontaneously. Thus you can deal with them and clear them.

Home and family are where the focus should be this month. The night side of your Horoscope, though not dominant, is as strong as it will ever be this year. So it is good to shift some attention here. The day side of the Horoscope is still dominant, but not as much as at the beginning of the year. The image that comes to me is that it is now midnight in your year; you should be sleeping and engaged in the activities of night. But you keep waking up – you keep being preoccupied with day activities. You sleep for a while and then wake up. You dream for a while and wake up. This goes on and on.

Love seems stressful from the 23rd onwards. You and the beloved seem distant – perhaps not physically but psychologically. You see things in opposite ways. There is a need to bridge your differences.

November

Best Days Overall: 5, 6, 15, 16, 24, 25
Most Stressful Days Overall: 1, 2, 7, 8, 22, 23, 28, 29
Best Days for Love: 1, 2, 3, 4, 7, 8, 13, 17, 18, 23, 24, 26, 27, 28, 29
Best Days for Money: 3, 4, 13, 14, 17, 18, 23, 24, 25
Best Days for Career: 3, 4, 7, 8, 13, 23, 24

The main headline this month is a very powerful lunar eclipse on the 8th. It has a strong effect on you and on the world in general: it is not only a total eclipse, but it impacts many other planets. Thus it shakes up many areas of your life. So take it nice and easy during that period. Do what needs to be done, but anything non-essential is better off being rescheduled. Spend more quiet time at home. Read a book or watch a movie. Best of all, meditate.

The eclipse occurs in your 10th house of career, and so brings career changes. People don't often change their entire career under this kind of eclipse – though sometimes they do – but they pursue things in a different way. There can be shake-ups in the hierarchy of your company, or shake-ups in your industry, that change things. Sometimes the government changes the rules and regulations for your industry. Sometimes there are dramas in the lives of bosses – personal dramas – and this changes things. (Parents and parent figures are also having personal dramas, and they should take a nice easy schedule too.)

The Moon is your spiritual planet, and so the eclipse is announcing spiritual changes. You change your practice, perhaps your teachings or teachers – more importantly, you change your attitudes. There are dramas and shake-ups in spiritual or charitable organizations that you're involved with. There are dramas in the lives of guru figures. Friends are making important financial changes.

As mentioned, other planets are affected by this eclipse – Venus, Mercury and Uranus. The impact on Venus reinforces what we mentioned earlier about career changes. But it also affects siblings and sibling figures in your life. They are having personal dramas. There can be disruptions in your neighbourhood and with neighbours. Students below college level have dramas at school and can change their educational plans.

The impact on Uranus shows that love is getting tested. There can be dramas in the personal life of the spouse, partner or current love. Be patient with the beloved during this period.

The impact on Mercury indicates that there are important financial changes happening for you. Your financial thinking was not realistic. You had assumptions that were not correct. A course correction is necessary.

December

Best Days Overall: 2, 3, 12, 13, 21, 22, 29, 30
Most Stressful Days Overall: 4, 5, 6, 19, 20, 25, 26
Best Days for Love: 2, 3, 4, 5, 14, 15, 23, 24, 25, 26
Best Days for Money: 1, 2, 3, 11, 14, 15, 16, 20, 21, 23, 24, 29
Best Days for Career: 2, 3, 4, 5, 6, 14, 23, 24

Now that the excitement of last month's eclipse is somewhat abated, you can focus on the joy of life. You're in the midst of a yearly personal pleasure peak this month until the 22nd. Leo is naturally very creative, and this period even more so.

Health is good – especially until the 22nd. If you want to enhance it further do so in the ways mentioned in the yearly report. Joy is of itself a powerful healing force, and you have plenty of joy this month.

Three planets are 'out of bounds' this month. Mars has been 'out of bounds' since October 24 and will remain so all this month. Venus is 'out of bounds' from the 2nd to the 24th and Mercury from the 1st to the 22nd. This is highly unusual and seems to be a trend in the world. People are going outside the box – outside their normal orbit. It seems fashionable these days. For you personally it shows a need to go outside your normal sphere in finance, career, and in your religious studies. There are no answers to be found within your normal orbit and you must seek them elsewhere.

Foreign travel seems to be happening this month as Jupiter moves into your 9th house on the 21st – this time for the long haul. However, there can be delays involved as Mars, the ruler of your 9th house, is retrograde. Next month seems better for travelling than this one.

Your 6th house of health and work becomes a house of power once again on the 22nd – though you will feel it even before then. This is a great period for jobseekers – there are many opportunities. Even those already employed will have opportunities for overtime and second jobs. You're in a work mood this month. So, it is good to harness this urge to do those boring, detail-oriented jobs that you keep putting off.

Finances are basically good this month, but get complicated after the 24th as Mercury goes retrograde. This retrograde won't be nearly as strong in its effect as the last one as most of the planets are moving forward. Still, it can bring delays or glitches in the financial life. The good thing here is that Mercury will be in the sign of Capricorn from the 7th onwards. So your financial judgement is sound and down to earth – until the 24th.

Virgo

♍

THE VIRGIN

Birthdays from
22nd August to
22nd September

Personality Profile

VIRGO AT A GLANCE

Element – Earth

Ruling Planet – Mercury
  Career Planet – Mercury
  Love Planet – Neptune
  Money Planet – Venus
  Planet of Home and Family Life – Jupiter
  Planet of Health and Work – Uranus
  Planet of Pleasure – Saturn
  Planet of Sexuality – Mars

Colours – earth tones, ochre, orange, yellow

Colour that promotes love, romance and social harmony – aqua blue

Colour that promotes earning power – jade green

Gems – agate, hyacinth

Metal – quicksilver

Scents – lavender, lilac, lily of the valley, storax

Quality – mutable (= flexibility)

Quality most needed for balance – a broader perspective

Strongest virtues – mental agility, analytical skills, ability to pay attention to detail, healing powers

Deepest needs – to be useful and productive

Characteristic to avoid – destructive criticism

Signs of greatest overall compatibility – Taurus, Capricorn

Signs of greatest overall incompatibility – Gemini, Sagittarius, Pisces

Sign most helpful to career – Gemini

Sign most helpful for emotional support – Sagittarius

Sign most helpful financially – Libra

Sign best for marriage and/or partnerships – Pisces

Sign most helpful for creative projects – Capricorn

Best Sign to have fun with – Capricorn

Signs most helpful in spiritual matters – Taurus, Leo

Best day of the week – Wednesday

Understanding a Virgo

The virgin is a particularly fitting symbol for those born under the sign of Virgo. If you meditate on the image of the virgin you will get a good understanding of the essence of the Virgo type. The virgin is, of course, a symbol of purity and innocence – not naïve, but pure. A virginal object has not been touched. A virgin field is land that is true to itself, the way it has always been. The same is true of virgin forest: it is pristine, unaltered.

Apply the idea of purity to the thought processes, emotional life, physical body and activities and projects of the everyday world, and you can see how Virgos approach life. Virgos desire the pure expression of the ideal in their mind, body and affairs. If they find impurities they will attempt to clear them away.

Impurities are the beginning of disorder, unhappiness and uneasiness. The job of the Virgo is to eject all impurities and keep only that which the body and mind can use and assimilate.

The secrets of good health are here revealed: 90 per cent of the art of staying well is maintaining a pure mind, a pure body and pure emotions. When you introduce more impurities than your mind and body can deal with, you will have what is known as 'dis-ease'. It is no wonder that Virgos make great doctors, nurses, healers and dieticians. They have an innate understanding of good health and they realize that good health is more than just physical. In all aspects of life, if you want a project to be successful it must be kept as pure as possible. It must be protected against the adverse elements that will try to undermine it. This is the secret behind Virgo's awesome technical proficiency.

One could talk about Virgo's analytical powers – which are formidable. One could talk about their perfectionism and their almost superhuman attention to detail. But this would be to miss the point. All of these virtues are manifestations of a Virgo's desire for purity and perfection – a world without Virgos would have ruined itself long ago.

A vice is nothing more than a virtue turned inside out, misapplied or used in the wrong context. Virgos' apparent vices come from their inherent virtue. Their analytical powers, which should be used for healing, helping or perfecting a project in the world, sometimes get misapplied and turned against people. Their critical faculties, which should be used constructively to perfect a strategy or proposal, can sometimes be used destructively to harm or wound. Their urge to perfection can turn into worry and lack of confidence; their natural humility can become self-denial and self-abasement. When Virgos turn negative they are apt to turn their devastating criticism on themselves, sowing the seeds of self-destruction.

Finance

Virgos have all the attitudes that create wealth. They are hard-working, industrious, efficient, organized, thrifty, productive and eager to serve. A developed Virgo is every employer's dream. But until Virgos master some of the social graces of Libra they will not even come close to fulfilling their financial potential. Purity and perfectionism, if not handled correctly or gracefully, can be very trying to others. Friction in human relationships can be devastating not only to your pet projects but – indirectly – to your wallet as well.

Virgos are quite interested in their financial security. Being hard-working, they know the true value of money. They do not like to take risks with their money, preferring to save for their retirement or for a rainy day. Virgos usually make prudent, calculated investments that involve a minimum of risk. These investments and savings usually work out well, helping Virgos to achieve the financial security they seek. The rich or even not-so-rich Virgo also likes to help his or her friends in need.

Career and Public Image

Virgos reach their full potential when they can communicate their knowledge in such a way that others can understand it. In order to get their ideas across better, Virgos need to develop greater verbal skills and fewer judgemental ways of expressing themselves. Virgos look up to teachers and communicators; they like their bosses to be good communicators. Virgos will probably not respect a superior who is not their intellectual equal – no matter how much money or power that superior has. Virgos themselves like to be perceived by others as being educated and intellectual.

The natural humility of Virgos often inhibits them from fulfilling their great ambitions, from acquiring name and fame. Virgos should indulge in a little more self-promotion if they are going to reach their career goals. They need to push themselves with the same ardour that they would use to foster others.

At work Virgos like to stay active. They are willing to learn any type of job as long as it serves their ultimate goal of financial security. Virgos may change occupations several times during their professional lives, until they find the one they really enjoy. Virgos work well with other people, are not afraid to work hard and always fulfil their responsibilities.

Love and Relationships

If you are an analyst or a critic you must, out of necessity, narrow your scope. You have to focus on a part and not the whole; this can create a temporary narrow-mindedness. Virgos do not like this kind of person. They like their partners to be broad-minded, with depth and vision. Virgos seek to get this broad-minded quality from their partners, since they sometimes lack it themselves.

Virgos are perfectionists in love just as they are in other areas of life. They need partners who are tolerant, open-minded and easy-going. If you are in love with a Virgo do not waste time on impractical romantic gestures. Do practical and useful things for him or her – this is what will be appreciated and what will be done for you.

Virgos express their love through pragmatic and useful gestures, so do not be put off because your Virgo partner does not say 'I love you' day-in and day-out. Virgos are not that type. If they love you, they will demonstrate it in practical ways. They will always be there for you; they will show an interest in your health and finances; they will fix your sink or repair your video recorder. Virgos deem these actions to be superior to sending flowers, chocolates or Valentine cards.

In love affairs Virgos are not particularly passionate or spontaneous. If you are in love with a Virgo, do not take this personally. It does not mean that you are not alluring enough or that your Virgo partner does not love or like you. It is just the way Virgos are. What they lack in passion they make up for in dedication and loyalty.

Home and Domestic Life

It goes without saying that the home of a Virgo will be spotless, sanitized and orderly. Everything will be in its proper place – and don't you dare move anything about! For Virgos to find domestic bliss they need to ease up a bit in the home, to allow their partner and children more freedom and to be more generous and open-minded. Family members are not to be analysed under a microscope, they are individuals with their own virtues to express.

With these small difficulties resolved, Virgos like to stay in and entertain at home. They make good hosts and they like to keep their friends and families happy and entertained at family and social gatherings. Virgos love children, but they are strict with them – at times – since they want to make sure their children are brought up with the correct sense of family and values.

Horoscope for 2022

Major Trends

Love is the main headline this year for you, Virgo. The love and social life is going to be very active and happy. Singles are likely to be involved in a serious relationship or even marriage. Those already in a relationship are meeting new people and having more romance within the relationship. The importance of love – of relationship – is seen in other ways too. *All* the long-term planets are in the Western, social sector of your chart this year. And, while the Eastern sector of self will gain strength at different times of the year, it will never dominate the West. So the year ahead is about others – relationship. More on this later.

Saturn has been in your 6th house since last year and he will be there in the year ahead. This shows someone who enjoys dealing with health and health issues (you're even more Virgo than usual) and someone who explores the healing power of joy. More on this later on.

Jupiter will enter your 8th house of regeneration on May 11 and stays there until October 29. Then he will return to the 8th house on December 21 and be there for the rest of the year and well into next year. This shows a sexually active kind of period. Whatever your age or stage in life, libido is stronger than usual. It also shows some dramas with the family and family members. More on this later.

Uranus has been in your 9th house for some years now, and will remain there for many more to come. This is bringing important changes to your religious, philosophical and theological beliefs. They are being challenged by science. Some of your beliefs will get modified and some will get discarded. This is very important, for your personal philosophy – your personal metaphysics – determines how you live your life. It has profound consequences. College-level students can be changing schools and educational plans.

Your most important interests this year are children, fun and personal creativity; health and work; love and romance; sex, personal transformation and occult studies (from May 11 to October 29 and from December 21 onwards); religion, philosophy, theology, higher education and foreign travel; and career (from August 20).

Your paths of greatest fulfilment this year are love and romance (until May 11 and from October 29 to December 21); sex, personal transformation and occult studies (from May 11 to October 29 and from December 21 onwards); and religion, philosophy, theology, higher education and foreign travel.

Health

(Please note that this is an astrological perspective on health and not a medical one. In days of yore there was no difference, both these perspectives were identical. But these days there could be quite a difference. For a medical perspective, please consult your doctor or health practitioner.)

Health needs some attention until May 11 and from October 29 to December 21. You will have two long-term planets in stressful alignment with you. The good news is that you are on the case, and not just because you're Virgo – who has a natural passion for health – but also because your 6th house of health is very strong. So I feel health will be good overall. You're paying attention. You're doing the right things and not taking things for granted.

You will see a big improvement in health and energy when Jupiter moves away from his stressful aspect with you when he moves into your 8th house (May 11 to October 29 and December 21 onwards). By the end of the year you'll be healthier than you were at the beginning.

You can do much to enhance your health. Give more attention to the following – the vulnerable areas of your Horoscope this year (the reflex points are shown in the chart below):

- The heart. This is vulnerable until May 11 and from October 29 to December 21. The reflex point is shown above. Chest massage – especially of the breastbone and upper rib cage – helps the heart too. The important thing with the heart is to avoid worry and anxiety, the two emotions that stress it out. Cultivate faith rather than worry.

Important foot reflexology points for the year ahead

Try to massage all of the foot on a regular basis – the top of the foot as well as the bottom – but pay extra attention to the points highlighted on the chart. When you massage, be aware of 'sore spots' as these need special attention. It's also a very good idea to massage the ankles and below them.

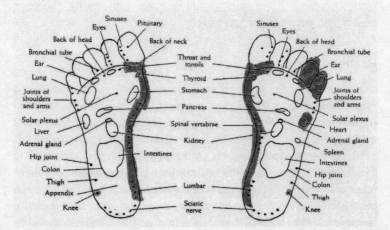

- The spine, knees, teeth, bones and overall skeletal alignment have become important areas since last year, and are still important in the year ahead. Regular back and knee massage will be wonderful. Regular visits to a chiropractor or osteopath will also be good. You need to keep the vertebrae in right alignment. Make sure you have enough calcium for the bones, and if you're out in the sun use a good sunscreen. Regular visits to the dental hygienist are a good idea too.
- The ankles and calves are always important for Virgo, and both areas should be massaged regularly. Give the ankles more support when exercising. A weak ankle can knock the spine and skeleton out of alignment and this will cause all kinds of other problems.
- The neck and throat. These have only become important in recent years, when your health planet moved into Taurus. The reflexes are shown above. Regular neck and throat massage will be very beneficial. Tension tends to collect in the neck and needs to be released. You might find craniosacral therapy helpful here too.

Saturn, the ruler of your creative 5th house, is in your 6th house of health, signalling the importance of staying happy and creative. A creative hobby will not only be fun, but therapeutic as well. Avoid depression like the plague. A simple rule for good health – stay happy. This transit would also indicate that you might be more involved with the health of children and children figures than you are with your own health. Do your best to keep relations with children positive.

Home and Family

Your 4th house of home and family is not a house of power this year. Not prominent. In addition, most of the long-term planets are in the upper half of your Horoscope – the day side. Thus, home and family are not a big issue this year. The year ahead is more about love and outer achievement. If you are in love or achieving your outer goals you feel 'emotionally well'. It also shows that you serve your family (or those who are like family to you) through outer success. Being a good provider, being successful in your career and job will help the family more than the more mundane kinds of things.

You seem distant with the family this year. Since you are socializing more with them, I read this more as psychological distance rather than physical. Two people can occupy the same physical space and be in two totally different worlds psychologically and spiritually.

The year ahead will be a stable one. A move is not likely. The spouse, partner or current love seems unusually fertile this year.

If you're planning a major renovation or construction project in the home, January 1–25 would be a good time. But the year ahead seems more about beautifying the home – redecorating it. It's about making the home a thing of beauty. This will go on all year. The home is becoming a social centre as much as a home. Those of you in the creative arts will draw inspiration from the home – the physical surroundings – and from family members.

Renovations could also happen after May 11 and next year.

Beautifying the home is a long-term project and can happen until May 11 and from October 29 to December 21, but during this period November 16 to December 21 is especially good.

A parent or parent figure, if she is of childbearing age, seems fertile this year. Children seem very important and on her mind. Another parent figure is having a good financial year. He or she could be doing important home renovations this year – but an actual move is not likely.

Siblings and sibling figures in your life shouldn't move. They could feel cramped in their present space, but it would be more useful to make better use of the space than to move. Children or children figures are likely to move this year – after May 11. However, this move could happen next year too. They are also more fertile this year (and next year too).

Grandchildren, if you have them, are restless and moving around a lot. They might not formally move but could be in different places for long periods of time. They seem difficult to handle as they want freedom and independence.

Finance and Career

Because your money house is not prominent, not a house of power, finance doesn't seem a big deal. Only short-term planets will move though the house and their effect is short term. This, as regular readers know, tends to the status quo. It tends to a feeling of contentment with things as they are. There is no need to devote unusual focus on these things. (Love is much more important and more fun.)

However, if financial problems arise, it could be due to neglect – not paying enough attention. These problems will force you to focus more. While your personal finances are stable, it's a different story for the spouse, partner or current love. He or she is having a banner financial year – especially from May 11 onwards (although there is a brief lull from October 29 to December 21). This prosperity will more than make up for your stable situation, and he or she is likely to be more generous with you.

When Jupiter moves into your 8th house on May 11, it will be a good time to pay off debt or to take loans on – depending on your need. It is important to be more tax efficient now as well. Good tax planning can add to your income. It is a good time for buying insurance, and if you are of appropriate age, for estate planning. Inheritance often happens under this transit, although no one needs to actually die. You can be named in someone's will or be appointed to some administrative position in an estate. Those of you who deal with estates should have a good year.

If you have good business ideas, this is a good period to seek outside investors for your projects. They are out there. (Perhaps family members would invest or family connections.)

Saturn in your 6th house of health and work shows a fun kind of job. The job involves much work, but it seems enjoyable.

Career will become more important after August 20 when Mars moves into your 10th house of career and stays there for the rest of the year (and well into next year too). Mars in your 10th house shows much activity (and aggressiveness) in the career. You need to fight hard for your position or status (perhaps this is so for your company as well). Since Mars rules your 8th house of regeneration this would indicate that you are dealing with death and death issues this year. Perhaps bosses or a parent figure are having surgery or near-death kinds of experiences. This would create career transformation. Perhaps the government changes the rules and regulations for your industry or company. This would force important changes.

Mars, the ruler of your 8th house, in your career house, would show that your personal sex appeal is important, careerwise.

The planets that rule your finances and career – Venus and Mercury respectively – are both fast-moving planets that move through your entire chart in any given year. So there are many short-term financial and career trends that depend on where these planets are and the kinds of aspects they receive. These short-term trends are best dealt with in the monthly reports.

Love and Social Life

This is where the real action is this year. Your 7th house of love is very powerful until May 11 (and from October 29 to December 21). Overall, it is the strongest house in your chart this year.

Neptune, the most spiritual of the planets, and ruler of your 7th house to boot, has been in your house of love for many years now. Jupiter moved in at the end of last year. So, as we mentioned, this is a happy love year. Singles are likely to be involved in a serious relationship. Marriage (or a relationship that is like marriage) is very likely. Not only that but it seems very happy. Love has been idealistic for many years now; it is even more idealistic this year. There is a strong spiritual connection with the beloved. Your relationship fosters the spiritual growth of both of you.

Spiritual compatibility in love has been important for many years. This year you also want someone with strong family values. You would want someone that the family would approve of – someone who would fit in.

Love seems to be found close to home this year, with no need to travel far and wide in search of it. As we mentioned earlier, you socialize more from home and with family members. A romantic evening at home is preferable to a night out on the town.

Romantic opportunities happen in spiritual types of settings – the yoga studio, the prayer meeting, the meditation lecture, or charity event. They happen as you involve yourself in altruistic kinds of activities.

Romantic opportunities also come from the family, family connections and those who are 'like' family to you. These people like playing Cupid and making introductions. They seem very involved in your love life (in a good way).

Jupiter rules your past – your memory body. So, this year, old flames from the past can come back into the picture. It may not be the actual person, but it can be someone who has the same patterns as the old flame. This can lead either to a rekindling of the old relationship or to the resolution of old issues – or both.

This is a year where you experience the heights of love and passion. Peak experiences.

Those working towards second marriages should probably not marry. There is love – probably multiple relationships – but marriage is not advisable. Enjoy love for what is without projecting too far into the future. The love life will be very exciting though. If you are in your second marriage, it is being tested. More work is needed to hold things together.

Those in or working towards a third marriage will have an active social life, but love is status quo this year. Those of you who are married will tend to stay married and singles will tend to stay single.

Self-improvement

The year ahead will be sexually active as we have mentioned. The latter part of the year especially so. Not only will Jupiter be in your 8th house of regeneration, but your sex planet, Mars, will be prominent at the top of your chart. Good emotional intimacy, the sharing of feelings, will enhance the sexual experience all year. Emotional sex seems just as important as physical sex. However, after May 11 the physical side seems more important. It is will also be good to share ideas and have good communications. Good communication is an important part of foreplay – especially from August 20 onwards.

With Neptune in your 7th house for many years now, the Cosmos has been leading you to spiritual love. We have written of this in past reports, but the trend is still in effect. Even though you will have physical love this year – a physical partner or lover – this is part of the agenda. Yes, love will be happy. But still it is not up to your standards. It is not perfect. Your standards are ultra high, and this has been the case for many years. Even the best of humans cannot live up to them. Human love is, by definition, limited. Some people can love more than others, but always there is some limitation (the human condition and capacity). So it is good to remember that there is a power that loves you absolutely and perfectly. It is a wise kind of love – a love that understands your destiny and purpose. It is always there whether you are in a relationship or not. You feel the same. Being in a physical relationship brings certain pleasures; not being in a relationship brings other pleasures. With spiritual love, it is all the same. You are loved in every place and time. It is good to retreat to this love when you feel disappointments.

This love will always supply every need in love – and often the true need is not what you think. This supply will be seen later on.

Uranus, as we mentioned, is creating long-term change – sudden and dramatic – in your religious, philosophical and theological ideas. This is sometimes uncomfortable. Uranus will often challenge the core beliefs by which we govern our lives. These are the beliefs which give meaning to our lives, so this is very important. You are in a period of great philosophical and theological experimentation. Little by little you will find the system that works for you. There's nothing wrong with you if you feel drawn to foreign religions, or ancient ones that have long ago been discarded. You will find elements of truth there and perceive some of the errors as well. It is as if each system, ancient and modern, grasped some aspect of truth but ignored others. You will, through these processes, formulate your own system – one that works for you.

Month-by-month Forecasts

January

Best Days Overall: 2, 3, 11, 12, 21, 22, 29, 30
Most Stressful Days Overall: 1, 6, 7, 13, 14, 27, 28
Best Days for Love: 2, 3, 6, 7, 11, 12, 17, 21, 22, 26, 29, 30
Best Days for Money: 2, 3, 6, 11, 12, 16, 21, 22, 23, 24, 25, 29,
   30
Best Days for Career: 4, 5, 13, 14, 23

Your party season didn't end with the holidays. It continues until the
20th as you are deep into one of your yearly personal pleasure peaks.
The time for seriousness will come after the 20th; in the meantime
have some fun.

Health should be good all month. But it's probably better after the
25th when Mars leaves his stressful aspect with you. Uranus, your
health planet, starts to move forward on the 18th and receives very
nice aspects all month. You can enhance the health even further by
applying the methods in the yearly report.

Love is an important headline. Serious love is happening. For many
of you the love life is at a lifetime peak. There is more socializing with
the family and at home this month. Family and family connections are
involved in love. In many cases, an old flame from the past is coming
back into the picture – and it looks serious (usually it's not). Even if the
person is not the actual old flame, it can be someone with similar
personality traits.

Love and social opportunities happen through family and family
connections – perhaps at family gatherings or through introductions.
But love also happens in spiritual types of setting: at meditation
sessions, spiritual lectures, charity events, or through being involved
in altruistic kinds of activities. The beloved has to be on your spiritual
wavelength, but also has to have strong family values. Your family is
likely to approve of your beloved.

The problem in love is really you. Mercury, the ruler of your
Horoscope, goes retrograde on the 14th. Love is there, although you
seem hesitant and not sure of what you want. This will pass next month.

Though the month ahead seems prosperous, your financial planet Venus is retrograde almost all month – until the 29th. So take a wait-and-see attitude with finance. Avoid major purchases or investments until the 29th. Work to gain financial clarity instead. If you must make an important purchase, study things carefully. Read the small print in the contract. Make sure the store has a good returns policy. Protect yourself as best as you can.

February

Best Days Overall: 7, 8, 17, 18, 26, 27
Most Stressful Days Overall: 2, 3, 9, 10, 11, 24, 25
Best Days for Love: 2, 3, 7, 8, 12, 13, 17, 18, 22, 23, 27
Best Days for Money: 2, 3, 7, 8, 12, 13, 17, 18, 19, 20, 21, 22, 27
Best Days for Career: 8, 9, 10, 11, 19, 20, 28

Most Virgos are always working. Unemployment is the cruellest form of torture for them. But if you are one of those rare Virgos who are unemployed this is a good month to find work. Those of you who are already employed (the vast majority) will have opportunities for over-time or second jobs.

Health is still good, but after the 18th it needs a little attention. There is nothing serious afoot – only short-term stress caused by short-term planets. After the 18th rest and relax more. Listen to the messages that your body gives. Enhance the health in the ways mentioned in the yearly report.

Love is still the headline this month. As the Sun moves into your 7th house on the 18th you begin a yearly (and for many of you a lifetime) love and social peak. The Sun's move into your 7th house reinforces the importance of spiritual compatibility – the Sun is your spiritual planet. So being on the same spiritual wavelength is the most impor-tant thing. This is not a month for going to bars or clubs in search of love. You might find sex there but not love. The spiritual lecture, the yoga studio, the meditation seminar or charity event is where love awaits you.

The choices you have are either spiritual or more spiritual.

Mercury will move forward on the 4th. This too helps love. You are clearer as to what you want.

Being in a state of love (and many of you are) enhances your spiritual practice and brings a strong connection with the Divine. Those of you on a spiritual path will get good results from chanting, singing, drumming and dancing. Ecstatic kinds of practices – the Bhakti path.

Finances are much better than last month. For a start, your financial planet Venus is moving forward, bringing clarity and confidence. Venus will be in the sign of Capricorn all month – also good for finances. You have sound financial judgement. You get value for your money and you manage your money well. You have a long-term perspective on wealth and are conservative in money matters. This is a very good time to start regular savings and investment plans.

March

Best Days Overall: 6, 7, 8, 16, 17, 25, 26
Most Stressful Days Overall: 2, 3, 9, 10, 23, 24, 30, 31
Best Days for Love: 2, 3, 9, 11, 12, 18, 19, 21, 22, 27, 28, 30, 31
Best Days for Money: 2, 3, 9, 11, 12, 18, 19, 21, 22, 27, 28, 30, 31
Best Days for Career: 8, 9, 10, 19, 20, 28

You're still in a yearly love and social peak this month, until the 20th. In fact, the social life is even stronger than last month as Mercury will also be in your 7th house, from the 10th to the 27th. So you are attending more parties and gatherings. Weddings can be happening in the family circle. All the planets are in the Western, social sector of your chart (except for the Moon, and that only occasionally). Your 7th house is powerful, while your 1st house of self is empty (only the Moon will visit there on the 16th and 17th). Thus, the month ahead is all about other people. It is about cultivating the social graces and putting others ahead of yourself. You are unusually popular and glamorous this month. People feel that you are there for them and this is appreciated. Your good will come through the graces of others, not through self-assertion or personal action.

This is a month where you think more like a Libra than a Virgo. Relationship is everything. It is the meaning and reason for life. One cannot know oneself except through relationship with others. (This will pass, but right now this is how you feel.)

Serious love – and even marriage – is in the air.

Venus travels with Mars until the 12th, indicating good financial cooperation with the beloved. It also shows a positive ability to pay down debt or to take it on (depending on your need). You have good access to outside capital. This is a good transit for tax and insurance planning and, for those of you of an appropriate age, for estate planning. You could be named in someone's will or be appointed to some administrative position in an estate. Sometimes an actual inheritance happens.

Venus (and Mars) move into your 6th house of health and work on the 6th and spend the rest of the month there. This would show earning the old-fashioned way – through your job – through work and practical service.

Health needs watching this month. As always, make sure to get enough rest and to maintain high energy levels. Enhance the health in the ways mentioned in the yearly report. Also pay more attention to the heart. Chest massage and massage of the heart reflex will be beneficial.

On the 20th the Sun moves into your 8th house. So sexual activity will increase. More importantly, it is a time to give birth to the you that you want to be – the you that you could be – your ideal you. To do this, you need to get rid of – eliminate – the old habits, thought and feeling patterns that hold you back. A good psychic purging would be wonderful. This period is good for weight loss and detox regimes.

April

Best Days Overall: 3, 4, 13, 14, 21, 22, 30
Most Stressful Days Overall: 5, 6, 19, 20, 25, 26
Best Days for Love: 8, 9, 17, 18, 25, 26, 27
Best Days for Money: 8, 9, 15, 16, 17, 18, 26, 27
Best Days for Career: 1, 2, 5, 6, 12, 13, 21, 22

Health still needs watching this month. Short-term planets are joining with two long-term planets to increase the stress on you. Happily the impact here is only temporary, but make sure to rest and relax as much as possible, and enhance the health in the ways mentioned in the yearly report.

Sexual activity is even stronger than last month. Mars, your sex planet, enters your 7th house of love on the 15th, while your 8th house remains strong until the 20th. Mars in your 7th house can lead to power struggles in love. If you can avoid these things, love should still be happy.

You're still in a period for personal transformation; for giving birth (or making progress towards) the ideal you, the you that you aspire to be. Keep in mind our discussion of this last month.

The month ahead is socially active, both on a romantic love (your 7th house) and on a friendship level (the 11th house). Friends and social connections can help you with your job and in your health situation. You're attracted to spiritual types of people, both romantically and as friends.

A solar eclipse on the 30th has a relatively mild effect on you. (However, if it hits important points in your personal, Natal horoscope – the one cast specifically for you – it can be powerful indeed.) But it won't hurt to take it easy over that period. Also keep in mind that while it can be relatively kind to you, it might not be so kind for other people around you.

The solar eclipse occurs in your 9th house and impacts college-level students. They make changes in their educational plans and often change schools or courses of study. There can be shake-ups in the college they attend. There can be dramas with students who are applying to college as well. Legal issues, if you're involved with those things, can take a dramatic turn one way or another. There are shake-ups in your place of worship and dramas in the lives of your worship leaders.

Since the Sun is your spiritual planet this eclipse brings spiritual changes, and not just changes of teachers, teachings and practice, but of attitudes as well. There are shake-ups in spiritual and charitable organizations that you're involved with. There are dramas in the lives of guru figures.

Parents and parent figures are making important financial changes. Siblings and sibling figures have important career changes.

May

Best Days Overall: 1, 10, 11, 19, 25, 26
Most Stressful Days Overall: 2, 3, 4, 16, 17, 23, 24, 30, 31
Best Days for Love: 6, 7, 8, 15, 16, 17, 23, 24
Best Days for Money: 6, 7, 8, 12, 13, 16, 17, 25
Best Days for Career: 2, 3, 4, 12, 13, 18, 19, 28, 30, 31

The planetary power is now in the upper half of your chart – the day side. Not only that but your 10th house of career becomes very powerful, from the 21st onwards. Mercury, the ruler of your Horoscope, has been in your 10th house since April 30 and will remain here until the 24th. You seem very successful. This is a month (especially from the 21st onwards – the beginning of a yearly career peak) to focus on your outer objectives and let home, family and emotional issues go for a while. Emotional harmony is always important, but outward success will bring you emotional harmony these days rather than the reverse. The only issue with the career this month is Mercury's retrograde from the 10th onwards. This introduces indecisiveness in you and weakens your self-esteem and self-confidence. But you seem successful nevertheless.

The Sun's entry into your 10th house on the 21st shows that you can enhance the career and your professional status by being involved in charities and altruistic causes. This burnishes your public image and brings important career connections. However, there is another way to read this transit. In many cases, your spiritual practice is the real career – the real mission – from the 21st onwards.

A lunar eclipse occurs on the 16th, which is also relatively mild in its effects on you. It occurs in your 3rd house of communication and impacts students below the college level. (Last month's eclipse affected college-level students.) Thus there are disruptions at school. The school hierarchy can get shaken up. Students often change their educational plans, even schools. Cars and communication equipment get tested and often need repairs. It would be prudent to drive more carefully over this time. This eclipse impacts Saturn, your planet of children. So children and children figures are affected and should take things easy during this period. The same is true for siblings and sibling figures. Children and siblings need to redefine themselves – how they think of themselves and how they want others to think of them. This will lead to new wardrobes and new looks – new presentations to the world – in the coming months.

Since the Moon rules your 11th house, friends are impacted here too. Friendships can be tested – often because of dramas in their own lives. Computers and high-tech gadgetry can behave erratically. Often repairs or replacements are necessary. Keep important files backed up and don't open suspicious emails.

June

Best Days Overall: 6, 7, 15, 16, 23, 24, 25
Most Stressful Days Overall: 13, 14, 19, 20, 26, 27
Best Days for Love: 2, 3, 6, 7, 12, 16, 19, 20, 26, 29, 30
Best Days for Money: 4, 6, 7, 9, 10, 13, 16, 21, 26
Best Days for Career: 6, 7, 17, 26, 27

Success will be even greater this month than last. Your 10th house is even stronger than it was last month, and you're still in the midst of a yearly career peak. Perhaps more importantly, Mercury will start to move forward again on the 4th and enters your 10th house on the 14th (in forward motion). So your personal confidence and self-esteem is back. Mercury at the top of the chart shows that you are on top of your world. People look up to you. In the case of younger Virgos, this tends to signal an aspiration to be on top (but they can be on top in their sphere too).

Health needs watching until the 21st. As always, don't allow yourself to get overtired. Listen to the messages of your body. Enhance the health in the ways mentioned in the yearly report. You will see dramatic improvement after the 21st.

Jupiter left your 7th house on May 11. (This also helps the health.) By now your social and romantic goals have been achieved and Jupiter will expand your 8th house activities. It is time to focus on personal transformation – becoming the person that you want to be, that you aspire to be. Parents or parent figures can be having surgery these days. Children and children figures can move. They are unusually fertile (if they are of an appropriate age). You're in a sexually active kind of period now. Libido is expanding.

On the 21st as the Sun enters your 11th house you become more social – but not so much romantically (that seems settled) as on a friendship level. You're meeting spiritual types of friends. Your knowledge of science, technology, astronomy and astrology will expand (you have more of a head for these things now). Your friendships become an important part of your spiritual path.

Finance is not a big deal this month – career is much more important. Venus will travel with Uranus on the 10th and 11th and this brings some financial changes. Often unexpected money comes, but sometimes this transit brings an unexpected expense. Still, the money to cover it will come too. Avoid speculations on the 17th and 18th. Basically, the month ahead is stable on the financial level. Your status and prestige will increase but your finances not so much.

July

Best Days Overall: 4, 5, 12, 13, 21, 22, 31
Most Stressful Days Overall: 10, 11, 16, 17, 23, 24
Best Days for Love: 6, 7, 9, 15, 16, 17, 26, 27
Best Days for Money: 1, 2, 6, 7, 10, 11, 15, 18, 19, 26, 28, 29
Best Days for Career: 8, 16, 17, 23, 24, 28, 29

Health is much improved over last month. There is only one long-term planet in stressful alignment with you. And the short-term planets are mostly in harmonious aspect. However, Mars will make a dynamic aspect with Uranus, your health planet, on the 30th and 31st. This can bring a medical procedure or surgery – or it is recommended to you. It will be a good idea to be more mindful on the physical plane during that period too. This mindfulness and care on the physical plane are important on the 1st and 2nd as well, as Mars makes a stressful aspect with Pluto.

Love, as we mentioned in the previous month, seems settled. There's no need to overly focus on it. But friendships and group activities still seem active until the 23rd. Mercury's trine with Neptune on the 16th and 17th brings romantic opportunity – either with your current love or with someone new.

On the 23rd, the Sun moves into your 12th house of spirituality – his own sign and house. He is very strong here. So this is an intense spiritual period (Mercury, the ruler of your Horoscope, will enter there as well, on the 19th), and the focus is on spiritual matters. These two beneficent planets in your 12th house show much spiritual advancement and much satisfaction from your spiritual practice. The dream life will be hyperactive and revelatory. Be sure to make a note of them. There will be all kinds of supernatural-type experiences. Your personal ESP and spiritual faculties will be much enhanced. The invisible world is letting you know that it is around and ready to help.

Though your money house is empty – only the Moon moves through there on the 6th and 7th – finances will be good. Until the 18th Venus, your financial planet, will be in your 10th house – a most powerful position. This shows focus and aspiration. It shows the financial favour of bosses, parents, parent figures and elders. Pay rises – official or unofficial – happen. Your good career reputation leads to increased earnings. On the 18th Venus enters your 11th house – a beneficent house. This indicates rich friends and friends who bring financial opportunity. It also favours earning from the online world. The 11th house is where 'fondest hopes and wishes' come true. And this will happen financially.

August

Best Days Overall: 1, 9, 10, 17, 18, 27, 28
Most Stressful Days Overall: 7, 8, 13, 14, 20, 21
Best Days for Love: 4, 5, 13, 14, 15, 23, 25, 26
Best Days for Money: 2, 3, 4, 5, 7, 15, 25, 26, 29, 30
Best Days for Career: 9, 17, 18, 20, 21, 29

The month ahead is very spiritual. As in life, first there is interior growth before outer growth materializes. On the 23rd, your spiritual progress becomes visible to yourself and the world.

Your ruler, Mercury, has his solstice from the 22nd to the 24th. He pauses in his latitudinal motion, and then changes direction. So it is with you. There is a pause in your personal desires and in the career and then a change of direction. This is all very natural and normal and there's no need to be alarmed.

By the 20th, when Mars moves to the Eastern sector – the sector of self – this sector will be as strong as it will ever be this year. It is not dominant, to be sure, just stronger than it has been. Thus, although other people are still very important, and your social graces are still important, now you can shift some attention to number one – to your personal happiness. You need to balance your personal interests with those of others – and especially with those of the spouse, partner or current love. If there are changes to be made to improve your happiness, now is the time to make them. Later on, when the planets move westwards again, it will be more difficult.

Planetary retrograde activity increases this month; 40 per cent of the planets are moving backwards until the 24th, and the percentage increases to 50 per cent after the 24th. (And we are not yet at the maximum for the year – that happens next month.) The pace of life slows down. Patience is necessary to deal with this.

Health is still good – in spite of the fact that Mars moves into a stressful aspect with you from the 20th. When the Sun moves into your sign on the 23rd, you begin another yearly personal pleasure peak. Since not much is happening in the world, you may as well enjoy yourself. The Sun's move into your 1st house on the 23rd brings charisma and a supernatural glamour to the image. Knowledge of how to mould, shape and sculpt your body by spiritual means will come to you as well. A good period for getting the body in the shape that you want.

Love is more complicated this month. Neptune, your love planet, is retrograde and receives stressful aspects after the 23rd. This can indicate a pause in a current relationship. It can cast doubt about it. If love is real, the relationship will survive. You and the beloved seem distant – far apart – from the 4th to the 26th. This might not mean physical distance but psychological distance. You see things in opposite ways and your challenge will be to bridge the differences.

Finance seems good this month. Venus, your financial planet, is moving forward all month. Until the 12th she is in the 11th house – a beneficent house, signalling good family support and support and financial opportunities that come from friends. After the 12th Venus moves into your 12th house of spirituality. Intuition is very important financially.

September

Best Days Overall: 5, 6, 13, 14, 15, 23, 24
Most Stressful Days Overall: 3, 4, 9, 10, 16, 17, 30
Best Days for Love: 2, 4, 5, 9, 10, 13, 14, 15, 19, 20, 29
Best Days for Money: 3, 7, 8, 11, 16, 21, 24, 26, 27, 30
Best Days for Career: 7, 8, 16, 17, 24

Mercury, the ruler of your Horoscope, goes retrograde on the 10th. This brings retrograde activity to its maximum extent for the year. Mercury retrograde will be a lot stronger in its effects than the previous ones this year, as there is a cumulative effect caused by so many other retrogrades.

Mercury's retrograde complicates the love life even more than last month. Now both you and the beloved are indecisive and not sure what you want. Avoid making important love decisions this month.

Mars entered your 10th house of career on August 20 and will remain here until the end of the year. So, career demands are strong. Perhaps you're dealing more with death and death-related issues. Perhaps there is necessary surgery, or near-death kinds of experience to do with bosses, elders, parents or parent figures. The need to confront death seems high on the agenda.

Venus, your financial planet, has her solstice from September 30 to October 3. This shows a pause in your financial affairs and then a change of direction – it mirrors Venus's behaviour in the heavens.

Finances, however, are excellent this month. Venus is moving forward all month. On the 5th she enters your own sign and 1st house and stays there until the 30th. This is wonderful for finances: she brings financial windfalls. Happy financial opportunities will come. The money people in your life are devoted to you. Money (and opportunity) pursue you.

You look good this month. The Sun in your own sign until the 23rd brings charisma, star quality and a spiritual glamour. Venus brings beauty and conventional grace. You dress expensively and stylishly. You display your prosperity. This month is a good time to buy clothing or accessories as your taste is excellent.

Health is very good this month too – especially until the 23rd. A Grand Trine in the Earth signs is very comfortable for you, as Earth is your native element. You are even more organized than usual.

October

Best Days Overall: 2, 3, 11, 12, 21, 22, 30
Most Stressful Days Overall: 1, 7, 13, 14, 27, 28
Best Days for Love: 4, 5, 6, 7, 8, 13, 14, 17, 25, 26
Best Days for Money: 4, 5, 8, 9, 13, 14, 18, 23, 24, 25, 26, 27
Best Days for Career: 2, 3, 13, 14, 23, 24

A prosperous month ahead, Virgo. The Sun entered your money house on the 23rd of last month and is there until the 23rd of this one. Mercury moves into your money house on the 11th and stays there until the 30th. Most importantly Venus, your financial planet, entered the money house on September 30 and will be there until the 23rd. Venus will be very strong in her own sign and house and this signals increased earnings. Greater financial power. You are in the midst of a yearly financial peak until the 23rd. With the Sun in your money house you're more charitable these days. But you're earning more and can afford to be charitable.

Health is still good this month. You can enhance it further in the ways mentioned in the yearly report.

A solar eclipse occurs in your 3rd house of communication on the 25th. This eclipse only has a mild effect on you but it won't hurt to reduce your schedule anyway. It might not be so mild on others around you (and, if it hits a sensitive point in your personal Natal horoscope – cast especially for you – it can be a lot more powerful than we say). This eclipse impacts students below the college level. There can be disturbances at school, shake-ups in the hierarchy there. It often brings changes in educational plans and sometimes actual changes of school. Siblings and sibling figures in your life are affected. They have career and personal dramas. They need to redefine themselves these days and change their self-concept – how they think of themselves and how they want others to think of them. This will lead to a new presentation – a new look – in the coming months. The money people in your life are making important financial changes. Every solar eclipse affects your spiritual life and this one is no different. (This one will also affect the spiritual life of a parent or parent figure as well.) There are changes in teaching, teachers and overall practice. There are shake-ups in a spiritual or charitable organization that you or the parent figure are involved with. There are dramas in the lives of guru figures. Intuition needs to be verified carefully during this period.

The good news about this eclipse is that it occurs as planetary retrograde activity is lessening. Things are starting to move forward again, and the eclipse is a big factor in this.

November

Best Days Overall: 7, 8, 17, 18, 26, 27
Most Stressful Days Overall: 3, 4, 10, 11, 24, 25, 30
Best Days for Love: 3, 4, 13, 14, 23, 24, 30
Best Days for Money: 3, 4, 13, 14, 19, 20, 23, 24
Best Days for Career: 3, 4, 10, 11, 13, 14, 24, 25

A very powerful total lunar eclipse on the 8th is the main headline this month. This 'Blood Moon' eclipse impacts many other planets, which is why it is so strong – it impacts on many areas of life.

The eclipse occurs in your 9th house, thus it affects college-level students or those seeking entry to college. (The previous eclipse impacted students below college level.) There are shake-ups in their institutions – shake-ups in the hierarchy of the institutions. Courses and professors can be changed. One college (perhaps your favourite) can reject you while another accepts you. (This is probably for the best.) Often educational plans change. Students often change their courses of study and even colleges. There are shake-ups at your place of worship and dramas in the lives of your worship leaders too. Your own religious and theological beliefs will get tested, and often some revision is necessary. Often old beliefs need to be discarded. Since the Moon rules your 11th house, friendships get tested and there are likely to be dramas in the lives of friends. Computers and other high-tech equipment get tested; often repair or replacement is necessary.

The impact of the eclipse on Mercury – a very important planet in your chart – brings career changes and shake-ups in the hierarchy of your company or industry. There are life-changing dramas in the lives of bosses, elders, parents or parent figures. The impact on Mercury also forces you to redefine yourself, your image and self-concept. You need to define yourself for yourself or others will do it for you, and this will not be so pleasant. In the coming months you will change your wardrobe, hairstyle and overall 'look'.

The impact on Uranus, your health and work planet, can signal job changes and changes in your health regime. If you employ others, there can be unusual employee turnover rates.

The impact of this lunar eclipse on Venus brings financial changes. The events of the eclipse will show where your financial thinking and strategy have been unrealistic, enabling you to make course corrections.

December

Best Days Overall: 4, 5, 6, 14, 15, 16, 23, 24
Most Stressful Days Overall: 1, 7, 8, 21, 22, 27, 28
Best Days for Love: 1, 2, 3, 10, 11, 14, 20, 23, 24, 27, 28
Best Days for Money: 1, 2, 3, 11, 14, 17, 18, 20, 21, 23, 24, 29
Best Days for Career: 2, 3, 7, 8, 14, 15, 23, 24

Health still needs attention until the 22nd. Short-term planets are in stressful alignment with you. Most of this stress passes by the 22nd, however, and you'll see a dramatic improvement in health. In the meantime, pay more attention to the heart – massage the reflex point and the chest and ribs. Make sure to get enough rest and review the discussion in the yearly report.

Career seems active as Mars is still in your 10th house. But home and family issues are stronger now. Do what you can careerwise, but focus on the home, family and your emotional wellness. Your spiritual planet the Sun is in your family house until the 22nd. This shows that your spiritual path this period is about resolving old issues from the past – they hold you back. Venus, your financial planet, is in the 4th house until the 10th, signalling good family support, and that you're earning money from home and through family and family connections. You probably spend more on the home and family as well. On the 10th, Venus moves into Capricorn, your house of fun and creativity. Though you become more speculative, it will not be out of control. The financial planet in Capricorn tends to be sober and judicious in money matters. If you do speculate, it will be well hedged and well thought out. You earn in happy ways and spend on happy things. You spend more on the children and children figures in your life.

Jupiter moves into your 8th house of regeneration on the 21st – this time for the long haul. This can signal an inheritance, although in many cases no one has to actually die. You can be named in someone's will or be appointed to some administrative position in an estate. With Mars, the ruler of your 8th house, still at the top of the chart in your 10th house, you are dealing with death and death issues, however. Perhaps surgery or a near-death experience. It makes you more serious about life.

Love is good this month, especially from the 7th onwards. Neptune, your love planet, starts to move forward on the 4th and receives positive aspects after the 22nd. The real issue in love is you – Mercury goes retrograde on the 29th and you seem undecided about things.

The month ahead is a party period. Your 5th house of fun, creativity and children gets gradually stronger as the month progresses. On the 22nd, as the Sun moves into this house, you begin a yearly personal pleasure peak. Time to let go of worries and cares and just enjoy life. Take a vacation from worry. You'll find that many problems just solve themselves.

The planetary momentum is overwhelmingly forward this month. Events are moving forward. The pace of life quickens.

An unusual number of planets are 'out of bounds' this month. Usually there are one or two planets 'out of bounds', but this month there are three. So, it is something in the air. Going outside boundaries seems trendy. Many people are doing it – you included.

Libra

⎯

THE SCALES

Birthdays from
23rd September to
22nd October

Personality Profile

LIBRA AT A GLANCE

Element – Air

Ruling Planet – Venus
   Career Planet – Moon
   Love Planet – Mars
   Money Planet – Pluto
   Planet of Communications – Jupiter
   Planet of Health and Work – Neptune
   Planet of Home and Family Life – Saturn
   Planet of Spirituality and Good Fortune – Mercury

Colours – blue, jade green

Colours that promote love, romance and social harmony – carmine, red, scarlet

Colours that promote earning power – burgundy, red-violet, violet

Gems – carnelian, chrysolite, coral, emerald, jade, opal, quartz, white marble

Metal – copper

Scents – almond, rose, vanilla, violet

Quality – cardinal (= activity)

Qualities most needed for balance – a sense of self, self-reliance, independence

Strongest virtues – social grace, charm, tact, diplomacy

Deepest needs – love, romance, social harmony

Characteristic to avoid – violating what is right in order to be socially accepted

Signs of greatest overall compatibility – Gemini, Aquarius

Signs of greatest overall incompatibility – Aries, Cancer, Capricorn

Sign most helpful to career – Cancer

Sign most helpful for emotional support – Capricorn

Sign most helpful financially – Scorpio

Sign best for marriage and/or partnerships – Aries

Sign most helpful for creative projects – Aquarius

Best Sign to have fun with – Aquarius

Signs most helpful in spiritual matters – Gemini, Virgo

Best day of the week – Friday

Understanding a Libra

In the sign of Libra the universal mind – the soul – expresses its genius for relationships, that is, its power to harmonize diverse elements in a unified, organic way. Libra is the soul's power to express beauty in all of its forms. And where is beauty if not within relationships? Beauty does not exist in isolation. Beauty arises out of comparison – out of the just relationship between different parts. Without a fair and harmonious relationship there is no beauty, whether in art, manners, ideas or the social or political forum.

There are two faculties humans have that exalt them above the animal kingdom: their rational faculty (expressed in the signs of Gemini and Aquarius) and their aesthetic faculty, exemplified by Libra. Without an aesthetic sense we would be little more than intelligent barbarians. Libra is the civilizing instinct or urge of the soul.

Beauty is the essence of what Librans are all about. They are here to beautify the world. One could discuss Librans' social grace, their sense of balance and fair play, their ability to see and love another person's point of view – but this would be to miss their central asset: their desire for beauty.

No one – no matter how alone he or she seems to be – exists in isolation. The universe is one vast collaboration of beings. Librans, more than most, understand this and understand the spiritual laws that make relationships bearable and enjoyable.

A Libra is always the unconscious (and in some cases conscious) civilizer, harmonizer and artist. This is a Libra's deepest urge and greatest genius. Librans love instinctively to bring people together, and they are uniquely qualified to do so. They have a knack for seeing what unites people – the things that attract and bind rather than separate individuals.

Finance

In financial matters Librans can seem frivolous and illogical to others. This is because Librans appear to be more concerned with earning money for others than for themselves. But there is a logic to this financial attitude. Librans know that everything and everyone is connected and that it is impossible to help another to prosper without also prospering yourself. Since enhancing their partner's income and position tends to strengthen their relationship, Librans choose to do so. What could be more fun than building a relationship? You will rarely find a Libra enriching him- or herself at someone else's expense.

Scorpio is the ruler of Libra's solar 2nd house of money, giving Libra unusual insight into financial matters – and the power to focus on these matters in a way that disguises a seeming indifference. In fact, many other signs come to Librans for financial advice and guidance.

Given their social grace, Librans often spend great sums of money on entertaining and organizing social events. They also like to help others when they are in need. Librans would go out of their way to help a friend in dire straits, even if they have to borrow from others to do so. However, Librans are also very careful to pay back any debts they owe, and like to make sure they never have to be reminded to do so.

Career and Public Image

Publicly, Librans like to appear as nurturers. Their friends and acquaintances are their family and they wield political power in parental ways. They also like bosses who are paternal or maternal.

The sign of Cancer is on Libra's 10th career house cusp; the Moon is Libra's career planet. The Moon is by far the speediest, most changeable planet in the horoscope. It alone among all the planets travels through the entire zodiac – all twelve signs and houses – every month. This is an important key to the way in which Librans approach their careers, and also to what they need to do to maximize their career potential. The Moon is the planet of moods and feelings – Librans need a career in which their emotions can have free expression. This is why so many Librans are involved in the creative arts. Libra's ambitions wax and wane with the Moon. They tend to wield power according to their mood.

The Moon 'rules' the masses – and that is why Libra's highest goal is to achieve a mass kind of acclaim and popularity. Librans who achieve fame cultivate the public as other people cultivate a lover or friend. Librans can be very flexible – and often fickle – in their career and ambitions. On the other hand, they can achieve their ends in a great variety of ways. They are not stuck in one attitude or with one way of doing things.

Love and Relationships

Librans express their true genius in love. In love you could not find a partner more romantic, more seductive or more fair. If there is one thing that is sure to destroy a relationship – sure to block your love from flowing – it is injustice or imbalance between lover and beloved. If one party is giving too much or taking too much, resentment is sure to surface at some time or other. Librans are careful about this. If anything, Librans might err on the side of giving more, but never giving less.

If you are in love with a Libra, make sure you keep the aura of romance alive. Do all the little things – candle-lit dinners, travel to exotic locales, flowers and small gifts. Give things that are beautiful, not necessarily expensive. Send cards. Ring regularly even if you have nothing in particular to say. The niceties are very important to a Libra. Your relationship is a work of art: make it beautiful and your Libran lover will appreciate it. If you are creative about it, he or she will appreciate it even more; for this is how your Libra will behave towards you.

Librans like their partners to be aggressive and even a bit self-willed. They know that these are qualities they sometimes lack and so they like their partners to have them. In relationships, however, Librans can be very aggressive – but always in a subtle and charming way! Librans are determined in their efforts to charm the object of their desire – and this determination can be very pleasant if you are on the receiving end.

Home and Domestic Life

Since Librans are such social creatures, they do not particularly like mundane domestic duties. They like a well-organized home – clean and neat with everything needful present – but housework is a chore and a burden, one of the unpleasant tasks in life that must be done, the quicker the better. If a Libra has enough money – and sometimes even if not – he or she will prefer to pay someone else to take care of the daily household chores. However, Librans like gardening; they love to have flowers and plants in the home.

A Libra's home is modern, and furnished in excellent taste. You will find many paintings and sculptures there. Since Librans like to be with friends and family, they enjoy entertaining at home and they make great hosts.

Capricorn is on the cusp of Libra's 4th solar house of home and family. Saturn, the planet of law, order, limits and discipline, rules Libra's domestic affairs. If Librans want their home life to be supportive and happy they need to develop some of the virtues of Saturn – order, organization and discipline. Librans, being so creative and so intensely in need of harmony, can tend to be too lax in the home and too permissive with their children. Too much of this is not always good; children need freedom but they also need limits.

Horoscope for 2022

Major Trends

Health and energy began improving last year. You came through a few rough years from 2018–2020, but now two important planets which were stressing you out are either in harmonious aspect to you or leaving you alone. Health should continue to be good this year. Perhaps the improvement was credited to some doctor or therapy or new regime, but the truth is that the planetary power shifted in your favour. More on this below.

Though health is good, you still seem focused on it – especially until May 11. However, this is a year where you land a dream kind of job. Ideal. Perfect. More on this later.

The love life is excellent this year – especially after May 11. Jupiter will be in your 7th house of love then and this will lead to serious relationships for singles. Perhaps even marriage. This trend will continue well into next year too. More details later.

Pluto has been in your 4th house for twenty or so years now. This has been transforming the whole family and home situation. During this time there have probably been deaths in the family, and perhaps surgery or near-death kinds of experiences in the lives of family members. This trend is still in effect in the year ahead. But family life seems happier since last year. More on this later.

Saturn has been in your 5th house since very late in 2020. This indicates a need to discipline the children and children figures in your life – to set some kind of limits on them. It is challenging as it can't be overdone. Discipline has to be applied 'just so'.

Neptune has been in your 6th house of health for many years and will be there for many more to come. This transit shows someone going deeper into the laws of spiritual healing. The spiritual aspects of physical health are being revealed. More on this later.

Uranus has been in your 8th house for some years now and will be there for a few more. This signals sexual experimentation. This is basically a good thing, so long as it isn't destructive. The spouse, partner or current love is experimental in his or her finances.

Your most important interests this year are home and family; children, fun and creativity; health and work; love and romance (from May 11 to October 29 and from December 21 onwards); sex, personal transformation and occult studies; and foreign travel, religion, philosophy, theology and higher learning (from August 20 onwards).

Your paths of greatest fulfilment this year will be health and work (until May 11 and from October 29 to December 21); love and romance (from May 11 to October 29 and from December 21 onwards); and religion, philosophy, theology, foreign travel and higher learning (from August 20 onwards).

Health

(Please note that this is an astrological perspective on health and not a medical one. In days of yore there was no difference, both these perspectives were identical. But these days there could be quite a difference. For a medical perspective, please consult your doctor or health practitioner.)

Health is good this year, as we mentioned. Until May 11 there is only one long-term planet in stressful alignment with you (and most of you won't even feel this: those of you born late in the sign of Libra – October 17–22 – will feel it the most strongly). After May 11 Jupiter will make stressful aspects – but Jupiter's stresses tend to be mild. Health is good.

Your 6th house of health is very prominent this year. So, you are focused on this area. Generally this is a good thing, but this year you could be overdoing it. The tendency is to magnify little things into big things. Be careful of such hypochondria. It is probably better to focus on healthy lifestyles and regimes than to over-focus on minor ailments.

Good though your health is you can make it better. Give more attention to the following – the vulnerable areas of your Horoscope this year (the reflex points are shown in the chart below):

- The kidneys and hips are always important for Libra, and regular hip massage should be part of your normal health regime. It will not only strengthen the kidneys and hips but the lower back as well.
- The feet too are always important for Libra. Regular foot massage is always beneficial for you. See our chart below.
- The liver and thighs. These have only become important since December 30 last year, when Jupiter entered your 6th house. They

Important foot reflexology points for the year ahead

Try to massage all of the foot on a regular basis – the top of the foot as well as the bottom – but pay extra attention to the points highlighted on the chart. When you massage, be aware of 'sore spots' as these need special attention. It's also a good idea to massage the ankles and below them.

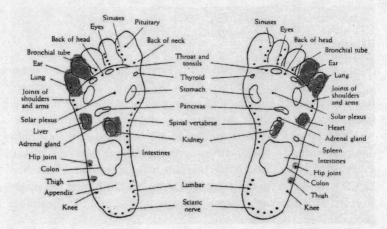

remain an important area until May 11 (and also from October 29 to December 21). The reflexes are shown above. Regular thigh massage will not only strengthen the liver and thighs but the lower back (and colon) as well.

- The heart is always very important for those of you born late in the sign of Libra – October 17 to 22. For the rest of you, the heart becomes important from May 11 to October 29 and from December 21 onwards, and it will be important next year too. The reflex is shown above. Chest massage – especially of the breastbone and upper rib cage – strengthens the heart. The important thing with the heart is to avoid worry and anxiety, the two emotions that stress it out. Replace worry with faith. Meditation is a big help here.

With Neptune as your health planet you respond very well to spiritual-healing techniques. If you feel under the weather, try seeing a spiritual healer. Many of you are exploring spiritual healing these days too – and if not, you should. More on this later.

Your health planet is in a Water sign – and this has been the case for the past ten years. Thus you have a good connection to the healing powers of the Water element – and these are considerable. If you feel under the weather, take a long leisurely bath. It would be good to soak in natural waters – in oceans, rivers, lakes or springs. Water applied to any area of the body that bothers you should be effective. Let the water – from the tap or the shower – flow over the afflicted area.

Home and Family

Your 4th house has been a house of power for the past twenty or so years and is still prominent in the year ahead. Pluto has been occupying this house and Pluto's job is to transform – to renew things through death and new birth. By now (Pluto is getting ready to move out of this house and his job seems to be done) most of you are in new home and family conditions. There have been deaths in the family – literally and figuratively. There have been many life and death dramas over the years. The purpose was to give birth to your ideal home and ideal domestic situation.

There have been deaths in the family but also new births to balance things out. Nature always compensates. If it takes something it replaces it with something else. Home and family (and your overall emotional life) are much better now.

Pluto is your financial planet, and his presence in the 4th house shows many things. You earn money from home, through family and family connections. There is good family support. You spend on the home but can also earn from here. Over the years you've been making the home as much a place of business as a home. Home offices have been set up, and perhaps home-based businesses as well.

Your emotional life has been undergoing a detox for many years as well. And by now it is much more pure – more clean – than it has been.

Pluto in the 4th house indicates that there have been many renovations of the home over the years, and more could happen this year too. If you're planning such work, January 25 to March 6 would be a good time.

A move was more likely in 2020 than now. There is nothing against it though – but nothing that especially supports it.

A parent or parent figure in your life has faced many near-death kinds of experiences over the years, and January 25 to March 6 could bring more of the same. This parent or parent figure will have a good financial year – this is his or her focus. This parent or parent figure could move (or enjoy the fortunate purchase or sale of a home) from May 11 onwards. (This move could also happen next year.) If the parent or parent figure is of childbearing age, there is greater fertility after May 11.

Siblings or sibling figures could move this year. Often it is not a literal move but the acquisition of another home, or the expansion or renovation of the existing home, or buying expensive items for the home. The effect is 'as if' they have moved. Their marriages or existing relationships gets tested from August 20 onwards.

Children and children figures in your life are difficult to handle as they seem very rebellious and on edge this year. They could have moved multiple times in recent years, and it can happen in coming years too. They are restless, have an intense desire for change and for breaking with the status quo. Their emotional lives are not stable. Meditation will be a big help for them.

Grandchildren, if you have them, are having a quiet, stable home and family year.

Finance and Career

Your money house is not prominent this year – not a house of power. This has been the case for some years now and tends to the status quo. You are basically content with things as they are and have no special need to make dramatic changes or to overly focus here. The financial upheavals of 2020 don't seem to have affected you too much, and probably led to greater wealth.

Pluto, your financial planet, has been in Capricorn (and your 4th house) for decades now, and will remain there in the year ahead. The financial planet in Capricorn signals sound financial judgement. It gives a long-term perspective on wealth. You have a good sense of what an investment will be worth many years down the road. You take a methodical step-by-step approach to wealth. You are thinking long term and are not especially interested in the 'fast buck'. You manage what you have efficiently. This money-management skill is perhaps just as important as increased earnings. You make good use of what you have.

This position favours long-term savings and investment plans. You have a disciplined approach to money. If you still haven't set up such a plan, the year ahead is still good for it.

Pluto rules inheritance. And many of you have received an inheritance over the past years. But in many cases no one has to actually die: you can be named in someone's will or be appointed to some administrative position in an estate. Many Libras are involved in the arts and antiques business. Thus, many deal with estates. These still seem profitable in the year ahead.

Pluto in your 4th house of home and family shows that you spend much on the home and family and earn from here as well. We discussed this earlier. Family support has been good. Family and family connections are important financially.

Jupiter has been in your 6th house of health and work since the end of 2021. This shows a fabulous job opportunity happening. A dream job.

This is not an especially strong career year. Your 10th house is basically empty. Only short-term planets move through there and their impact is temporary. Your 4th house of home and family is stronger than your 10th house of career. In addition, most of the long-term planets are in the night side – the bottom half – of your chart. So this is a year for cultivating emotional wellness and harmony and for dealing with home and family issues. However, you can succeed in your career from your point of emotional harmony. The problem is that the interest – the desire – for outward success is not there.

The Moon as your career planet reinforces this reading. Generically, the Moon rules home and family. So for most of you this is your real career (even if you are involved in worldly things) – home and family come first.

Love and Social Life

The year ahead – especially the latter part of the year – is going to be a great love year. Benevolent Jupiter will enter your 7th house on May 11. He will be there until October 29 and then return on December 21, spending approximately half the year in your 7th house of love.

So, singles are likely to marry or be involved in a relationship that is 'like' a marriage. This is especially so for those working on the first marriage. In general your social circle will expand. You will be meeting new and significant people. You will meet interesting people in your neighbourhood – people who were always there, but you've never met. There will be more socializing with neighbours, siblings and sibling figures.

Generically Jupiter rules foreigners, religious people and academics. You find these people alluring now. You like people you can learn from. We see this in other ways too. Mars, your love planet, will spend a lot of time (over four months) in your 9th house, reinforcing what we say here.

You have the aspects this year of someone who falls in love with their professor, minister, priest or imam – your worship leader or teacher. Love opportunities could happen in foreign lands or at religious or educational functions. People at school or in your place of worship can play Cupid. Siblings, sibling figures and neighbours could also play Cupid.

The physical aspects of love are always important, but you need more than that these days. There has to be a meeting of minds. You don't have to agree on every point but you should at least be on the same page. More relationships fail because of philosophical incompatibility than for any other reason. The other reasons are just the 'excuses' that mask the philosophical problems.

For those in or working on the second marriage this is also a good social year. If you are single, marriage could happen. If you are already married, there is more romance in the marriage.

Those in or working on the third marriage will have an expansive social life, but the love life is quiet. Those who are married will tend to stay married, and singles will tend to stay single.

You tend to be a love-at-first-sight kind of person by nature, and this year even more so. You go after what you want. You don't play games. If you like someone they know about it.

Those already in a relationship can enhance their relationship by taking courses – in subjects that interest you – as a couple. A foreign trip will also enhance an existing relationship. Worshipping together as a couple will also do much to deepen your relationship.

Self-improvement

Neptune has been in your 6th house of health for many years, so you are in a cycle for exploring the spiritual dimensions of health. There is a very strong and intimate connection between the two things. The body is only the place where disease happens, but it never originates there. Always, without exception, it has its origins in the more subtle regions – the realms of thought and feeling. So, while it is good to relieve symptoms (it relieves suffering) we shouldn't confuse this with a cure. Cure only happens when both the symptoms *and* their underlying root causes are dealt with. These root causes can only be dealt with spiritually. This is the realm of spiritual healing.

Spiritual disconnection – disconnection from the source of life, the Divine – is the root cause of all disease, for all people. In your case it is more dramatic, so it is very important for you to stay in a state of grace. This is good for its own sake, but for you it is an actual health issue.

There is nothing that spirit can't cure if allowed in.

By now you understand much more about this. But there is always more to learn. And this is a good year for doing so (even more than in previous years). Read all you can on the subject. The works of Ernest Holmes and Emmet Fox are good places to start. This will lead you to other books. There is much literature on this subject. (There is a lot of this kind of information on my blog www.spiritual-stories.com, for those interested in learning more.)

Uranus, as we mentioned earlier, has been in your 8th house of regeneration for some years now, leading you to be experimental in sexual matters. This has good points and dangers. The good points are that everyone responds sexually in different ways. Everyone is wired up in a unique way. What pleasures one, displeases another. There is no 'one way' to enjoy sex. So the object is to learn about ourselves and our partners and see what works for us. This requires letting go of the rule books and experimenting in real life. This is how real knowledge is attained. The dangers here are also real. Sometimes this experimentation can turn destructive. The act of sex is an act of love, not of pain and destruction. So experiment by all means, but keep it constructive.

Month-by-month Forecasts

January

Best Days Overall: 4, 5, 13, 14, 23, 24, 31
Most Stressful Days Overall: 2, 3, 8, 9, 16, 17, 29, 30
Best Days for Love: 1, 2, 3, 8, 9, 11, 12, 19, 21, 22, 29, 30
Best Days for Money: 3, 6, 12, 16, 22, 25, 26, 30
Best Days for Career: 2, 3, 11, 12, 16, 17, 23

Health needs watching this month. Basically, the health is good, but there are short-term stresses caused by the short-term planets. Much of this will pass after the 20th, but you still need to pay attention. The good news is that your 6th house of health is very strong and you are on the case. You can enhance the health with foot massage, spiritual-healing techniques, chest and rib massage and massage of the heart reflex. Perhaps most importantly, rest when tired. Don't allow yourself to get overtired.

Home and family are where the action is this month. At least 80 per cent (sometimes 90 per cent) of the planets are below the horizon of your chart in the night side of the Horoscope. Your 10th house of career is empty – only the Moon will move through there on the 16th and 17th. So we have a clear message. Focus on the domestic situation – your emotional wellness – and let career issues go. You are building the infrastructure upon which a successful career can be built. You're building the foundations for it. This is interior work. It happens behind the scenes.

This is a month for important psychological-type breakthroughs. Those involved in therapy will make much progress. Even if you're not involved in professional therapy, you will still make progress here as the Cosmos will become your therapist. Old, long-forgotten memories will arise, spontaneously, allowing you to look at them from your present state of consciousness. This, of itself, brings healing. Things that traumatized you as a child now bring a smile.

Venus, your ruling planet, is retrograde until the 28th. So you need to get clearer on personal goals. Be sure of what you really want before you act.

Finances are good this month. Your financial planet Pluto is receiving positive aspects. Also, with Jupiter in your 6th house of work you have wonderful job aspects. Dream job opportunities are coming to you.

Mars, your love planet, is 'out of bounds' from the 12th to the 31st. So, singles are looking for love outside their usual spheres. Those already in relationships find that the spouse, partner or current love is also operating outside the normal boundaries.

Love is close to home until the 25th. It is found in the neighbour-hood and perhaps with neighbours. Siblings and sibling figures like to play Cupid. There are romantic opportunities at schools, lectures, seminars, the library or bookstore. After the 25th Mars moves into your 4th house. Love is still close to home but can happen through family or family connections. There will be more socializing at home. Family values seem important in love. Emotional intimacy can be just as important as physical intimacy. Mars likes to be aggressive in love

– Mars is a love-at-first-sight kind of planet. But in the sign of Capricorn (from the 25th onwards) he is more restrained. This is a good thing. You look before you leap.

February

Best Days Overall: 1, 9, 10, 11, 19, 20, 28
Most Stressful Days Overall: 5, 6, 12, 13, 26, 27
Best Days for Love: 5, 6, 7, 8, 17, 18, 26, 27
Best Days for Money: 2, 3, 8, 12, 13, 18, 21, 22, 23, 27
Best Days for Career: 1, 9, 10, 12, 13, 22, 23

A happy month ahead, Libra. You're still in a yearly personal pleasure peak until the 18th (it began on January 20). Health is improving day by day, but still needs watching. You are in a party period. Time to enjoy life. Time to take a vacation from worry and care and let the magic of joy do its work. Sure, you will work hard this month – your 6th house is very powerful – but you will enjoy your work; it won't feel like work.

Health still needs some attention, but you are on the case. That's good news. It would be more dangerous if you were ignoring things. Jupiter in your 6th house shows that you will get best-case scenarios with any health issue. Continue to enhance the health in the ways mentioned last month. On the 18th, as the Sun enters your 6th house, you gravitate to alternative kinds of healing. Even if your stay with orthodox medicine, you favour new cutting-edge technologies.

Personal pleasure – the enjoyment of life – is not only good in its own right but will assist in your spiritual practice. Stress is one of the biggest blockages to spiritual growth. The Divine is not stressed, is not labouring; it does everything easily and powerfully. Personal creativity will be very inspired during this period, until the 18th.

Prosperity is still strong this month. Venus, the ruler of your Horoscope, is travelling near Pluto, your financial planet. (The aspect will be more exact next month, but you're feeling it even now.) This shows financial increase and closeness to the money people in your life. You look and feel more prosperous. Family support is good.

Mars, your love planet, is still 'out of bounds' until the 10th. So, like last month, you are outside your normal boundaries in the search for love. Those already in relationships find that the spouse, partner or current love is outside his or her normal orbit. But in spite of this (or perhaps because of this) love seems happy. Venus and Mars are travelling together from the 25th to the 28th. This indicates a romantic relationship. It shows a closeness with the beloved.

The planetary momentum is overwhelmingly forward this month. Indeed, after the 4th all of them are moving forward. So, the pace of life quickens. Events move fast, in your personal world and in the world at large. Babies born during this period will be fast developers in life.

The power in your 6th house (strong all year) becomes even stronger after the 18th. Jobseekers have multiple job opportunities, and they are good ones. You're a hot commodity in the jobs market these days. New job opportunities can come to those of you already employed as well. This can be with other companies or opportunities for overtime or second jobs. Children and children figures in your life are having a banner financial month. Guru figures in your life seem involved in a serious romantic relationship.

March

Best Days Overall: 1, 9, 10, 18, 19, 27, 28
Most Stressful Days Overall: 4, 5, 11, 12, 13, 25, 26
Best Days for Love: 4, 5, 9, 18, 19, 27, 28
Best Days for Money: 2, 3, 8, 11, 12, 18, 21, 22, 26, 30, 31
Best Days for Career: 2, 3, 11, 12, 13, 23

There are a lot of positive signals for love this month. Mars, your love planet, is travelling with Venus, the ruler of your Horoscope, until the 12th, showing a romantic relationship and high social grace (more than usual). On the 20th the Sun enters your 7th house and you begin a yearly love and social peak. (Love will get even better next month.) Romance is in the air. Singles might not be single for too much longer. Those already in relationships are unusually close to the beloved (especially until the 12th). Both Mars and Venus change signs this month – they leave Capricorn and enter Aquarius on the 6th and they stay there for the rest of the month. This shows a more experimental attitude to love. It shows the enjoyment of love. A playful attitude.

You're having fun with the beloved. Romantic opportunities happen for singles in the usual places – parties, gatherings, the theatre, resorts and places of entertainment. The online world and social media also seem a venue for romance.

Health is much improved this month – especially after the 6th. Although later on, after the 20th, it will need keeping an eye on again. The good news is that your 6th house is still very powerful all month and you are on the case. Enhance the health in the ways mentioned in the yearly report. There is nothing seriously amiss; it is only short-term stress caused by the transit of short-term planets.

Jobseekers still have excellent job prospects this month, and this applies even to those already employed. You're still a hot commodity in the jobs market. Those of you who employ others have good job applicants. Not only that, but you're expanding the workforce.

Both Mars and Venus travel with Pluto, your financial planet, from the 2nd to the 4th. This brings financial increase to both you and the beloved. It often brings opportunities for a business type of partnership or joint venture. You and the beloved are cooperating financially and seem on the same page – in agreement. The Sun and Jupiter also travel together, from the 4th to the 6th. This too brings financial increase. Friends are also prospering and can bring opportunity.

By the 6th finance doesn't seem such a big deal. Your money house is empty (only the Moon will move through there on the 21st and 22nd). Finances will tend to be stable. There is a feeling of content-ment with things as they are.

Children and children figures are still having a strong financial month. (The whole year so far has been good financially for them). Parents and parent figures are also prospering, and you seem very involved in this. Aunts and uncles are having a good month too. They are prospering as well.

April

Best Days Overall: 5, 6, 15, 16, 23, 24
Most Stressful Days Overall: 1, 2, 8, 9, 21, 22, 28, 29
Best Days for Love: 1, 2, 5, 6, 8, 17, 18, 25, 26, 27, 28, 29
Best Days for Money: 4, 8, 9, 14, 17, 18, 26, 27, 28
Best Days for Career: 1, 2, 8, 9, 10, 11, 20, 21, 30

Though health still needs watching until the 20th the month ahead seems happy and prosperous. With your 6th house still very strong this month you're paying attention to health, and that is good. Enhance the health in the ways mentioned in the yearly report. You will see dramatic improvement after the 20th.

All the planets are in the Western, social sector of your chart this month. The only exception is the Moon, which will occasionally visit the East (from the 8th to the 20th). Your 7th house of love is very powerful until the 20th, while your 1st house of self is basically empty. So the focus is on others and their needs – this is natural to you anyway. The focus on the Western sector is very comfortable for you. Personal independence is not strong, but you are used to getting your way through consensus and cooperation.

You're still in a yearly love and social peak until the 20th, so love is going well. Mars, your love planet, makes an important move into Pisces, your 6th house, on the 15th, signalling some changes in love attitudes. First, you seem more serious about love; it's not just fun and games as it has been recently. Love is now idealistic and spiritual. Spiritual compatibility is very important. Also, you show love in practical ways – through practical service to the beloved. Service is love in action. The workplace becomes a venue for romance. Jobseekers look at the social aspects of a job as much as the other factors. There are love opportunities with co-workers and people involved in your health. Health professionals are alluring these days.

Your 8th house of regeneration becomes powerful from the 20th. It becomes even more pronounced due to a solar eclipse on the 30th which occurs there. Eclipses in the 8th house tend to be dramatic, so take it nice and easy during that period. This eclipse can bring confrontations with death – generally only psychological confrontations.

Sometimes there is a near-death experience or close call. Sometimes surgery is recommended. Friends can have near-death kinds of experiences as well. These are kindly cosmic reminders to get more serious about life; it is short and can end at any time, so it is important to knuckle down to the work that you came here to do.

This eclipse brings financial changes to the spouse, partner or current love. He or she has been making important changes for years now, but this eclipse accelerates things. Friendships get tested and there are dramas in the lives of friends. Computers and high-tech gadgetry behave erratically.

May

Best Days Overall: 2, 3, 4, 12, 13, 21, 30, 31
Most Stressful Days Overall: 5, 6, 19, 25, 26
Best Days for Love: 7, 8, 9, 16, 17, 18, 25, 26
Best Days for Money: 1, 6, 11, 16, 14, 15, 20, 25, 28
Best Days for Career: 5, 6, 10, 11, 20, 30

An eventful month. Jupiter makes a major move from your 6th house into your 7th house on the 11th. The love life is blooming even more than it has been. Venus enters your 7th house on the 3rd and Mars on the 25th. So though technically you're not in a yearly love and social peak, the social life is very active and happy.

Like last month all the planets (with the exception of the Moon) are in your favourite sector, the Western social sector. So the month ahead, like last month, is about others and their needs. Your normal Libra tendencies are very much enhanced. Your normal social grace – always strong – is even stronger.

The other headline of the month is the lunar eclipse of the 16th. This occurs in your money house and shows a need for course corrections in finance. Your financial thinking, planning and strategies, your financial assumptions, haven't been realistic and you're forced to change things. This eclipse impacts Saturn, so parents and parent figures are affected as well. They should reduce their schedules over this period. The Moon, the eclipsed planet, is your career planet and also rules the parent or parent figure. So parents are having personal dramas. Career changes are also afoot. There are dramas in the lives of bosses and shake-ups in the hierarchy of your company and industry. Sometimes people change their career paths under such an eclipse, but most of the time they merely need to change the way that they pursue that path. Siblings and sibling figures make changes to their finances. There are dramas in the lives of family members and repairs can be needed in the home.

The planetary power is now mostly above the horizon – the day side of your chart; 60 per cent, sometimes 70 per cent of the planets are on the day side. This is a time for focusing on your career and outer objectives. (The eclipse will force some attention on the home, but when that is over, focus on your career.)

June

Best Days Overall: 9, 10, 17, 18, 26, 27
Most Stressful Days Overall: 1, 2, 3, 15, 16, 21, 22, 28, 29, 30
Best Days for Love: 4, 6, 7, 13, 14, 16, 21, 22, 26
Best Days for Money: 4, 7, 11, 12, 13, 16, 21, 25
Best Days for Career: 1, 2, 3, 9, 10, 18, 28, 29, 30

Your 7th house is still very strong this month. Jupiter is there along with Mars. Mars in his own sign and house is more powerful on your behalf. The social grace is unusually strong. Your love planet in Aries makes you a love-at-first-sight kind of person. You know immediately when someone is for you. You are aggressive in love and jump into relationships quickly. You're developing a fearlessness about love. Even if rejection happens, you pick yourself up and get back into the race – as the expression goes. As long as you overcome the fear you are successful. Singles are in a marriage kind of period. You're in the mood for serious love, for commitment. You may or may not get married in a legal way, but you will be involved in a relationship that is 'like' a marriage.

The month ahead is happy. The power is in your 9th house – a beneficent house – until the 21st. Travel – foreign travel – is likely. College-level students are doing well in their studies. There is a strong interest in religion, philosophy and theology, and philosophical breakthroughs are likely.

The month ahead is successful for you, Libra. On the 21st the Sun enters your 10th house and you begin a yearly career peak. With your family planet Saturn retrograde from the 4th onwards, you may as well focus on the career. Family issues will need time to resolve; there are no quick solutions there. Friends seems successful too, and they are opening doors for you. Good technology skills seem important.

Health should be watched this month – especially from the 21st. As always, make sure to get enough rest. Enhance the health in the ways mentioned in the yearly report.

Finances are more complicated now as Pluto, your financial planet, is retrograde. This won't stop earnings, only slow things down a bit. Venus makes beautiful aspects with Pluto on the 20th and 21st and this brings some happy financial event.

July

Best Days Overall: 6, 7, 14, 15, 23, 24
Most Stressful Days Overall: 12, 13, 18, 19, 20, 26, 27
Best Days for Love: 2, 3, 6, 7, 12, 13, 15, 18, 19, 20, 21, 22, 26
Best Days for Money: 1, 2, 5, 8, 9, 10, 11, 13, 18, 19, 22, 28, 29
Best Days for Career: 8, 9, 17, 26, 27, 28, 29

Continue to focus on the career. Nothing much has changed since last month. Your family planet is still retrograde, while your 10th house of career is even stronger than last month. You're in a period of outer success. Ride the wave. On the 18th, as Venus moves into your 10th house, this success is even greater. You are on top of your world. People look up to you. You are recognized not just for professional achievements, but for who you are and your overall demeanour. Your personal appearance plays an important role in your career success from the 18th onwards.

Health still needs some care. You need to rest whenever possible and listen to the messages the body gives you. The demands of the career can't be avoided, but you can work more steadily and focus on the really important things in your life. Let the trivia go. If possible, spend time in a health spa, or schedule more massages or health treatments. Enhance the health in the ways mentioned in the yearly report.

Your love planet moves out of your 7th house on the 5th and enters your 8th house, signalling more changes in your love attitude. Sexual magnetism seems the primary allurement now for singles. In general, the month ahead is more sexually active.

Personal finances are more stressful until the 23rd. Pluto is stressfully aspected and in retrograde motion. Earnings will happen, but with more challenges and more delays. The good news is that the spouse, partner or current love is having a strong financial month and he or she will pick up the slack. Your personal finances should improve after the 23rd, but they still occur with delays.

Your social life is active and happy in two ways - romantically and in the area of friendships. On the 23rd the Sun moves into your 11th house and you become more involved with groups and group activities. You seem successful here as the Sun rules your 11th house and he is strong in his own sign and house. This is a good time to enhance your knowledge of science, technology, astronomy and astrology too. Many people have their personal horoscopes done under these kinds of transits. It is also auspicious for buying high-tech equipment or gadgetry. Your choices will tend to be good.

Planetary retrograde activity increases this month. Until the 28th 30 per cent of the planets are retrograde; after that it is 40 per cent. The good news is that your career planet, the Moon, never goes retrograde, so the career is not affected.

August

Best Days Overall: 2, 3, 11, 12, 20, 21, 29, 30
Most Stressful Days Overall: 9, 10, 15, 16, 22, 23
Best Days for Love: 1, 4, 5, 9, 10, 15, 16, 18, 19, 25, 26, 29
Best Days for Money: 4, 5, 7, 10, 15, 18, 25, 28
Best Days for Career: 7, 8, 16, 22, 23

Health is much improved, and after the 12th it will improve even further. You have plenty of energy to achieve your goals.

Social activity is still strong this month. Your 7th house of romance is still strong - Jupiter is there - and your 11th house of friends, groups and group activities is even stronger than last month. You have both love and friendships. Your love planet Mars moves into your 9th house on the 20th and stays there for the rest of the year. This changes the love attitudes and needs once again. Before the 20th sex and sexual magnetism seemed paramount in love. But after the 20th you want more intellectual and philosophical compatibility. Though other things generally get the blame, most relationships break up because of philosophical differences – different world views and different core values. So although you don't need to agree on every point with the beloved, you do need to be on the same page philosophically. The love planet in the 9th house favours people from foreign lands, highly educated and refined people and religious-minded people. Love and social opportunities will happen at university or university functions, at your place of worship or religious functions or in foreign lands. Those in a current relationship can bolster it with a foreign trip.

College-bound students will weigh the social aspects of the institution as much as the academic ones.

Mars travels with Uranus on the 1st and 2nd and this brings an opportunity for a love affair (not necessarily something serious). This is a dynamic aspect so be more mindful on the physical plane. This goes for the spouse, partner or current love as well.

Finances seem stressed on the 8th and 9th. You seem 'distant' from money and from the money people in your life. Career, status and prestige are much more important these days than mere money. You still seem very successful until the 12th. After that career goals, the short-term ones at least, appear to be attained and you can focus on other things.

Finances will improve after the 12th as the stressful aspects to Pluto leave. But Pluto is still retrograde and your money house is still empty. Finance is just not a big deal at the moment. (Finances will improve next month.)

Though the Eastern sector of self is not dominant, it is about as strong as it will get this year, and you are in a period of stronger personal independence (which will get stronger in the next two months). So, while keeping in mind the needs of others, make the changes that need to be made for your personal happiness. You can be a bit more personally assertive than you have been this past year. (You definitely won't overdo it.)

September

Best Days Overall: 7, 8, 16, 17, 26, 27
Most Stressful Days Overall: 5, 6, 11, 12, 18, 19, 20
Best Days for Love: 4, 5, 7, 8, 11, 12, 13, 14, 15, 16, 17, 26, 27
Best Days for Money: 1, 2, 3, 6, 11, 14, 15, 21, 24, 28, 29, 30
Best Days for Career: 5, 6, 14, 15, 18, 19, 20, 25, 26

Your spiritual life became important on August 23 and is still important until the 23rd of this month. You are a social creature by nature, but now more solitude might be in order. Have no fear, you're not becoming a recluse, you're just getting more in touch with yourself and your own aura. This is normal when the 12th house is strong. Spiritual growth, which is what this period is about, happens best in solitude with no outer distractions.

With retrograde activity hitting its maximum extent for the year you might as well withdraw and develop your spiritual life. Nothing much is happening in the world. The pace of life is at its slowest for the year. When doors are closed on the physical plane, it is best to work spiritually. The spiritual doors are always open.

On the 23rd, as the Sun enters your 1st house, you begin a yearly personal pleasure peak. The sensual delights will open up to you. The body gets more pampering. The physical appearance and overall health and energy will also improve. The Sun brings star quality and charisma to the image.

With your 1st house strong from the 23rd onwards, make those changes that need to be made for your happiness. Love others, but take care of number one as well.

Health is good this month and improves further after the 23rd. A rare Grand Trine in the Air signs, your native element, further enhances your health. But it will also enhance your intellectual and communication faculties. Those of you involved in writing, teaching, sales, marketing, advertising and PR will do well. One of the problems with this much Air – and especially for you – is that the mind can get overstimulated very easily. It goes round and round to no avail, thinking the same thoughts over and over. There is also a tendency to talk too much. These consume energy that the body needs for other things – healing, cell repair, digestion, etc. So be careful about this.

A Grand Trine in the Earth signs (we have two Grand Trines in one month) will boost finances. Pluto is still retrograde, but he will receive nice aspects from the Sun on the 17th and 18th and from Venus on the 25th and 26th. These should be nice paydays. But the Grand Trine will help finances in other ways. It brings a down-to-earth attitude to life. It enhances your management skills. It gives the ability to create ease on the material plane.

Love is as we have described last month. Mars remains in Gemini, your 9th house, all month.

October

Best Days Overall: 4, 5, 13, 14, 23, 24
Most Stressful Days Overall: 2, 3, 9, 10, 16, 17, 30
Best Days for Love: 4, 5, 9, 10, 13, 14, 15, 24, 25
Best Days for Money: 3, 8, 9, 12, 18, 22, 25, 26, 27
Best Days for Career: 4, 5, 13, 14, 16, 17, 25

A happy and prosperous month, Libra, enjoy.

You're still in the midst of a yearly personal pleasure peak until the 23rd. And though retrograde activity is less than last month it is still intense. You may as well enjoy yourself. Enjoy all the pleasures of the senses. Pamper the body. Reward it for its yeoman service to you. With Venus in your own sign until the 23rd it is a good time for beautifying the body and for purchasing clothing and accessories. You were born with good aesthetic taste, but this month it is even stronger – your purchases will be good.

Love also looks happy. You look great. Self-esteem and self-confidence are as strong as they will be this year. The social grace is very strong. Venus is making nice aspects with Mars, your love planet. And although you are more independent than usual, it doesn't seem to affect love. The only issue with love is Mars's retrograde on the 30th. But for most of the month there is no problem.

On the 23rd, as the Sun (and Venus) enter your money house, you begin a yearly financial peak. It should be a prosperous period. Your money planet Pluto receives nice aspects too after the 23rd. Earnings will happen before the 23rd, but with more difficulty.

A solar eclipse on the 25th occurs in your money house. Thus you will be making important financial changes. The events of the eclipse will show you where your financial thinking and assumptions were unrealistic and enable you to make course corrections. These will work out well over the long haul, but they are not so comfortable while they are happening. This eclipse has only a mild effect on you, but it won't hurt to reduce your schedule a bit. It seems stronger on the money people in your life and those involved in your finances. They need to take a reduced schedule. Every solar eclipse brings dramas with friends and the testing of friendships and this one is no different. It will also test your computers and high-tech equipment. They can behave errat-ically. (There is no question that planetary phenomena affect physical things - especially delicate things like computers and software; the only issue is *how* this happens.)

November

Best Days Overall: 1, 2, 10, 11, 19, 20, 28, 29
Most Stressful Days Overall: 5, 6, 12, 13, 26, 27
Best Days for Love: 1, 2, 3, 4, 5, 6, 10, 11, 13, 19, 20, 23, 24, 28, 29
Best Days for Money: 4, 8, 9, 14, 18, 22, 23, 27
Best Days for Career: 3, 4, 12, 13, 14, 23

The consensus among astrologers is that a solar eclipse is stronger than a lunar one. But this is a big generalization and is not always the case. Take the lunar eclipse of the 8th as an example. Because it affects many more planets than the solar eclipse last month, it is definitely stronger. It is not only the Moon that is impacted, but Mercury, Uranus and Venus (particularly important for you). Also, this eclipse is total, while the last solar eclipse was partial. It impacts you personally and the world at large.

This is the main headline this month.

This eclipse occurs in your 8th house and can bring confrontations (generally on a psychological level) with death. It can bring near-death experiences and dreams of death. Since the Moon is your career planet, it brings career changes. Generally it brings shake-ups in the hierarchy of your company or industry. It can bring shake-ups in the rules and regulations governing your industry. And, sometimes, it actually changes the career path. Parents, parent figures, bosses and elders have personal dramas. The impact on Mercury brings spiritual changes – changes in teachings, teachers and practice. There are shake-ups in a spiritual or charitable organization that you're involved with. There are dramas in your place of worship. Dramas in the lives of worship leaders. Your religious and philosophical beliefs will get tested and some will have to be revised, while others will be discarded. You will live your life differently after this eclipse. College-level students are also affected and may change their educational plans – perhaps suddenly. Sometimes they change schools. Children and children figures are impacted as well. They should relax more over this period, and stay out of harm's way.

In spite of the eclipse you seem prosperous. The changes you make will be good. You're still in the midst of a yearly financial peak until the 22nd.

Health also looks good.

December

Best Days Overall: 7, 8, 17, 18, 25, 26
Most Stressful Days Overall: 2, 3, 9, 10, 11, 23, 24, 29, 30
Best Days for Love: 2, 3, 7, 8, 14, 17, 18, 23, 24, 25, 26, 29, 30
Best Days for Money: 1, 6, 11, 15, 16, 19, 20, 21, 24, 29
Best Days for Career: 2, 3, 9, 10, 11, 13, 22, 23

Your love planet is still retrograde this month, but love is gradually getting better and better. It's just not wise to make important, long-term love decisions right now. Things are not what they seem. Jupiter, which had retrograded back into your 6th house on October 29, now moves back into your 7th house on the 21st. He will be there well into next year. So, romance (perhaps even marriage) is happening. Siblings and sibling figures seem involved in your love life. Perhaps neighbours as well. You are attracted to foreigners, but these people can be living next door. You don't need to travel to find love.

Your 3rd house of communication and intellectual interests is powerful until the 22nd. So this is a good period for students; they are focused on their studies and should do well. And, even if you're not a student, your intellectual faculties are stronger than usual and it is a good month to read and study more, or to take courses in subjects that interest you.

On the 22nd, the Sun moves into your 4th house and you enter the midnight period of your year. You can let go of career issues for a while and focus on the home and family. If you want to advance your career, do so by the methods of night rather than the methods of day. Dream more. Visualize where you want to be careerwise. Get into the feeling of 'being there'. Later, when the planets shift to the top of your chart again, overt actions will happen spontaneously (and powerfully).

Finances will be good this month. Pluto, your financial planet, started to move forward again on October 8 and this month will receive good aspects. (Next month the aspects will be even better.) There is financial confidence and enhanced earning power.

Health needs watching after the 22nd, but this is merely temporary stress caused by the short-term planets and is not really serious. Still, make sure to rest and relax more. Low energy can make you vulnerable to opportunistic infections. Enhance the health in the ways mentioned in the yearly reports.

Scorpio

ᛗ

THE SCORPION

Birthdays from
23rd October to
22nd November

Personality Profile

SCORPIO AT A GLANCE

Element – Water

Ruling Planet – Pluto
  Co-ruling Planet – Mars
  Career Planet – Sun
  Love Planet – Venus
  Money Planet – Jupiter
  Planet of Health and Work – Mars
  Planet of Home and Family Life – Uranus

Colour – red-violet

Colour that promotes love, romance and social harmony – green

Colour that promotes earning power – blue

Gems – bloodstone, malachite, topaz

Metals – iron, radium, steel

Scents – cherry blossom, coconut, sandalwood, watermelon

Quality – fixed (= stability)

Quality most needed for balance – a wider view of things

Strongest virtues – loyalty, concentration, determination, courage, depth

Deepest needs – to penetrate and transform

Characteristics to avoid – jealousy, vindictiveness, fanaticism

Signs of greatest overall compatibility – Cancer, Pisces

Signs of greatest overall incompatibility – Taurus, Leo, Aquarius

Sign most helpful to career – Leo

Sign most helpful for emotional support – Aquarius

Sign most helpful financially – Sagittarius

Sign best for marriage and/or partnerships – Taurus

Sign most helpful for creative projects – Pisces

Best Sign to have fun with – Pisces

Signs most helpful in spiritual matters – Cancer, Libra

Best day of the week – Tuesday

Understanding a Scorpio

One symbol of the sign of Scorpio is the phoenix. If you meditate upon the legend of the phoenix you will begin to understand the Scorpio character – his or her powers and abilities, interests and deepest urges.

The phoenix of mythology was a bird that could recreate and reproduce itself. It did so in a most intriguing way: it would seek a fire – usually in a religious temple – fly into it, consume itself in the flames and then emerge a new bird. If this is not the ultimate, most profound transformation, then what is?

Transformation is what Scorpios are all about – in their minds, bodies, affairs and relationships (Scorpios are also society's transformers). To change something in a natural, not an artificial way, involves a transformation from within. This type of change is radical change as opposed to a mere cosmetic make-over. Some people think that change means altering just their appearance, but this is not the kind of thing that interests a Scorpio. Scorpios seek deep, fundamental change. Since real change always proceeds from within, a Scorpio is very interested in – and usually accustomed to – the inner, intimate and philosophical side of life.

Scorpios are people of depth and intellect. If you want to interest them you must present them with more than just a superficial image. You and your interests, projects or business deals must have real substance to them in order to stimulate a Scorpio. If they haven't, he or she will find you out – and that will be the end of the story.

If we observe life – the processes of growth and decay – we see the transformational powers of Scorpio at work all the time. The caterpillar changes itself into a butterfly; the infant grows into a child and then an adult. To Scorpios this definite and perpetual transformation is not something to be feared. They see it as a normal part of life. This acceptance of transformation gives Scorpios the key to understanding the true meaning of life.

Scorpios' understanding of life (including life's weaknesses) makes them powerful warriors – in all senses of the word. Add to this their depth, patience and endurance and you have a powerful personality. Scorpios have good, long memories and can at times be quite vindictive

– they can wait years to get their revenge. As a friend, though, there is no one more loyal and true than a Scorpio. Few are willing to make the sacrifices that a Scorpio will make for a true friend.

The results of a transformation are quite obvious, although the process of transformation is invisible and secret. This is why Scorpios are considered secretive in nature. A seed will not grow properly if you keep digging it up and exposing it to the light of day. It must stay buried – invisible – until it starts to grow. In the same manner, Scorpios fear revealing too much about themselves or their hopes to other people. However, they will be more than happy to let you see the finished product – but only when it is completely unwrapped. On the other hand, Scorpios like knowing everyone else's secrets as much as they dislike anyone knowing theirs.

Finance

Love, birth, life as well as death are Nature's most potent transformations; Scorpios are interested in all of these. In our society, money is a transforming power, too, and a Scorpio is interested in money for that reason. To a Scorpio money is power, money causes change, money controls. It is the power of money that fascinates them. But Scorpios can be too materialistic if they are not careful. They can be overly awed by the power of money, to a point where they think that money rules the world.

Even the term 'plutocrat' comes from Pluto, the ruler of the sign of Scorpio. Scorpios will – in one way or another – achieve the financial status they strive for. When they do so they are careful in the way they handle their wealth. Part of this financial carefulness is really a kind of honesty, for Scorpios are usually involved with other people's money – as accountants, lawyers, stockbrokers or corporate managers – and when you handle other people's money you have to be more cautious than when you handle your own.

In order to fulfil their financial goals, Scorpios have important lessons to learn. They need to develop qualities that do not come naturally to them, such as breadth of vision, optimism, faith, trust and, above all, generosity. They need to see the wealth in Nature and in life, as well as in its more obvious forms of money and power. When they develop generosity their financial potential reaches great heights, for Jupiter, the Lord of Opulence and Good Fortune, is Scorpio's money planet.

Career and Public Image

Scorpio's greatest aspiration in life is to be considered by society as a source of light and life. They want to be leaders, to be stars. But they follow a very different road than do Leos, the other stars of the zodiac. A Scorpio arrives at the goal secretly, without ostentation; a Leo pursues it openly. Scorpios seek the glamour and fun of the rich and famous in a restrained, discreet way.

Scorpios are by nature introverted and tend to avoid the limelight. But if they want to attain their highest career goals they need to open up a bit and to express themselves more. They need to stop hiding their light under a bushel and let it shine. Above all, they need to let go of any vindictiveness and small-mindedness. All their gifts and insights were given to them for one important reason – to serve life and to increase the joy of living for others.

Love and Relationships

Scorpio is another zodiac sign that likes committed, clearly defined, structured relationships. They are cautious about marriage, but when they do commit to a relationship they tend to be faithful – and heaven help the mate caught or even suspected of infidelity! The jealousy of the Scorpio is legendary. They can be so intense in their jealousy that even the thought or intention of infidelity will be detected and is likely to cause as much of a storm as if the deed had actually been done.

Scorpios tend to settle down with those who are wealthier than they are. They usually have enough intensity for two, so in their partners they seek someone pleasant, hard-working, amiable, stable and easy-going. They want someone they can lean on, someone loyal behind them as they fight the battles of life. To a Scorpio a partner, be it a lover or a friend, is a real partner – not an adversary. Most of all a Scorpio is looking for an ally, not a competitor.

If you are in love with a Scorpio you will need a lot of patience. It takes a long time to get to know Scorpios, because they do not reveal themselves readily. But if you persist and your motives are honourable, you will gradually be allowed into a Scorpio's inner chambers of the mind and heart.

Home and Domestic Life

Uranus is ruler of Scorpio's 4th solar house of home and family. Uranus is the planet of science, technology, changes and democracy. This tells us a lot about a Scorpio's conduct in the home and what he or she needs in order to have a happy, harmonious home life.

Scorpios can sometimes bring their passion, intensity and wilfulness into the home and family, which is not always the place for these qualities. These traits are good for the warrior and the transformer, but not so good for the nurturer and family member. Because of this (and also because of their need for change and transformation) the Scorpio may be prone to sudden changes of residence. If not carefully constrained, the sometimes inflexible Scorpio can produce turmoil and sudden upheavals within the family.

Scorpios need to develop some of the virtues of Aquarius in order to cope better with domestic matters. There is a need to build a team spirit at home, to treat family activities as truly group activities - family members should all have a say in what does and does not get done. For at times a Scorpio can be most dictatorial. When a Scorpio gets dictatorial it is much worse than if a Leo or Capricorn (the two other power signs in the zodiac) does. For the dictatorship of a Scorpio is applied with more zeal, passion, intensity and concentration than is true of either a Leo or a Capricorn. Obviously this can be unbearable to family members - especially if they are sensitive types.

In order for a Scorpio to get the full benefit of the emotional support that a family can give, he or she needs to let go of conservatism and be a bit more experimental, to explore new techniques in childrearing, be more democratic with family members and to try to manage things by consensus rather than by autocratic edict.

Horoscope for 2022

Major Trends

Health and energy will be better than last year, but will still need watching, Scorpio. Two powerful long-term planets are in stressful alignment with you, so make sure you get enough rest. More on this later.

The year ahead seems happy, however – a fun kind of year. Your 5th house is very powerful – especially until May 11, and from October 29 to December 21. So roughly half the year. This is a time for exploring the fun side of life. Good for creative hobbies. Those of you who are of childbearing age are more fertile than usual. In general, it is good (and fulfilling) to be involved with children.

Finances are excellent this year – especially until May 11 and from October 29 to December 21. From May 11 to October 29, and then again from December 21, there are excellent job opportunities. Unemployed Scorpios will not be unemployed for long. Even those already employed can be offered better job opportunities, either with their present employer or with a new one. More details later.

Saturn has been in your 4th house since December 2020, and remains there for the year ahead. Thus the home and family situation seems burdensome. You're taking on more responsibility at home. More on this later.

Uranus has been in your 7th house of love for some years now and will be there for some more to come. This is testing marriages and long-term relationships. As if this wasn't enough, the four eclipses in the year ahead also impact here. Love can be stormy. Details later.

Mars spends an unusual amount of time in your 8th house of regeneration this year – over four months. (Generally, he spends a month and a half in a sign.) This is giving a strong message. It can show surgery for you – or it can be recommended – and financial changes for children and children figures in your life. More on this later.

Pluto has been in your 3rd house for twenty or so years – a very long-term transit. He will be there for the year ahead but is getting ready to leave. This impacts on siblings, sibling figures and neighbours. Your neighbourhood has undergone radical transformation over the years. Siblings and sibling figures have led stormy, tumultuous lives.

For students below college level, learning has been slower, but what was learned was deeper.

Your most important interests this year are communication and intellectual interests; home and family; children, fun and creativity; health and work (from May 11 to October 29 and from December 21 onwards); and love and romance.

Your paths of greatest fulfilment this year are children, fun and creativity (until May 11 and from October 29 to December 21); health and work (from May 11 to October 29 and December 21 onwards); and love and romance.

Health

(Please note that this is an astrological perspective on health and not a medical one. In days of yore there was no difference, both these perspectives were identical. But these days there could be quite a difference. For a medical perspective, please consult your doctor or health practitioner.)

Health, as we mentioned, is much improved over last year but still needs attention. The good news is that your 6th house becomes very powerful after May 11. So you will be focused here. On the case. Watchful.

There is much you can do to enhance your health and prevent problems from developing. Give more attention to the following – the vulnerable areas of your Horoscope this year (the reflex points are shown in the chart opposite):

- The heart became especially important last year and is still important in the year ahead. The reflex is shown above. Chest massage – especially of the breastbone and upper rib cage – will also strengthen the heart. The important thing with the heart is to cultivate faith rather than worry and anxiety. The consensus among spiritual healers is that worry and anxiety are the root causes of heart problems.
- The liver and thighs become an important area after May 11 when Jupiter enters your 6th house. They will be important next year too. The reflexes are shown above. Regular thigh massage will not only strengthen the liver, but the lower back and colon as well.

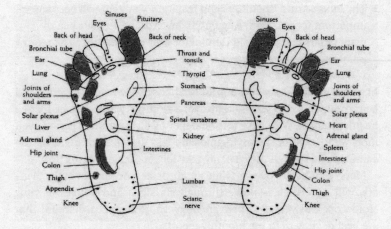

Important foot reflexology points for the year ahead

Try to massage all of the foot on a regular basis – the top of the foot as well as the bottom – but pay extra attention to the points highlighted on the chart. When you massage, be aware of 'sore spots' as these need special attention. It's also a good idea to massage the ankles – and especially below them.

- The colon, bladder and sexual organs are always important areas for Scorpio and this year is no different. Safe sex and sexual moderation continue to be priorities.
- The head and face. Regular scalp and face massage should be part of your normal health regime. This will not only strengthen the head and face but the entire body as well. Craniosacral therapy is an excellent treatment for you.
- The adrenals. These too are always important for Scorpio, and the reflexes are shown above. The vital thing here is to avoid anger and fear, the two emotions that stress them out. Meditation is a big help here.
- The musculature. You don't need to be a body-builder with bulging muscles. You only need good muscle tone. Weak or flabby muscles can knock the spine and skeleton out of alignment, which can cause all kinds of other problems. So vigorous physical exercise is important for you – according to your age and stage in life.

- The lungs, arms, shoulders and respiratory system will become important for you from August 20 onwards, when your health planet Mars camps out in Gemini for over four months. The reflex points are shown above.

Mars's unusually long stay in your 8th house shows that surgery could be recommended to you. Perhaps you see surgery as the quick fix to a health problem. (You have this tendency by birth, but this period even more so.) However, detox regimes are less drastic and might do the same things, though they usually take longer. Explore detox first.

Mars, your health planet, while not the fastest or slowest of the planets, will nevertheless move through six signs and houses of your Horoscope this year. So, there are many short-term health trends that are best dealt with in the monthly reports.

Home and Family

Your 4th house has been prominent since last year and is a house of power this year too. Many of you moved last year, but it was complicated. A move in the year ahead is not likely – or advisable. You might feel cramped where you are but it is better to make more efficient use of the space that you have than to move.

The family situation seems stressful. You seem bound by duty and obligation, not by love and joy. There are disappointments here. You are taking on more responsibility with family matters and thus it seems a burden. You sort of have to grit your teeth and endure it: there's no way to escape. This seems a karmic situation. Handling this will lead to much spiritual growth.

Saturn in the 4th house gives a tendency to depression. You need to avoid this as it never helps. Meditation will be very useful here. Learn to enjoy your burdens rather than chafe at them.

Saturn rules your 3rd house of communication and intellectual interests. Thus you are making the home as much a place of learning as a home. You're building up the library, installing computers and software. Many of you are involved in home schooling. Many of you will hold classes or lectures at home. You're probably installing new communications equipment too.

The 3rd house also rules siblings, sibling figures and neighbours. Siblings could be moving in with you or spending much time in your home. The neighbours seem unusually involved in the home and family matters.

If you're planning a major renovation or construction project in the home, March 6 to April 15 would be a good time. The latter half of July also seems good. If you're redecorating or otherwise beautifying the home, March 6 to April 5 and June 9–12 are good times.

A parent or parent figure is having a rough time this year. He or she seems unduly pessimistic and feel older than their years. Sudden mood changes afflict him or her. There is a tendency to multiple moves these days – this has been going on for some years. Sometimes it's not an actual move, but he or she is living in different places for long periods of time. The other parent figure has a quiet kind of family year.

Siblings and sibling figures are very focused on finance and will tend to prosper. A move could happen after May 11. (It could happen next year too.) Children and children figures in your life could be undertaking serious renovations in the home from August 20 onwards, but a physical move is not likely. Children need to watch the temper from August 20 onwards. Grandchildren, if you have them, are having a stable kind of family year.

Finance and Career

Your financial planet, Jupiter, behaves unusually this year. Normally he will spend nearly all the year in one sign. This year he spends approximately half the year in Pisces and half the year in Aries. This would tend to show important financial changes happening this year, a shift in financial attitudes. But finances look good – especially until May 11 and from October 29 to December 21, when Jupiter will be in your 5th house of fun, children and personal creativity. He will also be travelling with Neptune, the most spiritual of all the planets. This gives many messages. You are more speculative this year and tend to be lucky. You spend more on children and can earn from them as well. When they are younger they can inspire you – motivate you – to earn more. Sometimes they inadvertently give you profitable ideas. If they are older, the financial support can be more tangible. This transit also shows happy money: money that is earned in happy ways and that is spent on happy things. There is financial joy during this period. Jupiter travelling with Neptune shows a fabulous financial intuition – the shortcut to wealth. Good intuition is worth more than many years of hard labour.

Those of you involved in the creative arts will find your work more marketable this year. Your personal creativity is also very much enhanced.

You spend on the children and can earn from them as well, as we mentioned. But you can also profit from entertainment and music. Companies and industries that cater to youth are interesting investments. Oil, natural gas, shipping, shipbuilders, fisheries, water bottling or purifying companies and certain pharmaceuticals are all interesting investments this year.

On May 11 Jupiter moves into Aries, your 6th house. Jupiter is stronger in your 5th house than he is in your 6th, so you will work harder for earnings, but they will come. You still seem to take risks after May 11 as well. You make quick financial judgements and perhaps jump into things – investments and purchases – too quickly. But when the intuition is good these things work out. Jupiter in Aries likes the 'quick buck' – fast money. Be careful here as there are predators out there who exploit this tendency.

Jupiter in Aries favours earning the old-fashioned way – through hard work and productive service. Very nice job opportunities are coming in this period too. This position favours the health industry – pharmaceuticals, health foods, health products and companies that supply doctors and surgeons. You might be spending more on health, but you can earn from it too.

This doesn't seem a particularly strong career year. Home and family seem much more important. Your 10th house of career is basically empty (only short-term planets move through there) while your 4th house of home and family is prominent all year. In addition, almost all of the long-term planets (with the exception of Uranus) are in the night side, the bottom half of your chart. So the year ahead is about dealing with the family and your emotional wellness. Once this is in order, the career will fall into place.

Love and Social Life

As we mentioned earlier, love is very challenging this year. Uranus in
your 7th house is testing current relationships. Even friendships of the
heart are being tested. By the time Uranus is finished with you in a few
years, you will be in a whole new social circle. You are being liberated
socially – though it might not feel that way while it's happening.

So, those of you who are married or involved in serious relationships
will need to work harder to keep things together this year. I have seen
marriages weather a Uranus transit, but much, much work (and sacrifice) was involved in this. Most people are not willing to pay the price.
This will be a good test of your commitment to each other.

If you are single it's probably not wise to marry this year. Things are
too unstable. Enjoy love for what it is, no need to get into commit-
ments that might not hold up.

Though love is unstable this year it is, nevertheless, very exciting. All
your assumptions about it are blown to smithereens. Love and romantic opportunity can happen any time in any place. You could be doing
a mundane task like taking out the garbage and Mr or Ms Right
happens by. The only problem is the stability of these things. Love can
come unexpectedly and end just as unexpectedly. But no matter,
tomorrow is another day and more love can happen. While you yourself might be more stable in your affections, you tend to attract people
who are like that. They want freedom.

This, as we have mentioned in past reports, favours serial love affairs
rather than marriage.

Uranus is your family planet. His position in your house of love has
many meanings. You are socializing more from home and with the
family. You are attracted to people with strong family values. Family
members or family connections can be important in love. In some
cases, the family is meddling too much in your love life, and not in a
good way. Family disputes can be one of the causes for the problems
in your relationship.

Fast-moving Venus is your love planet, and in the course of a year
she will move through your entire chart. Thus, there are many short-
term trends in love that depend on where Venus is and the kinds of
aspects she receives. These are best dealt with in the monthly reports.

Self-improvement

Saturn has been in your 4th house since last year, and this creates a tendency to repress your feelings. Generally, you don't feel safe expressing your true feelings and so they are bottled up inside. This can't go on for too long. (It is like trying to repress a bowel movement.) Control of the emotional nature is a great thing, and it is one of the spiritual lessons for the year ahead. But control has nothing to do with repression. One directs the emotions through the attention and the will. This is often hard to do when one is boiling over with negativity. So, what is needed is a positive way to release negative emotion in a way that is harmless to you and the people around you. In my book *A Technique for Meditation* we give some ways to achieve this. There is also information on my website, www.spiritual-stories.com.

Once the negative feelings are released, it is then very easy to change the mood to something positive and constructive. You can repeat positive affirmations, chant mantras, pray and meditate. All these things will change the mood.

Uranus has been in your 7th house of love for some years now and will be there for some more to come. Aside from the worldly phenomena that this produces, there are spiritual lessons happening that will last for the rest of your life. The purpose is to get comfortable with romantic change and instability. Embrace it. Roll with the punches. Nature always compensates: if one thing is taken away something else will come to replace it – and often better. But as long as you are in turmoil about it, you won't experience it. Instead, learn to accept what comes.

This is a year where many of you will experience heightened creativity. Many of you will discover creative talents that you never knew you had. Spirit is inspiring you in this area. Expressing this inspiration will not only bring more joy into your life but will enhance your bottom line as well.

Month-by-month Forecasts

January

Best Days Overall: 6, 7, 16, 17, 25, 26
Most Stressful Days Overall: 4, 5, 11, 12, 18, 19, 31
Best Days for Love: 2, 3, 11, 12, 21, 22, 29, 30
Best Days for Money: 1, 6, 16, 25, 27, 28
Best Days for Career: 2, 3, 11, 12, 18, 19, 23

Health is good this month until the 20th but afterwards becomes more stressful. Make sure to get enough rest after that date. Enhance the health with thigh massage and massage of the liver reflex until the 25th. After the 25th back and knee massage will be helpful. Good to focus on dental hygiene after the 20th as well.

Though health and energy could be better, there are many nice things happening. Jupiter in your 5th house of fun and creativity brings pleasure and leisure activities. You manage to enjoy life more. You're in the mood for fun and it comes to you. Finances also seem good. Your financial planet in your 5th house indicates happy money – money that is earned in happy ways and spent on happy things. Speculations are favourable. You can experience 'miracle money' this month (and for the next few months as well).

You begin your year with the 3rd house very strong. So the focus is on intellectual interests and communication. This is excellent for students, below college level, as it shows success in their studies. Your own mental and communication faculties are very much enhanced – even if you are not in school. You read more. You speak more than usual. You absorb information. Siblings and sibling figures are having a good month too. They have good self-esteem and confidence; their health also looks good. They have been having financial stresses for the past year, but after the 20th finances improve.

On the 20th, as the Sun moves into your 4th house of home and family, this is where the focus is, and on your emotional wellness (which needs work). Since the Sun is your career planet, the message of the Horoscope is very clear: your mission for the month ahead (from the 20th onwards) is your home, your family and your emotional wellness.

Many of you will be pursuing your career from the home – perhaps in a home office or via remote working. But on a metaphysical level this transit shows that it is good to pursue your career goals by the methods of night – through meditation, creative visualization and by getting into the feeling, the mood, of being where you want to be in your career. Later, when the planets shift to the day side of your chart, exterior actions will happen spontaneously, for the interior ground has been prepared.

Love is complicated this month, as both the planets involved in your love life are retrograde – Uranus is retrograde until the 18th and Venus, your actual love planet, is retrograde until the 29th. So there is a lot of indecision and confusion about this. Perhaps there will be delays and glitches as well. Love will improve next month.

February

Best Days Overall: 2, 3, 12, 13, 21, 22, 23
Most Stressful Days Overall: 1, 7, 8, 14, 15, 16, 28
Best Days for Love: 7, 8, 17, 18, 27
Best Days for Money: 2, 3, 12, 13, 21, 22, 24, 25
Best Days for Career: 1, 9, 10, 14, 15, 22, 23

Your health planet, Mars, has been 'out of bounds' since January 12, and remains so until the 10th. This shows that in health matters you're going outside your normal orbit. You're exploring therapies that are outside your normal experience. This is probably a good thing. With health still delicate until the 18th, you need 'outside the box' therapies. Health will improve after the 18th, but still needs watching. You still have two powerful long-term planets in stressful alignment with you.

In spite of this the month ahead is happy. The Sun's move into your 5th house initiates a yearly personal pleasure period. In fact, having fun, enjoying life, is your mission from the 18th onwards. Joy itself will cure many problems. The Sun in the 5th house after the 18th shows that you are enjoying your career path. Perhaps you are entertaining clients and customers – showing them a good time. Perhaps you make important contacts as you indulge in leisure activities.

This transit would also show a strong focus on children and children figures in your life. Being there for them – guiding them and helping them – is your mission during this period.

Children and children figures in your life are having an excellent month. They look good and have self-confidence and self-esteem. Health and energy should be good. They seem prosperous as well (and very fertile).

Love is much improved over last month. Marriage is not in the stars this year, as we've said, but love is happening. Your love planet Venus spends the month in Capricorn, your 3rd house. Thus love is close to home – in the neighbourhood or with neighbours. Romantic opportunities can happen at schools, lectures, seminars, the library or bookshop – as you pursue your intellectual interests. Venus in Capricorn signals slow love. It takes time. Love needs to be tested to see if it is real. But once someone has passed the various tests, love tends to endure. However, with Uranus in your 7th house love is still unstable – even with people who have passed the tests.

Finances are excellent this month. Review our discussion of this last month.

March

Best Days Overall: 2, 3, 11, 12, 13, 21, 22, 30, 31
Most Stressful Days Overall: 1, 6, 7, 8, 14, 15, 27, 28
Best Days for Love: 6, 7, 8, 9, 18, 19, 27, 28
Best Days for Money: 2, 3, 11, 12, 21, 22, 23, 24, 30, 31
Best Days for Career: 2, 3, 11, 12, 14, 15, 23

Mars and Venus began travelling together on February 25, and they journey on together until the 12th. This has many good points and some challenging ones. On the positive side this shows a romantic involvement with someone at work. This person could also be a therapist, or someone involved in your health. You seem attracted to health professionals during this period. The downside of this transit is that you can be (and the person you attract as well) a bit of a perfectionist in love – critical and nit-picky. You need to be careful about this. Venus travels with Pluto, too, on the 2nd and 3rd, bringing a happy romantic experience.

Mars and Venus enter your 4th house on the 6th and spend the rest of the month there. This has many messages. You are socializing more from home. There is more harmony with the family. Family and family connections are important in love. Perhaps an old flame reappears in your life. This seems more therapeutic than romantic; you will be able to resolve old issues. Mars in your 4th house shows the importance of emotional health this month. Very important to keep the moods positive and constructive. Diet also seems important healthwise. Calf and ankle massage also enhance health. Health needs attention this month.

The planetary power shifts to the Western, social sector of your chart this month. After the 6th, 80 per cent, sometimes 90 per cent of the planets are in the West. So other people are important. It is time to cultivate your social graces. Selfishness – although there is nothing wrong with it per se – won't cut it these days. Good comes to you through the good graces of others.

The Sun travels with Jupiter from the 4th to the 6th. This is a harbinger of career success and brings a nice payday. From the 11th to the 13th the Sun travels with Neptune, bringing fun, happiness, close relations with children or children figures and career opportunity. Being involved with charities and altruistic activities boost the career. Children seem successful too. They are having a banner financial month.

You're still in the midst of a yearly personal pleasure peak until the 20th. So life is fun these days. Like last month, career opportunities come as you're having fun.

April

Best Days Overall: 8, 9, 17, 18, 25, 26
Most Stressful Days Overall: 3, 4, 10, 11, 23, 24, 30
Best Days for Love: 3, 4, 8, 17, 18, 25, 26, 27, 30
Best Days for Money: 8, 9, 17, 18, 19, 20, 26, 27
Best Days for Career: 1, 2, 10, 11, 20, 21, 30

Last month all the planets were moving forward, and life proceeded swiftly. This is the case for the month ahead as well. But on the 29th a very important planet, Pluto, the ruler of your Horoscope, goes retrograde, and this will last for many months. So the need is to be clear about your personal goals and about the image that you want to project to the world.

We will also have a solar eclipse on the 30th that occurs in your 7th house of love. Health needs watching most of the month and your schedule should be reduced, especially around the eclipse period. A current relationship gets tested. There can be dramas in the life of the spouse, partner or current love. There are career changes happening and dramas in the lives of parents, parent figures, bosses and elders – the authority figures in your life. They too should reduce their schedules. Children and children figures should drive more carefully – cars and communication equipment will get tested. Siblings and sibling figures have issues with their own children or children figures.

A relationship can break down this month, but your love life is still active and exciting. On the 20th the Sun moves into your 7th house and you begin a yearly love and social peak. Singles will date more and have all kinds of romantic opportunities, but the issue is the stability of these things. Instability is the price we pay for excitement. Venus will travel with Neptune from the 26th to the 28th. This brings opportunities for love affairs. Then she travels with Jupiter on the 30th, which also brings love opportunities as well as financial increase.

Jupiter, your financial planet, travels with Neptune from the 1st to the 17th. This brings excellent financial intuition, spiritual guidance on money matters and luck in speculations. It should be a good financial period.

Your health planet Mars will be in your 4th house until the 15th. So, like last month, enhance the health with calf and ankle massage, right diet and maintaining good emotional health. On the 15th Mars moves into your 5th house. This favours foot massage, spiritual-healing techniques and plain joy. Joy is a powerful healing force.

May

> Best Days Overall: 5, 6, 14, 15, 23, 24
> Most Stressful Days Overall: 1, 7, 8, 9, 21, 27, 28
> Best Days for Love: 1, 7, 8, 16, 17, 27, 28
> Best Days for Money: 6, 16, 17, 25
> Best Days for Career: 7, 8, 9, 10, 11, 20, 30

The lunar eclipse of the 16th occurs in your own sign and thus has a strong effect on you. Take things nice and easy. Things that must be done should be done. But non-essentials – especially if they are stressful – are better off rescheduled. This eclipse forces you to re-evaluate yourself; it forces some soul-searching. You need to update your self-concept, your image and how you want others to see and think of you. Usually this happens because people are talking badly about you. You must define yourself for yourself, or they will do it for you. So, in the coming months you will change your look, your wardrobe, hairstyle, etc.

Every lunar eclipse tests your religious and philosophical views – your theology too. This is basically a good thing. Some of your beliefs will be discarded, some will merely be revised and updated. The events of the eclipse will show you what is what.

Since this eclipse impacts Saturn, the ruler of your 3rd house, siblings and sibling figures are affected. They too need to redefine themselves. They will have dramas with their friends and friendships will be tested. With you, cars and communications equipment get tested (it's a good idea to drive more carefully).

Love is still unstable (and perhaps you like it that way) but there is plenty of opportunity. Singles are dating more. Those in a relationship are attending more social functions and meeting new people. You're still in the midst of a yearly love and social peak until the 21st.

Your financial planet, Jupiter, makes a major move out of your 5th house on the 11th and enters your 6th house. This signals earnings achieved the old-fashioned way through work and practical service. The health field seems interesting as an investment or business opportunity. You still take risks in finance, but your hard work and diligence will create your good luck.

Health and energy improve after the 21st. In the meantime, enhance the health with foot massage and spiritual-healing techniques until the 25th. After then face, scalp and head massage – massage of the adrenal reflexes – will enhance the health. Increase your exercise time after the 25th.

June

Best Days Overall: 1, 2, 3, 11, 12, 19, 20, 28, 29, 30
Most Stressful Days Overall: 4, 5, 17, 18, 23, 24, 25
Best Days for Love: 6, 7, 16, 23, 24, 25, 26
Best Days for Money: 4, 13, 14, 21
Best Days for Career: 4, 5, 9, 10, 18, 28, 29

Mars, your health planet, began his solstice on May 27 and this continues until the 2nd. He pauses in the heavens and then changes direction (in his latitudinal motion). So it is with you in health matters and in your work. There is a pause and then a change of direction.

Mars and Jupiter are both in your 6th house all month. This shows earnings from work – the old-fashioned way. It also favours the athletic industry and companies that supply them, and the health field as well. You spend on health but can earn from it as well. Jupiter travelling with Mars in your house of health is a positive for health. It shows best-case scenarios in health issues. Jobseekers have excellent prospects too. Those who employ others have good applicants for positions and seem to be enlarging the workforce.

Health is much improved over last month. Much of the short-term stress caused by the short-term planets is dissipating, and by the 23rd it will all have gone. Energy is good.

Your 8th house – your favourite house – is powerful this month until the 21st. This favours all of Scorpio's natural interests – sex, personal transformation, detox and purging regimes. You are very much at home now, psychologically speaking. The Cosmos impels you to do that which you most love.

Love will be good, but unstable still. This is especially so on the 10th and 11th as Venus travels with Uranus. You don't know where you stand with your current love interest from one moment to the next.

There can be shake-ups in love, but they seem short term. Until the 23rd love and love opportunities happen in the usual ways – at parties, gatherings and through introductions from friends or family members. After the 23rd, as Venus enters your 8th house love becomes more erotic, more sexual. Sexual magnetism is paramount. (It is a sexually active kind of period anyway.) Love opportunities can happen in strange ways (although not strange for Scorpio) – at funerals, wakes or as you visit a bereaved person or family. It can happen as you visit someone in hospital as well. There is an allurement to wealthy people too. Those of you already in a relationship will find that the spouse, partner or current love is having a very strong financial month.

On the 21st your 9th house becomes powerful and this favours the career. There is success and expansion. Career is becoming ever more important now as the planetary power shifts to the upper, day side of your chart. It is not dominant, but much stronger than it has been all year. There is a need to balance home and family with career goals. There is foreign travel related to the career after the 21st. Your willingness to travel is a big factor in career success. The Sun's entry into your 9th house is good for college-level students and shows focus on their studies: focus brings success. Your interest in religion, philosophy and theology will increase during this period as well. A juicy theological discussion or the visit of a spiritual teacher or theologian can be more interesting than a night on the town.

July

Best Days Overall: 8, 9, 16, 17, 26, 27
Most Stressful Days Overall: 1, 2, 14, 15, 21, 22, 28, 29
Best Days for Love: 6, 7, 15, 21, 22, 26
Best Days for Money: 1, 2, 10, 11, 18, 19, 28, 29
Best Days for Career: 1, 2, 8, 9, 17, 28, 29

Health is good until the 23rd but afterwards will need more attention. Your health planet Mars will move into Taurus, your 7th house, on the 5th and stay there for the rest of the month. Thus, good health means a healthy love and social life. If problems arise, restore social harmony as quickly as possible. Heath can also be enhanced through neck and throat massage and through craniosacral therapy. With your health planet in the 7th house you might be more involved in the health of friends and that of the beloved than with your own health. The good news here is that with benevolent Jupiter in your 6th house of health you'll likely get best-case scenarios with health issues.

Mars in your 7th house complicates the love life. It can make you too perfectionist in love – too critical – too prone to search for flaws. This will destroy romantic moments, so be careful. On the other hand, this transit indicates an attraction to health professionals and people involved in your health. A visit to the therapist can turn out to be much more than that.

Mars will make dynamic aspects with Pluto, the ruler of your chart, on the 1st and 2nd, so be more mindful on the physical plane. The same holds true on the 30th and 31st when Mars travels with Uranus. Family members also need to be more mindful now.

Mars's move into Taurus on the 5th shifts the planetary balance to the upper half, the day side of your Horoscope. The day side is now dominant. Add to this the power in your 10th house from the 23rd onwards and we have a clear message – focus on the career.

Health and energy could be better, but you're very successful this month. On the 23rd you begin a yearly career peak. The Sun, your career planet, will be in his own sign and house, where he is most powerful. This spells success.

Your career planet will make very beautiful aspects to Jupiter, your financial planet, on the 30th and 31st. This brings both financial and career success. It can bring pay rises – official or unofficial – and good parental support. Bosses are kindly disposed to your financial goals. If you have issues with the government, this will be a good time to deal with that.

Until the 23rd, with your 9th house very strong, you will be travelling. Like last month it seems career related. Like last month too, there is a strong interest in religion, philosophy and theology. College students are successful in their studies.

Pluto, your ruling planet, is still retrograde this month (along with three other planets). And most of the planets are still in the social Western sector. Perhaps it is good that self-confidence and self-esteem are not as strong as usual. This is a month where the focus is on others and their needs. Your way (and you're not sure what that is at the moment) is probably not the best way. Let others have their way, so long as it isn't destructive.

August

Best Days Overall: 4, 5, 13, 14, 22, 23
Most Stressful Days Overall: 11, 12, 17, 18, 25, 26
Best Days for Love: 4, 5, 15, 17, 18, 25, 26
Best Days for Money: 7, 8, 15, 25
Best Days for Career: 7, 8, 16, 25, 26

Mars is still travelling with Uranus on the 1st and 2nd so, like last month, be more mindful on the material plane. This goes for family members as well. There can be changes in your health regime as well.

Health still needs some attention until the 23rd but after that you will see dramatic improvement. Mars moves away from his stressful aspect, as do the Sun and Mercury. In the meantime, make sure to rest and relax more. Don't allow yourself to get overtired. Make sure to maintain social harmony with friends and the beloved. Neck and throat massage and craniosacral therapy are helpful until the 20th. After then, enhance health with arm and shoulder massage. Massage of the lung and bronchial reflexes will also be good. Make sure to get enough fresh air and breathe deeply. Hand reflexology (you can google this) will be especially effective. Mars in your 8th house from the 20th onwards favours detox and weight-loss regimes. Sometimes surgery is recommended, although it doesn't mean that you have to undergo it.

You're still in a very successful period. You're in the midst of your yearly career peak until the 23rd. So the focus needs to be on the career and your outer objectives. (Emotional health is important on the 1st and 2nd, but its importance wanes after that.) Succeed in the outer world and you'll feel in emotional harmony. Outer success is the best way to serve your family.

You still seem distant with the beloved this month. You might not be distant physically but psychologically. This goes on until the 12th. Your challenge is to bridge your differences. Neither of you is right or wrong – you just have different perspectives on things. Sometimes one perspective is right, sometimes the other. Venus makes nice aspects to Neptune on the 6th and 7th – this brings an opportunity for a love affair, although it doesn't seem serious. After the 12th Venus moves into your 10th house of career. This gives many messages. Singles are attracted to people of power and prestige. There are romantic opportunities with (and perhaps overtures from) bosses and people above you in social or professional standing. The danger is getting involved in relationships of convenience rather than real love. You will enhance your career by social means – by attending or hosting the right kinds of parties and gatherings. Your social connections are playing a big role in the career and much of your socializing is career related. Venus makes nice aspects to Jupiter on the 17th and 18th. This is wonderful for both love and finance.

Planetary retrograde activity is high this month, so the pace of life slows down. But your career seems unaffected. Your career planet, the Sun, never goes retrograde.

Though your financial planet is retrograde all month, finances look good until the 23rd in spite of this. Things might be slower and there are more delays, but earnings look strong.

When the Sun enters your 11th house on the 23rd you can further the career through your technological expertise and through online activities. Social connections are important after the 23rd as well.

September

Best Days Overall: 1, 2, 9, 10, 18, 19, 20, 28, 29
Most Stressful Days Overall: 7, 8, 13, 14, 15, 21, 22
Best Days for Love: 4, 5, 13, 14, 15
Best Days for Money: 3, 4, 11, 21, 30
Best Days for Career: 5, 6, 14, 15, 21, 22, 25, 26

Health is now much improved. Although there are two long-term planets in stressful alignment with you, the short-term planets are either helping you or leaving you alone. You can enhance the health with arm and shoulder massage, fresh air and deep breathing, massage of the lung and bronchial reflexes and detox regimes. Health during this period is not about adding things to the body but about getting rid of what doesn't belong there.

Venus, your love planet, moves into your 11th house of groups and friends on the 5th and stays there until the end of the month. (She enters Libra on the 30th.) So, power and prestige are less alluring after the 5th. You want a relationship of equals. You want friendship with the beloved as well as passion.

Love should be good this month but there are some pitfalls. Venus in the sign of Virgo (your 11th house) can make you or the beloved (it impacts both of you) too critical and perfectionistic about love. There is a tendency to relate too much from the head rather than the heart. There is a tendency to be hypercritical of flaws. The motive is good. You want perfection and anything less needs to be corrected. But this can destroy romantic moments. It is good to want perfection, but analysis should come after, not during, romantic moments. And keep any criticism constructive. Another issue is that Pluto is still retrograde, and though the opportunities are there for you, you're not sure what you want. Self-confidence is not what it should be. Still, Venus is making nice aspects to Pluto from the 5th onwards, and especially on the 25th and 26th. So there is romantic opportunity. The online world seems important in love – social media or dating sites. It would also be good to be involved in professional or trade organizations. There can be romantic meetings in these venues.

Venus, your love planet, has her solstice from September 30 to October 3. She pauses in the heavens (in her latitudinal motion) and then changes direction. So it is with your love life. There is a pause and change of direction. This solstice is like a 'cosmic breather'. You take stock and change direction. It is basically good.

Finance is complicated this month. Your financial planet Jupiter is retrograde all month. (Overall, retrograde activity is at its maximum extent for the year.) Earnings are happening but more slowly than usual. Finance seems better before the 23rd than after. If possible, avoid major investments or purchases this month. However, if you must do these things, do more homework – more due diligence.

Your 11th house is strong until the 23rd which makes this a social period – but it's more about friendships and group activities than about romance (although romance can happen here as a side effect).

On the 23rd the Sun enters your spiritual 12th house and you begin a strong spiritual period. This is a good time for meditation, the study of sacred literature and being involved in charities and good causes – being involved in things that transcend yourself. As you connect deeper with the Divine within you and allow its power to operate, many problems in life will just dissolve.

October

Best Days Overall: 7, 16, 17, 25, 26
Most Stressful Days Overall: 4, 5, 11, 12, 18, 19
Best Days for Love: 4, 5, 11, 12, 13, 14, 25
Best Days for Money: 1, 8, 9, 18, 26, 27, 28
Best Days for Career: 4, 5, 13, 14, 18, 19, 25

Venus, your love planet, is still in her solstice period until the 3rd, so review our discussion of this last month. There is a healthy pause in your love life.

Jupiter has been in solstice since September 8. This will continue until the 16th. (Jupiter is a very slow-moving planet, so his solstices last a long time.) So there has been – and it continues – a pause in your financial life – a breather, a mini vacation – and then a change of direction. It's as if you are 'shifting gears' financially. (Jupiter is also changing signs this month; he is moving back into Pisces on the 29th, which adds to the 'shift of gears'.)

Retrograde activity is still substantial, but less than last month. And, in spite of a solar eclipse on the 25th, the month is basically happy. Your spiritual focus until the 23rd (and it will go on afterwards too) will help you go through the eclipse, which has a strong effect on you.

This eclipse occurs in your own sign and impacts you personally. (This is the second eclipse in your sign this year.) Once again you are forced to redefine yourself and your self-concept. You need to create a more correct concept of yourself. This will lead, in the coming months, to a change of wardrobe, hairstyle and overall presentation. As you change within, change happens without.

The Sun is your career planet, so every solar eclipse affects the career and brings changes and shake-ups. Sometimes the actual career path changes, but not always. Sometimes there are shake-ups in your corporate hierarchy or industry, and you have to change the way you pursue career advancement. Sometimes the government changes the rules and regulations for your industry. Often there are personal dramas in the lives of bosses, parents and parent figures – life-changing kinds of dramas. In your case (with the Sun in your 1st house) a new career opportunity comes to you and you take the opportunity. Spiritual or charitable organizations you're involved with are forced to make important financial changes. The money people in your life are having spiritual-type changes. Siblings and sibling figures have dramas with friends and perhaps near-death kinds of experiences. Children or children figures have job changes and changes in their health regime. If they are in college there are changes in their educational plans.

So, there is more excitement this month, but also more happiness. The Sun's entry into your own sign on the 23rd brings more energy and charisma. You look good. You have confidence and self-esteem. (Pluto, the ruler of your Horoscope, finally moves forward again on the 2nd and this also improves self-confidence and self-esteem.)

Venus moves into your sign on the 23rd too. This indicates that love is pursuing you. You just have to go about your daily business. It is a time for having love on your terms. If you are in a relationship, the beloved is devoted to you. He or she puts your interest ahead of their own. Marriage is not in the cards, but romance is.

November

Best Days Overall: 3, 4, 12, 13, 22, 23, 30
Most Stressful Days Overall: 1, 2, 7, 8, 15, 16, 28, 29
Best Days for Love: 3, 4, 7, 8, 3, 24
Best Days for Money: 4, 14, 23, 24, 25
Best Days for Career: 3, 4, 13, 14, 15, 16, 23

You are still in a yearly personal pleasure peak until the 22nd, so it is a good time to enjoy the pleasures of the senses and the body. It is good to reward and pamper the body for all the yeoman, selfless service it gives you. Very good to get the body in the shape that you want.

Personal appearance is excellent now. It's not just the physical appearance that improves, but you exude more energy – more life – the X factor, and people (especially the opposite sex) respond to this.

Though the Eastern sector of self is not dominant, it is as strong as it will get this year. So, other people are certainly very important, but you have more personal independence than usual. If there are changes to be made to improve your personal happiness, now is the time to make them.

The main headline this month is a powerful, total lunar eclipse on the 8th. Since it impacts many other planets – and thus many areas of your life – it is much stronger than the solar eclipse last month. It has a strong effect on you and on the world in general.

This eclipse occurs in your 7th house of love and thus tests a current relationship. As we mentioned previously, long-standing relationships have been tested for a few years now. This eclipse adds to the stress. A current relationship is on shaky ground. This eclipse also brings personal dramas and crises to the beloved. College-level students have shake-ups in their institutions and make changes to educational plans. There are shake-ups and crises in your place of worship and in the lives of worship leaders. Foreign travel is not advisable over this period.

Three planets are affected by this eclipse – Mercury, Uranus and Venus. The impact on Venus only reinforces the love dramas that we have written about. The impact on Mercury also tests friendships. There are dramas in the lives of friends. Computer and high-tech equipment will get tested and will often need repair or replacement. Parents or parent figures are making important financial changes. Since Mercury rules your 8th house there can be psychological encounters with death. Perhaps near-death experiences or close calls. The impact on Uranus brings dramas in the family circle and dramas in the lives of parents or parent figures. Often repairs are needed in the home.

However, overall the planets are kind to you this month, and you should get best-case outcomes to all these challenges.

You're still in the midst of a yearly personal pleasure period until the 22nd. After the 22nd, as the Sun enters your money house you begin a yearly financial peak. This should be better than usual as Jupiter, your financial planet, will move forward again on the 23rd. This is fortunate timing. Prosperity is happening, and whatever expenses are incurred because of the eclipse are easily handled.

December

Best Days Overall: 1, 9, 10, 11, 19, 20, 27, 28
Most Stressful Days Overall: 4, 5, 6, 12, 13, 25, 26
Best Days for Love: 2, 3, 4, 5, 6, 14, 23, 24
Best Days for Money: 1, 11, 20, 21, 22, 29
Best Days for Career: 2, 3, 12, 13, 22, 23

Mars, your health planet, has been 'out of bounds' since October 24 and remains so for the month ahead. (Other planets are also 'out of bounds' this month as well.) Mars is also retrograde all month. So in health matters you are going outside your normal orbit – exploring things that you normally wouldn't explore. However, with Mars retrograde, be very cautious about making important changes to the health regime. Health is good this month and there's no need to rush into important changes. This transit could also show you going outside your normal work. The job takes you into unknown places.

We see this tendency in love as well. You are outside the box in love – and perhaps the people you attract are also outside their normal orbits. The same is true in your spirituality. (In general, it seems to be a trend in the world at large – people are exploring outside their orbits.)

The month ahead is prosperous. You're still in a yearly financial peak until the 22nd. Jupiter, your financial planet, is moving forward. You have confidence and clarity. More importantly there is focus. By the spiritual law we get what we focus on. Jupiter changes signs this month on the 21st, returning to your 6th house for the long haul. Thus you earn from work. You will have excellent job opportunities, regardless of whether you are employed or unemployed. You can earn from the health field too and probably you will spend more on health. Children and children figures were prosperous this year and become even more prosperous under this transit.

On the 22nd the Sun enters your 3rd house and the focus shifts to intellectual interests. Financial goals, the short-term ones at least, seem to be attained and now you want to expand your mind and knowledge. Students will do well in their studies. There is great focus here. The intellectual faculties are enhanced and learning (and teaching) comes easily. Scorpios are not big talkers, but this month they talk more than usual. This is a good month to take courses in subjects that interest you. If you have expertise in a given area you might want to teach or blog about it. It is a good time for catching up on all those phone calls, emails or letters you owe to others.

Venus, your love planet, moves into your 3rd house on the 10th. She began the year here and now she comes full cycle. Thus love is close to home, in your neighbourhood or with neighbours. Intellectual compatibility is important in love. You like people with the gift of the gab – people who are easy to talk to. Good communication is part of foreplay these days. Romantic opportunities happen at school, lectures, seminars, the library or bookstore: educational-type settings. As we saw at the beginning of the year, Venus in Capricorn is slow to fall in love. There is caution here, which is generally a good thing. You like to test love these days. You want to be sure it is real. (And your partner could be the same way.)

Sagittarius

↗

THE ARCHER

Birthdays from
23rd November to
20th December

Personality Profile

SAGITTARIUS AT A GLANCE

Element – Fire

Ruling Planet – Jupiter
　Career Planet – Mercury
　Love Planet – Mercury
　Money Planet – Saturn
　Planet of Health and Work – Venus
　Planet of Home and Family Life – Neptune
　Planet of Spirituality – Pluto

Colours – blue, dark blue

Colours that promote love, romance and social harmony – yellow,
　yellow-orange

Colours that promote earning power – black, indigo

Gems – carbuncle, turquoise

Metal – tin

Scents – carnation, jasmine, myrrh

Quality – mutable (= flexibility)

Qualities most needed for balance – attention to detail, administrative and organizational skills

Strongest virtues – generosity, honesty, broad-mindedness, tremendous vision

Deepest need – to expand mentally

Characteristics to avoid – over-optimism, exaggeration, being too generous with other people's money

Signs of greatest overall compatibility – Aries, Leo

Signs of greatest overall incompatibility – Gemini, Virgo, Pisces

Sign most helpful to career – Virgo

Sign most helpful for emotional support – Pisces

Sign most helpful financially – Capricorn

Sign best for marriage and/or partnerships – Gemini

Sign most helpful for creative projects – Aries

Best Sign to have fun with – Aries

Signs most helpful in spiritual matters – Leo, Scorpio

Best day of the week – Thursday

Understanding a Sagittarius

If you look at the symbol of the archer you will gain a good, intuitive understanding of a person born under this astrological sign. The development of archery was humanity's first refinement of the power to hunt and wage war. The ability to shoot an arrow far beyond the ordinary range of a spear extended humanity's horizons, wealth, personal will and power.

Today, instead of using bows and arrows we project our power with fuels and mighty engines, but the essential reason for using these new powers remains the same. These powers represent our ability to extend our personal sphere of influence – and this is what Sagittarius is all about. Sagittarians are always seeking to expand their horizons, to cover more territory and increase their range and scope. This applies to all aspects of their lives: economic, social and intellectual.

Sagittarians are noted for the development of the mind – the higher intellect – which understands philosophical and spiritual concepts. This mind represents the higher part of the psychic nature and is motivated not by self-centred considerations but by the light and grace of a Higher Power. Thus, Sagittarians love higher education of all kinds. They might be bored with formal schooling but they love to study on their own and in their own way. A love of foreign travel and interest in places far away from home are also noteworthy characteristics of the Sagittarian type.

If you give some thought to all these Sagittarian attributes you will see that they spring from the inner Sagittarian desire to develop. To travel more is to know more, to know more is to be more, to cultivate the higher mind is to grow and to reach more. All these traits tend to broaden the intellectual – and indirectly, the economic and material – horizons of the Sagittarian.

The generosity of the Sagittarian is legendary. There are many reasons for this. One is that Sagittarians seem to have an inborn consciousness of wealth. They feel that they are rich, that they are lucky, that they can attain any financial goal – and so they feel that they can afford to be generous. Sagittarians do not carry the burdens of want and limitation which stop most other people from giving generously. Another reason for their generosity is their religious and philosophical idealism, derived from the higher mind. This higher mind is by nature generous because it is unaffected by material circumstances. Still another reason is that the act of giving tends to enhance their emotional nature. Every act of giving seems to be enriching, and this is reward enough for the Sagittarian.

Finance

Sagittarians generally entice wealth. They either attract it or create it. They have the ideas, energy and talent to make their vision of paradise on Earth a reality. However, mere wealth is not enough. Sagittarians want luxury – earning a comfortable living seems small and insignificant to them.

In order for Sagittarians to attain their true earning potential they must develop better managerial and organizational skills. They must learn to set limits, to arrive at their goals through a series of attainable sub-goals or objectives. It is very rare that a person goes from rags to riches overnight. But a long, drawn-out process is difficult for Sagittarians. Like Leos, they want to achieve wealth and success quickly and impressively. They must be aware, however, that this over-optimism can lead to unrealistic financial ventures and disappointing losses. Of course, no zodiac sign can bounce back as quickly as Sagittarius, but only needless heartache will be caused by this attitude. Sagittarians need to maintain their vision – never letting it go – but they must also work towards it in practical and efficient ways.

Career and Public Image

Sagittarians are big thinkers. They want it all: money, fame, glamour, prestige, public acclaim and a place in history. They often go after all these goals. Some attain them, some do not – much depends on each individual's personal horoscope. But if Sagittarians want to attain public and professional status they must understand that these things are not conferred to enhance one's ego but as rewards for the amount of service that one does for the whole of humanity. If and when they figure out ways to serve more, Sagittarians can rise to the top.

The ego of the Sagittarian is gigantic – and perhaps rightly so. They have much to be proud of. If they want public acclaim, however, they will have to learn to tone down the ego a bit, to become more humble and self-effacing, without falling into the trap of self-denial and self-abasement. They must also learn to master the details of life, which can sometimes elude them.

At their jobs Sagittarians are hard workers who like to please their bosses and co-workers. They are dependable, trustworthy and enjoy a challenge. Sagittarians are friendly to work with and helpful to their colleagues. They usually contribute intelligent ideas or new methods that improve the work environment for everyone. Sagittarians always look for challenging positions and careers that develop their intellect, even if they have to work very hard in order to succeed. They also work well under the supervision of others, although by nature they would rather be the supervisors and increase their sphere of influence. Sagittarians excel at professions that allow them to be in contact with many different people and to travel to new and exciting locations.

Love and Relationships

Sagittarians love freedom for themselves and will readily grant it to their partners. They like their relationships to be fluid and ever-changing. Sagittarians tend to be fickle in love and to change their minds about their partners quite frequently.

Sagittarians feel threatened by a clearly defined, well-structured relationship, as they feel this limits their freedom. The Sagittarian tends to marry more than once in life.

Sagittarians in love are passionate, generous, open, benevolent and very active. They demonstrate their affections very openly. However, just like an Aries they tend to be egocentric in the way they relate to their partners. Sagittarians should develop the ability to see others' points of view, not just their own. They need to develop some objectivity and cool intellectual clarity in their relationships so that they can develop better two-way communication with their partners. Sagittarians tend to be overly idealistic about their partners and about love in general. A cool and rational attitude will help them to perceive reality more clearly and enable them to avoid disappointment.

Home and Domestic Life

Sagittarians tend to grant a lot of freedom to their family. They like big homes and many children and are one of the most fertile signs of the zodiac. However, when it comes to their children Sagittarians generally err on the side of allowing them too much freedom. Sometimes their children get the idea that there are no limits. However, allowing freedom in the home is basically a positive thing – so long as some measure of balance is maintained – for it enables all family members to develop as they should.

Horoscope for 2022

Major Trends

The year ahead is not a strong career year. It is rather more about emotional wellness and resolving the past. Your 10th house of career is empty while your 4th house of home and family is easily the strongest in the Horoscope this year. More on this later.

Pluto has been in your money house for twenty or so years, and he will be there for the year ahead. This shows a fabulous financial intuition and someone who is charitable and giving (though you don't seem wildly so). Your financial planet Saturn has been in your 3rd house since last year. So you are spending on communications equipment and perhaps earning from this field. Finances are OK this year but will be even better in 2023. More later.

Health is basically good this year, but it will get even better after May 11. There is great experimentation going on in your health attitudes. More details below.

Jupiter's move into your 5th house of creativity on May 11 makes the year ahead a fun kind of year. Women of childbearing age are much more fertile all year.

Mars will spend an unusual amount of time in your 7th house of love this year. Usually he spends a month and a half in a sign or house. This year he spends more than four months in your 7th house. For singles this shows love affairs. For those who are married this can show power struggles in the relationship. More on this later.

Your most important areas of interest in the year ahead will be finance; communication and intellectual interests; home and family; fun, children and creativity (from May 11 to October 29 and from December 21 onwards); health and work; and love and romance (from August 20).

Your paths of greatest fulfilment will be home and family (until May 11 and from October 29 to December 21); fun, children and creativity (from May 11 to October 29 and from December 21 onwards); and health and work.

Health

(Please note that this is an astrological perspective on health and not a medical one. In days of yore there was no difference, both these perspectives were identical. But these days there could be quite a difference. For a medical perspective, please consult your doctor or health practitioner.)

Your 6th house has been prominent for some years now, and is prominent in the year ahead as well. Uranus – a slow-moving planet – is there. This indicates serial changes in your health regime. You are searching for the perfect regime and every time you feel you have found it, something new arises and you change.

There is much good to this. You're experimenting with therapies and different doctors. You are throwing out all the rule books and learning what works for you personally. You know that you are 'wired up' in a unique way and that things that work for others might not work for you. (And things that work for you might not work for others.) Learning how you function is the main job right now (and has been for the past few years). This is one of the greatest things a person can do – to know oneself. And this is what is going on now.

Uranus is creating change in your health regime, but he is helped by two eclipses in your 6th house in the coming year – a solar eclipse on April 30 and a lunar eclipse on November 8.

Your health is reasonable this year, and gets even better after May 11. In August, as Mars moves into stressful alignment with you, you will once again need to focus on health.

You can do much to enhance your health and prevent problems from developing. Give more attention to the following – the vulnerable areas

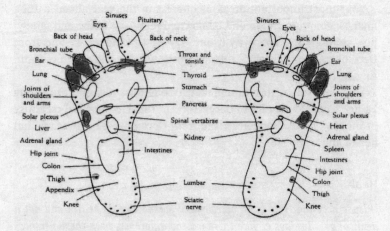

Important foot reflexology points for the year ahead

Try to massage all of the foot on a regular basis – the top of the foot as well as the bottom – but pay extra attention to the points highlighted on the chart. When you massage, be aware of 'sore spots' as these need special attention. It's also a very good idea to massage the ankles, and below them.

of your Horoscope this year (the reflex points are shown in the chart above):

- The heart became an important area last year when Jupiter moved into stressful alignment with you. It becomes even more important from August 20 onwards. Chest massage – especially of the breastbone and upper rib cage – will be beneficial. The important thing with the heart is to cultivate faith – the antidote to worry and anxiety. Avoid worry like the plague. Meditation will be a big help here.
- The neck and throat are always important for Sagittarius as Venus is your health planet. Tension tends to collect in the neck and needs to be released.
- The liver and thighs. These are also always important for Sagittarius (the reflexes are shown above). Regular thigh massage will not only strengthen the liver and thighs but the lower back as well.

- The ankles and calves. These have become important since 2019, when Uranus moved into your 6th house. These areas should be regularly massaged. Make sure the ankles are supported when exercising.

Your health planet is a fast-moving planet, as our regular readers know. In any given year Venus will move through every sign and house of your Horoscope. So there are many short-term trends in health that depend on where she is and the kinds of aspects she receives. These are best dealt with in the monthly reports.

Home and Family

Your 4th house of home and family is strong this year. It is a house of power. In contrast, your 10th house of career is empty. Not only that: *all* the long-term planets will be in the bottom half of your Horoscope this year, which just reinforces the focus on home and family and the need for emotional wellness.

This is a happy home and family year. Women of childbearing age are unusually fertile. The family circle will expand. Usually this happens through birth or marriage, but not always. Sometimes you meet people who are 'like' family to you. This is a good year to buy or sell a home. There is much good fortune here. Moves – and happy ones – are likely. Sometimes people don't actually move; they can acquire an additional home or property or have access to other homes. Sometimes they renovate the existing home or buy expensive items for the home. The whole effect is 'as if' they had moved.

'The past is not dead,' said William Faulkner, 'it's not even past.' This is a year where you see the truth of this. You will be very nostalgic, very into history – your personal and family history as well as world history. You will be digesting and reinterpreting past events and experiences.

Those of you undergoing psychological therapy will make much progress this year. There are many psychological breakthroughs happening. Even if you're not undergoing therapy, or are not an official therapist, you will be doing psychological therapeutics unofficially for friends and family. You have great insight into these matters these days.

If you're planning major renovations or construction projects around the home, April 15 to May 25 would be a good time. If you're merely redecorating or buying art objects for the home, April 5 to May 2 is a good time.

A parent or parent figure of childbearing age is fertile these days. A parent figure prospers greatly in the year ahead – next year also seems prosperous. He or she is making important renovations in the home.

Siblings and sibling figures in your life have been emotionally unstable for some years now. There could have been moves among them in recent years and the trend continues in the year ahead.

Children and children figures are having a quiet, stable family year.

Finance and Career

Your money house has been prominent for the past twenty years and remains so this year as well. This is soon to change, however. In the next two years, Pluto will leave the money house and finally enter your 3rd house.

The financial life has been undergoing a complete transformation under Pluto's influence. There have been crises – near-death financial experiences and, in some cases, actual financial deaths (bankruptcies or defaults and the like). Though these are not pleasant experiences, the Cosmos was leading you to the financial life of your dreams, and you are very close to manifesting it now. The financial travails were only the pangs of a new birth, not punitive.

Part of this transformation involved a financial detox, as detoxing is always the preliminary for new birth. So, there was (and still is) a need to get rid of financial waste – needless expenses, redundant bank or brokerage accounts and other wasteful expenditures. Less is more. It was also good to get rid of possessions that you didn't need or use.

Since Pluto is the slowest moving of all the planets, he stays in a sign for up to thirty-five years. Many of the trends we've written about in past reports are still in effect in the year ahead.

Pluto rules inheritance. This could have happened for many of you. But it also shows that earnings could come from estate issues. No one has actually to die, but you can be named in a will or be appointed to some administrative position in a will. There are people who deal with estates – they buy and sell them – which also seems good.

Those of you of an appropriate age have been doing estate planning, and this is still indicated in the year ahead. Good tax planning and general tax efficiency had been important and continue to be important.

Perhaps the most important trend is that many of you are getting involved in the spiritual dimensions of wealth – applying the spiritual laws and relying on intuition. More on this later on.

As we mentioned earlier, this is not a very strong career year. The Cosmos is focused on a balanced life. Sometimes home and family, emotional issues, children and personal creativity are more important than career. This is the case in the year ahead. There is nothing wrong with the career, there just seems a lack of interest. Your 10th house of career is basically empty, while your 4th house of home and family is very powerful. So, this is a year for dealing with family and emotional issues – getting the domestic life in order. This will build the infrastructure needed for future career success.

Your empty 10th house can be read as a good thing. It shows contentment with things as they are and thus no need to devote extra energy to it. It tends to the status quo.

Your career planet, Mercury, is a fast-moving planet, cycling through the whole Horoscope in a year. Thus there are many short-term career trends depending on where Mercury is and the kinds of aspects that he receives, and are best dealt with in the monthly reports.

Love and Social Life

Your love life seems stable until May 11 but picks up more speed from August 20 onwards.

This doesn't seem a year for marriage or serious relationships. But it is good year for love affairs – fun types of relationships. Singles don't seem in a marrying mood, and you seem to be attracting people who feel the same way.

We mentioned earlier that you are more fertile these days and a marriage could happen due to pregnancy – thus though neither you nor the partner are in the mood for permanence it could happen through extenuating circumstances.

Mars in your 7th house of love has various meanings. On the one hand it shows what we've just mentioned – a desire for fun and entertainment. Relationships are merely another form of entertainment and are not meant to be serious. They tend to become unstable when the tough times come – and they inevitably do.

The other problem with Mars in the 7th house is that it indicates power struggles within the relationship. This is a romance killer. If you can avoid this the relationship can survive.

This year you are attracted to people who can show you a good time. People who are fun to be around. You would be attracted to athletic types, and romantic opportunities can happen at the gym, the sports stadium, the theatre, resort or place of entertainment. Parties are also good venues. A night out on the town is a nice romantic evening.

Since Mercury, your love planet, is also the ruler of your 10th house of career, you would be attracted to successful people – people of power and prestige. Thus, romantic opportunity can happen as you pursue your career goals (though they don't seem a big interest this year) or with people involved in your career.

There are a lot of short-term love trends in the year ahead because your love planet is so fast-moving. During the year Mercury will move through your entire Horoscope. These short-term trends depend on where Mercury is at a given time and the kinds of aspects he receives. These are best dealt with in the monthly reports.

Self-improvement

The year ahead is a strong home and family year as we mentioned. But even more than that, it is a year for emotional healing. You will be confronting your past. You will have a very natural interest in it – not just your personal past but the family history as well. Many old feelings will arise. Most of them are not pertinent to the present, but events in the present can easily trigger them. Someone looked at you a certain way. Someone wore a certain perfume. Someone made a certain gesture or used a certain voice tone. These remind you of past experiences and they arise for a reason. For healing. For resolution. For reinterpreting them from your present standpoint. An event that was traumatic to a six-year-old might bring a smile to who you are now. Yes, the emotions are there, but you are not that six-year-old and you can see a whole different meaning to the event. In most cases, just neutral, non-judgemental observation is enough to bring resolution. If the event was extremely traumatic there are spiritual methods for clearing and discharging the negative emotions involved. My book *A Technique for Meditation* contains two chapters that deal with this. There is also much information on my website, www.spiritual-stories. com, for those who want to learn more. Cleaning the memory body is the job of many lifetimes according to the sages. So be patient. This is not an overnight solution. But every bit of progress brings improvement to the life. This is what matters, and this is a year where you make progress.

Jupiter, the ruler of your Horoscope, and Neptune, the most spiritual of the planets, travel together for a good part of the year. So there is a spiritual agenda behind all this. When you clean your memory body, your spiritual life will blossom as well.

Pluto, the ruler of your spiritual 12th house, has been in your money house for decades now. So you have been in a cycle for learning and applying the spiritual laws of affluence and supply. Here we have the true and lasting solution to poverty. It is the cure. A good spiritual definition of poverty is 'disconnection from the Divine Affluence'. This affluence is always there and is never diminished or lost. It is not dependent on any material condition. It doesn't care how much you have or don't have. It doesn't care whether you are employed, unemployed, in debt, or the victim of a bear market. It just is. When the Divine Affluence is contacted and understood, it will flow. It is never withheld. It has its laws, however. By now you understand much about it but there is always more to learn. My website has much information about this too.

Month-by-month Forecasts

January

Best Days Overall: 1, 8, 9, 18, 19, 27, 28
Most Stressful Days Overall: 6, 7, 13, 14, 21, 22
Best Days for Love: 2, 3, 4, 5, 11, 12, 13, 14, 21, 22, 23, 29, 30
Best Days for Money: 2, 3, 4, 5, 6, 13, 14, 16, 23, 24, 25, 29, 30, 31
Best Days for Career: 4, 5, 13, 14, 21, 22, 23

A happy and prosperous month, Sagittarius. Enjoy.

Health is excellent. Mars in your sign until the 25th gives energy, courage and a can-do spirit. You get things done quickly. You excel in sports and exercise regimes. You seem to be having fun as well. Children and children figures in your life are devoted to you. The only problem with Mars in your sign is haste and impatience, which can lead to accidents or injury. (You probably don't even realize that you're rushing – it's like being on drugs.) So make haste by all means, but in a mindful way. Also watch the temper. You don't suffer fools gladly these days and you can come across as more aggressive than usual.

You're in the midst of a yearly financial peak until the 20th. And even after the 20th there will be prosperity. Over half the planets are either in your money house or moving through there. That's a lot of energy. Money can come to you in many ways and through many people. For investors this favours a large, diversified portfolio. You've got your fingers in a lot of company and industry pies.

Though health is good, your health planet Venus is retrograde until the 29th. Avoid making major changes to the diet or health regime over this period. (Uranus, which is also involved in your health, is also retrograde until the 18th.) So, changes are best delayed.

There are job opportunities happening as well, but these too need more investigation. Resolve your doubts. Ask questions. Things are not what they seem. Clarity will come next month.

Love is complicated this month and there are a few reasons for it. Number one, most of the planets are in the Eastern sector of the chart – the sector of self. Your 1st house is strong until the 25th while your

7th house of love is empty (only the Moon moves through there, on the 13th and 14th). Add to this the retrograde of your love planet Mercury on the 14th and you have a recipe for a slowdown in love.

So relationships are just not that important these days. This is a 'me' oriented period. It's a time for developing personal initiative and independence – self-reliance. This doesn't mean that you are cruel to others – only that they are not that important. This is a time for taking responsibility for your own happiness. It is up to you. Happiness, spiritually speaking, is merely a choice. Make the choice. If changes need to be made to increase your happiness, now is the time to make them. You have the money and the drive. Later on, when the planets shift to the West, it will be more difficult to do.

Important love decisions, one way or another, shouldn't be made after the 14th. Gain clarity. Your love planet wavers back and forth between your 2nd and 3rd houses. Until the 2nd and from the 27th onwards there are romantic opportunities as you pursue your financial goals or with people involved in your finances. From the 2nd to the 27th there are romantic opportunities to be found in your neighbourhood, and perhaps with neighbours.

February

Best Days Overall: 5, 6, 14, 15, 24, 25
Most Stressful Days Overall: 2, 3, 9, 10, 11, 17, 18
Best Days for Love: 7, 8, 9, 10, 11, 17, 18, 19, 27, 28
Best Days for Money: 1, 2, 3, 9, 10, 11, 12, 13, 19, 20, 21, 22, 26, 27, 28
Best Days for Career: 8, 17, 18, 19, 20, 28

Love is starting to straighten out as Mercury moves forward on the 4th. Until the 15th he occupies your money house, so like last month there are romantic opportunities as you pursue your financial goals and perhaps with people involved in your finances. You socialize more with the money people in your life. Wealth is a romantic turn-on. You express love in practical ways and this is how you feel loved. On the 15th Mercury moves into Aquarius, your 3rd house. He is very powerful in this sign. It is the sign of his 'exaltation'. So the social grace is very strong, but the problem is lack of interest. Your 7th house of love is still empty (only the Moon moves through there, on the 9th, 10th and 11th) and this tends to the status quo. Singles will be attracted to intellectual people. Mental compatibility is important in love. You need to love the person's mind as much as his or her body.

You're still in a period of personal independence this month, so if you haven't made those changes for your happiness it is still a good time to make them. The planets are getting ready to shift to the West next month, so make those changes now.

Your 3rd house of communication and intellectual pursuits became powerful on January 20 and is still powerful until the 18th. This is wonderful for students – both college level and below. There is focus on their studies and this brings success. The mental and communication faculties are stronger than usual.

Your money house is still strong this month, though not as strong as the last. Earnings are still good and you have good financial intuition. Perhaps you're more speculative than usual too. The 3rd and 4th seem especially profitable. The new Moon of the 1st occurs near your financial planet, Saturn, and should also be a good financial day. Further finances will clarify as the month progresses. All the information you need to make a good decision will come to you. (This is so for intellectual and educational issues as well.)

Health needs more attention from the 18th. Enhance the health with chest massage and massage of the heart reflex. Back and knee massage will also be good.

The home and family situation seems very happy this year, and especially from the 18th onwards. Moves could happen. Pregnancies can happen. The family circle expands either through birth or marriage. Moods are optimistic these days. All the planets (with the exception of the Moon – and that only occasionally) are below the Horizon of your chart – the night side of your Horoscope. Your 10th house of career is basically empty, with only the Moon moving through there on the 17th and 18th. So the focus is on home and family and your emotional wellness. Many psychological breakthroughs are happening this month. The Cosmos is therapizing your feeling world.

March

Best Days Overall: 4, 5, 14, 15, 23, 24
Most Stressful Days Overall: 2, 3, 9, 10, 16, 17, 30, 31
Best Days for Love: 1, 9, 10, 11, 12, 18, 19, 22, 27, 28
Best Days for Money: 1, 2, 3, 9, 10, 11, 12, 18, 19, 21, 22, 25, 26, 27, 28, 30, 31
Best Days for Career: 8, 16, 17, 19, 20, 28

Mars and Venus have been travelling together since February 25 and this will go on until the 12th. It's as if they are in lock step – united as one. In general this improves the romantic life of the entire planet. There is a closeness between the sexes. In your chart this shows that children and children figures are prospering this month. They can be involved in a serious romance too.

The home seems the centre of everything this month. Even your love and career planet, Mercury, will be in your 4th house from the 10th to the 27th. So home and family is the mission – the career – this period. But this would also indicate pursuing the worldly career from home. In addition, the home is your social centre as well.

Health still needs watching until the 20th, but after then you will see dramatic improvement. Enhance the health as always with more rest. Until the 6th back and knee massage is beneficial. After the 6th ankle and calf massage will be good. After the 6th make sure to get plenty of fresh air and ensure you're breathing properly.

The Sun will travel with Jupiter from the 4th to the 6th. This could bring a foreign trip for you or the family as a whole. (A cruise would probably be most fun.) It also brings good news for college students, or those applying to college.

Mercury travels with your financial planet Saturn on the 1st and 2nd. This can bring pay rises and financial support from parents or parent figures. Perhaps there is an opportunity for a business partnership or joint venture as well. Mercury will travel with Jupiter on the 20th and 21st, which brings both career and romantic opportunities. The spouse, partner or current love has a good financial period.

Mercury's move through your 4th house – Pisces – brings idealism in both love and the career. You can further the career by being more involved in charities or altruistic causes. You will see the results of this later on – although probably not right away. This transit also shows that family values and spiritual compatibility are important in love. Emotional intimacy is perhaps as important as physical intimacy.

Finances in general look good. Your financial planet Saturn is moving forward and receives very nice aspects this month.

On the 20th, as the Sun moves into your 5th house of creativity, you begin one of your yearly personal pleasure peaks. It's time to enjoy life. As you have fun, career and love opportunities come to you very naturally (especially after the 27th).

April

Best Days Overall: 1, 2, 10, 11, 19, 20, 28, 29
Most Stressful Days Overall: 5, 6, 13, 14, 25, 26
Best Days for Love: 1, 2, 5, 6, 8, 12, 13, 17, 18, 21, 22, 25, 26, 27
Best Days for Money: 5, 6, 8, 9, 15, 16, 17, 18, 21, 22, 23, 24, 26, 27
Best Days for Career: 1, 2, 12, 13, 14, 21, 22

Health needs watching this month from the 15th onwards. There is nothing serious afoot, only temporary stress caused by the short-term planets. Enhance the health with more rest, as usual. Until the 5th calf and ankle massage will be good. Fresh air and deep breathing will also help. After the 5th enhance the health with foot massage and spiritual-healing techniques. If you feel under the weather, see a spiritual type of healer. Good emotional health is very important from the 5th onwards. Spiritual healing is especially powerful from the 26th to the 28th.

The planetary power shifts to the West on the 15th and you enter a more social period now. A time to cultivate your social skills. Personal initiative and assertiveness are not the way to go now. Now you attain your goals through consensus and your social grace. Put other people first and your own good will come to you naturally and normally. On the 30th Mercury will enter your 7th house, making it stronger.

A solar eclipse on the 30th occurs in your 6th house of health, and signals important changes in the health regime in the coming months.

Sometimes there is a health scare, but if this happens make sure to get a second opinion. (Sometimes when tests are taken when the planetary aspects are challenging they can show things that will disappear when the aspects change.) Job changes are afoot too. This can be within your present company or with another company. If you employ others there can be staff turnover and dramas in the lives of employees.

The Sun rules your 9th house, and so every solar eclipse impacts your 9th house. Thus college-level students experience disruptions at school, changes in educational plans and sometimes change of schools. There are shake-ups in your place of worship and dramas in the lives of worship leaders. You like to travel, but best to avoid it during this eclipse period. If you are involved in legal issues they will take a dramatic turn, one way or another.

Finances are better until the 20th than after. Earnings will come after the 20th but you'll have to work harder for them.

May

Best Days Overall: 7, 8, 9, 16, 17, 25, 26
Most Stressful Days Overall: 2, 3, 4, 10, 11, 23, 24, 30, 31
Best Days for Love: 2, 3, 4, 7, 8, 12, 13, 16, 17, 18, 19, 28, 30, 31
Best Days for Money: 3, 4, 6, 13, 16, 19, 21, 22, 25, 31
Best Days for Career: 2, 3, 4, 10, 11, 12, 13, 18, 19, 28

On an overall level health is good these days, although there is short-term stress caused by the short-term planets again this month. So overall energy is not what it should be – and will be. As always, make sure to get enough rest: high energy levels are the first defence against disease. Enhance the health with scalp, face and head massage from the 3rd to the 28th. Physical exercise will help you maintain good muscle tone, which is important. Avoid anger and fear, the two emotions that stress the adrenals (it will be a good idea to massage the reflex points for the adrenals too). After the 28th neck and throat massage will be useful. Craniosacral therapy will be beneficial all month. The good news is that your 6th house of health is very strong all this month so you're not ignoring things. You're focused on health.

Jupiter, the ruler of your Horoscope, makes a major move into your 5th house on the 11th. A major headline. So, you are more involved with children and children figures in your life. Those of you of child-bearing age are still very fertile. There is more fun in your life too. This is a trend for the year ahead and for next year. Personal creativity will be much stronger than usual.

A lunar eclipse on the 16th occurs in your 12th house of spirituality. It is relatively mild in its effect on you, but it won't hurt to reduce your schedule a little that period. (You should be taking things more easily all month, but especially around this period.) This eclipse brings changes in your spiritual practice, teachings and teachers. It changes your attitudes to your spiritual path. In some cases, people embark on a spiritual path with this kind of eclipse. In many others the eclipse brings inner revelations that cause changes in practice and attitudes. There are disruptions in charitable and spiritual organizations that you're involved with. (And since the Moon rules your 9th house, it brings disruptions at your place of worship as well.) Worship leaders and guru figures experience personal dramas. College-level students or those entering college are affected too: there are changes in educational plans and often changes of school. There can be shake-ups in the hierarchy of the school. Legal issues – if you're involved in these things – will take a dramatic turn one way or another. They move forward. Saturn, your financial planet, is hit by this eclipse, bringing a need for a financial change. Your thinking and assumptions have been amiss – as the events of the eclipse will show – and you are forced to adjust. There are dramas in the lives of the money people in your life as well. Friends are making important financial changes – their assumptions have also been unrealistic.

Love is active but complicated. The Sun moves into your 7th house on the 21st and you begin a yearly love and social peak. The only problem is the retrograde of your love planet Mercury on the 10th. This complicates things. Social confidence is not what it should be. Singles will date and attend parties, but there's no need for major decisions about love at the moment.

Jobseekers have many opportunities this month. Perhaps too many. Those already employed will have opportunities for overtime or second jobs. You're in the mood for work and employers pick up on this.

June

Best Days Overall: 4, 5, 13, 14, 21, 22
Most Stressful Days Overall: 6, 7, 19, 20, 26, 27
Best Days for Love: 6, 7, 16, 17, 26, 27
Best Days for Money: 2, 3, 4, 10, 13, 15, 16, 18, 21, 29, 30
Best Days for Career: 6, 7, 17, 26, 27

The planetary power is mostly in the West now – in fact it is at its most Western position. Your 7th house of love and social activities is chock-full of planets while your 1st house of self is empty (only the Moon moves through there, on the 13th and 14th). So we have a clear message. The month ahead is about other people and your relationship with them. Love and social activities – the needs of others – take priority over your own needs. You are cultivating your social skills this month. Personal skills, assertiveness and initiative are not as important as your social skills. Get your way through consensus and cooperation. Don't try to force your own way into your good: good will come through the good graces of others.

You're still in the midst of a yearly love and social peak. While marriage most likely won't happen – you don't seem in the mood for it – there are plenty of love opportunities. You are more in the mood for fun and games than anything serious. The love life is also helped by Mercury going forward on the 3rd. Social confidence returns. You are clearer as to what you want. A stalled relationship starts to move forward again.

Health still needs watching until the 21st. Your health is basically good, but you're feeling the short-term stresses caused by the short-term planets. Most of the stress will pass by the 21st. In the meantime, be sure to get enough rest and enhance the health with neck massage until the 23rd and craniosacral therapy. After the 23rd you can enhance the health with arm and shoulder massage and hand reflexology. Also, get plenty of fresh air and breathe deeply. After the 23rd social harmony is very important for health.

Although health and energy could be better, you're still having a good time. Your 5th house is strong and you're in party mode these days. Two very important planets occupy your 5th house – Jupiter, the ruler of your Horoscope, and Mars, the ruler of your 5th house. So, the goal of life these days is just happiness. Personal creativity is unusually strong. Women of childbearing age are still unusually fertile.

Finances are strong this month. Saturn receives wonderful aspects until the 21st. The 15th and 16th seem especially good for earnings. The only issue financially is the retrograde of your financial planet on the 4th, which will go on for many months. With such a long-term retrograde you can't stop your financial activity, but you can research things more thoroughly.

On the 21st, the Sun enters your 8th house of regeneration and stays there the rest of the month (and well into the next). This is a time to focus on personal transformation – giving birth to the you that you want to be. This entails purging yourself of old baggage – old thinking and emotional patterns that have no place in the new you. It is also a good transit for weight-loss and detox regimes. It is a time for expanding your horizons by getting rid of things that are no longer needed. We expand by eliminating, not by adding.

July

Best Days Overall: 1, 2, 10, 11, 18, 19, 20, 28, 29
Most Stressful Days Overall: 4, 5, 16, 17, 23, 24, 31
Best Days for Love: 6, 7, 8, 15, 16, 17, 23, 24, 26, 28, 29
Best Days for Money: 1, 2, 7, 10, 11, 12, 13, 15, 18, 19, 24, 28, 29
Best Days for Career: 4, 5, 8, 16, 17, 28, 29, 31

Health and energy are excellent this month, and will just get better as the month progresses. You have all the energy you need to achieve whatever you set your mind to. You can enhance it even further with arm and shoulder massage, hand reflexology and massage of the lung and bronchial reflexes until the 18th. After the 18th diet becomes more important. Massage of the stomach reflex and good emotional health will also be helpful.

Your 8th house is even stronger than it was last month. Thus, as we mentioned, this is a period for reinventing yourself – personal transformation – and detox and weight-loss regimes. Mercury, your love and career planet, will be in the 8th house for most of the month – from the 5th to the 19th. This shows that sexual magnetism is the predominant allurement for singles. In general, the month ahead is more sexually active, although this will change on the 19th when your love planet enters Leo, your 9th house. You realize that though sex is important, other things are perhaps equally important. You gravitate to highly educated and refined people. You look for philosophical compatibility. You are attracted to people you can learn from and look up to. You have the aspects of someone who falls in love with their professor or minister, priest or rabbi. Love and social opportunities happen at college or college functions or at your place of worship and religious functions. You find people from foreign lands alluring as well.

Mercury moves speedily this month. In general, although there is a lot of retrograde activity this month, it doesn't seem to affect love or the career. You have confidence and make quick progress.

Mars moves into your 6th house of health and work on the 5th. This favours exercise regimes. There is a need for good muscle tone (in addition to what we mentioned earlier). The transit shows that you might be more involved with the health of children and children figures than with your own health. A happy job opportunity comes to you.

Your 9th house becomes powerful on the 23rd. This will bring travel opportunities, and a lot of these seem career related. The 30th and 31st seem very good for foreign travel. This is also a good period for college students and for those entering or applying to college. The 30th and 31st bring good news on that front too.

August

Best Days Overall: 7, 8, 15, 16, 25, 26
Most Stressful Days Overall: 1, 13, 14, 20, 21, 27, 28
Best Days for Love: 4, 5, 9, 15, 17, 18, 20, 21, 25, 26, 29
Best Days for Money: 3, 7, 9, 10, 12, 15, 21, 25, 30
Best Days for Career: 1, 9, 17, 18, 27, 28, 29

Health needs more watching from the 23rd onwards. Again, this is due to temporary stresses caused by the short-term planets. Nothing major seems amiss. As always, do your best to maintain high energy levels.

Massage of the heart reflex and chest massage will be helpful. Diet is important until the 12th.

Love is interesting this month. Mars moves into your 7th house on the 20th and will stay there for the rest of the year. This doesn't seem to presage marriage, more like love affairs – fun and games. On the 4th your love planet moves into your 10th house of career, signalling an allurement to people of power and prestige. People who can help you careerwise. You are meeting these kinds of people this month. Your social grace is strong as Mercury is well placed – in his own sign and house and at the top of your chart, from the 4th to the 26th. The love life should be good. A lot of your socializing is career related (but not all of it). There are romantic opportunities with bosses and people above you in status. Also, with people involved in your career. Love attitudes change after the 26th when Mercury enters romantic Libra. Until the 26th love seems pragmatic – practical – a career move. But after that you want more romance.

The month ahead is successful. While the day side of the Horoscope is not dominant – the night side is still stronger – it is as strong as it will be this year. So, this is a good time to focus more on the career. The image that comes to me is that you are in the noon of your year and should be up and about, but you get drowsy and go to sleep, then you wake up, then go to sleep again. It's hard to shake off the night.

Career-related travel seems likely this month. Your willingness to travel and to mentor others seems important careerwise. Don't forget to attend or host the right kinds of parties and gatherings.

Finances seem stressful this month. Though you are successful in your career you might see the financial benefits only later. Your financial planet Saturn is still retrograde. In addition, he receives stressful aspects until the 23rd. Finances should improve after then, and next month will be a lot better.

September

Best Days Overall: 3, 4, 11, 12, 21, 22, 30
Most Stressful Days Overall: 9, 10, 16, 17, 23, 24
Best Days for Love: 4, 5, 7, 8, 13, 14, 15, 16, 17, 24
Best Days for Money: 3, 5, 6, 7, 8, 11, 16, 17, 21, 26, 27, 30
Best Days for Career: 7, 8, 16, 23, 24

Retrograde activity hits its maximum for the year. From the 10th onwards 60 per cent of the planets are retrograde. Children born this period – we don't even need to know their actual horoscope – will be late bloomers, late developers. Perhaps it is good that Jupiter has his solstice this month. It goes from the 8th of this month to October 16. (Jupiter moves very slowly, hence the solstice goes on much longer.) This is very important for you as Jupiter is the ruler of your Horoscope. There is a pause in your personal activities and, next month, a change of direction. This pause will work in your favour.

When planetary retrograde activity is this strong there is much we can do to use it to our advantage. First, we can review all the departments of our lives and see where improvements can be made. Then when the planets start moving forward, we are ready to move forward along with them. Secondly, with this many retrogrades we can work to become perfect in all that we do. Make sure all the details of life – financial, careerwise, etc. are done perfectly. There are no shortcuts now. Take the time and be perfect. This won't eliminate delays and glitches, but it will reduce them and their impact.

Health still needs watching until the 23rd. So rest and relax more and listen to the messages that your body sends you. If you're exercising and feel pain or discomfort, stop and rest and then go back to it. Enhance the health with massage of the heart reflex and the chest. After the 5th abdominal massage will be good. Health will improve dramatically after the 23rd.

You're still in a yearly career peak until the 23rd, so try to stay awake and focus on the career. It's OK to feel drowsy (there are still many planets in the night side of your chart) but snap out of it whenever possible.

Mercury's retrograde on the 10th complicates both love and the career. With both Jupiter and Mercury retrograde at the same time both you and the beloved lack direction and clarity. Neither of you is sure of what you want. Avoid making important love decisions from the 10th onwards.

Though your financial planet is still retrograde he is now receiving good aspects – so earnings are increasing and come with less effort.

October

Best Days Overall: 1, 9, 10, 18, 19, 27, 28
Most Stressful Days Overall: 7, 13, 14, 21, 22
Best Days for Love: 2, 3, 4, 5, 13, 14, 25
Best Days for Money: 2, 3, 4, 5, 8, 9, 13, 14, 18, 23, 24, 26, 27, 30
Best Days for Career: 2, 3, 13, 21, 22, 23, 24

A solar eclipse on the 25th is almost a replay of the lunar eclipse of May 16. It occurs in your 12th house and seems relatively mild in its effect on you. It produces spiritual changes. It produces changes behind the scenes – things that you might see later on. There are shake-ups and dramas in spiritual or charitable organizations that you're involved with. You make changes in your charitable giving. You change spiritual teachings, teachers and practices. (Often this comes from inner revelation and is very natural and normal.)

Friends are making important financial changes. Siblings and sibling figures are having love dramas. Relationships get tested now. Children and children figures can have psychological confrontations with death. Perhaps surgery is recommended to them.

The Sun rules your 9th house and every solar eclipse affects the affairs of this house. So college students experience dramas at school. They change their educational plans, or courses. Sometimes they change schools. College policy can change in a way that impacts educational plans. There are shake-ups in your place of worship as well. There are personal dramas – often life-changing kinds of dramas – in the lives of worship leaders. This is not a good time to be travelling. If you must, try to schedule your trip around the eclipse period. Legal decisions can be shocking.

The good news is that health is good this month. The home and family situation also seem happy and you are more focused here. A parent or parent figure prospers.

Finances are also improving. Saturn, your financial planet, starts to move forward on the 23rd. You have clarity in finance and are ready to move forward. However, you will probably have to work harder for earnings from the 23rd onwards. If you put in the effort, you will prosper.

You can enhance your health further through massage of the kidney reflex and the hips – until the 23rd. Afterwards, detox regimes are beneficial – also spiritual-healing techniques.

November

Best Days Overall: 5, 6, 15, 16, 24, 25
Most Stressful Days Overall: 3, 4, 10, 11, 17, 18, 30
Best Days for Love: 3, 4, 10, 11, 13, 14, 23, 24, 25
Best Days for Money: 1, 2, 4, 10, 11, 14, 19, 20, 23, 26, 27, 28, 29
Best Days for Career: 3, 4, 13, 14, 17, 18, 24, 25

Retrograde activity continues to decline this month, and by the end of the month only 20 per cent of the planets will be retrograde. Events in the world and in your life are moving forward. Blocked projects get unblocked.

Along with this we have a monster lunar eclipse on the 8th. (I feel this eclipse is part of the 'unblocking' of projects. It blasts away the hindrances.) This eclipse is strongly felt for many reasons. First, it is a total eclipse (these are always stronger than partial ones). Secondly, it impacts many other planets and thus many departments of life. So, it is strong personally and for the world at large. It affects Mercury, Venus and Uranus.

The eclipse occurs in your 6th house of health and work and impacts the ruler of that house, Venus. So job changes are afoot. The conditions of the workplace change. There could be a health scare (and if there is, schedule a second opinion for the end of the month – often tests will show one thing when the planetary energies are roiled up and another when there is more harmony). In the coming months you will be making important changes to the health regime. If you employ others, there will be dramas in the lives of your employees, and employee turnover is happening this month and in the months to come.

The Moon, the eclipsed planet, rules your 8th house. So there can be psychological encounters with death or near-death kinds of experiences. Perhaps surgery is recommended. (Get a second opinion.) The spouse, partner or current love has to make important financial changes. Their financial thinking and strategy have been unrealistic.

Aside from this, the spouse, partner or current love is having personal dramas. He or she has to redefine him or herself. There is a need to upgrade the image and presentation to others. Your relationship gets tested.

Career changes are also happening. Usually it is not a literal change – usually it stems from changes in company policy or changes in the industry or changes in government regulations. You have to approach the career in a different way. But sometimes it brings an actual change of the career path. There are dramas – often life-changing – in the lives of bosses, elders, parents and parent figures.

This eclipse happens when your spiritual 12th house is strong. You are in a more spiritual period until the 22nd. Spirituality – meditation and spiritual practice – is the best way to go through this kind of eclipse. It keeps you calm and reveals solutions.

On the 22nd as the Sun enters your 1st house you begin one of your yearly personal pleasure peaks – a happy period.

December

Best Days Overall: 2, 3, 12, 13, 21, 22, 29, 30
Most Stressful Days Overall: 1, 7, 8, 14, 15, 16, 27, 28
Best Days for Love: 2, 3, 7, 8, 14, 17, 18, 23, 24, 25, 26
Best Days for Money: 1, 7, 8, 11, 17, 18, 20, 21, 23, 24, 25, 26, 29
Best Days for Career: 2, 3, 14, 15, 16, 23, 24

A happy and prosperous month ahead, Sagittarius, enjoy.

The planetary power is now mostly in the Eastern sector of self – and at its maximum Eastern position. You are in a period of maximum personal independence. You can and should have things your way, and others seem eager to comply. Make the changes that need to be made for your happiness. They will happen easily now and you don't need the approval of others (though you will have it anyway). Take responsibility for your own happiness.

You're still in the midst of a yearly personal pleasure peak, which began last month on the 22nd. Health is good and will get even better after the 21st. This is a time to enjoy all the pleasures of the senses and body. It is good to pamper the body and show it appreciation for its yeoman and selfless service to you all these years. It is good to get the body in the shape that you want. It is also good for buying clothing and personal accessories as your taste is good now (Venus is in your 1st house until the 10th).

Happy travel opportunities are coming. Job opportunities as well. College-level students hear good news from school. The personal appearance shines and the opposite sex takes notice.

Your love planet, Mercury, has been in your sign since November 17 and is there until the 7th. This shows someone who has love on their own terms. Love pursues you. There's nothing special that you need to do. Career opportunities are also coming to you. And this happens without any special effort too.

On the 21st the Sun enters your 2nd money house and you begin a yearly financial peak. (You'll feel this even before the 21st, as Mercury enters the money house on the 7th and Venus on the 10th.)

Jupiter moves back into your 5th house on the 21st and you enter a strong party period. Moreover, you have the funds to sustain it.

Going outside boundaries – ignoring boundaries – seems to be the style in the world this month. Many people are doing this. Three planets are 'out of bounds' this month – Mars, Venus and Mercury. For you this shows being outside your normal orbit in love and career, in health and in the kinds of enjoyments you prefer.

Capricorn

♑

THE GOAT

Birthdays from
21st December to
19th January

Personality Profile

CAPRICORN AT A GLANCE

Element – Earth

Ruling Planet – Saturn
  Career Planet – Venus
  Love Planet – Moon
  Money Planet – Uranus
  Planet of Communications – Neptune
  Planet of Health and Work – Mercury
  Planet of Home and Family Life – Mars
  Planet of Spirituality – Jupiter

Colours – black, indigo

Colours that promote love, romance and social harmony – puce, silver

Colour that promotes earning power – ultramarine blue

Gem – black onyx

Metal – lead

Scents – magnolia, pine, sweet pea, wintergreen

Quality – cardinal (= activity)

Qualities most needed for balance – warmth, spontaneity, a sense of fun

Strongest virtues – sense of duty, organization, perseverance, patience, ability to take the long-term view

Deepest needs – to manage, take charge and administrate

Characteristics to avoid – pessimism, depression, undue materialism and undue conservatism

Signs of greatest overall compatibility – Taurus, Virgo

Signs of greatest overall incompatibility – Aries, Cancer, Libra

Sign most helpful to career – Libra

Sign most helpful for emotional support – Aries

Sign most helpful financially – Aquarius

Sign best for marriage and/or partnerships – Cancer

Sign most helpful for creative projects – Taurus

Best Sign to have fun with – Taurus

Signs most helpful in spiritual matters – Virgo, Sagittarius

Best day of the week – Saturday

Understanding a Capricorn

The virtues of Capricorns are such that there will always be people for and against them. Many admire them, many dislike them. Why? It seems to be because of Capricorn's power urges. A well-developed Capricorn has his or her eyes set on the heights of power, prestige and authority. In the sign of Capricorn, ambition is not a fatal flaw, but rather the highest virtue.

Capricorns are not frightened by the resentment their authority may sometimes breed. In Capricorn's cool, calculated, organized mind all the dangers are already factored into the equation – the unpopularity, the animosity, the misunderstandings, even the outright slander – and a plan is always in place for dealing with these things in the most efficient way. To the Capricorn, situations that would terrify an ordinary mind are merely problems to be managed, bumps on the road to ever-growing power, effectiveness and prestige.

Some people attribute pessimism to the Capricorn sign, but this is a bit deceptive. It is true that Capricorns like to take into account the negative side of things. It is also true that they love to imagine the worst possible scenario in every undertaking. Other people might find such analyses depressing, but Capricorns only do these things so that they can formulate a way out – an escape route.

Capricorns will argue with success. They will show you that you are not doing as well as you think you are. Capricorns do this to themselves as well as to others. They do not mean to discourage you but rather to root out any impediments to your greater success. A Capricorn boss or supervisor feels that no matter how good the performance there is always room for improvement. This explains why Capricorn supervisors are difficult to handle and even infuriating at times. Their actions are, however, quite often effective – they can get their subordinates to improve and become better at their jobs.

Capricorn is a born manager and administrator. Leo is better at being king or queen, but Capricorn is better at being prime minister – the person actually wielding power.

Capricorn is interested in the virtues that last, in the things that will stand the test of time and trials of circumstance. Temporary fads and fashions mean little to a Capricorn – except as things to be used for profit or power. Capricorns apply this attitude to business, love, to their thinking and even to their philosophy and religion.

Finance

Capricorns generally attain wealth and they usually earn it. They are willing to work long and hard for what they want. They are quite amenable to forgoing a short-term gain in favour of long-term benefits. Financially, they come into their own later in life.

However, if Capricorns are to attain their financial goals they must shed some of their strong conservatism. Perhaps this is the least desirable trait of the Capricorn. They can resist anything new merely because it is new and untried. They are afraid of experimentation. Capricorns need to be willing to take a few risks. They should be more eager to market new products or explore different managerial techniques. Otherwise, progress will leave them behind. If necessary, Capricorns must be ready to change with the times, to discard old methods that no longer work.

Very often this experimentation will mean that Capricorns have to break with existing authority. They might even consider changing their present position or starting their own ventures. If so, they should be willing to accept all the risks and just get on with it. Only then will a Capricorn be on the road to the highest financial gains.

Career and Public Image

A Capricorn's ambition and quest for power are evident. It is perhaps the most ambitious sign of the zodiac – and usually the most successful in a worldly sense. However, there are lessons Capricorns need to learn in order to fulfil their highest aspirations.

Intelligence, hard work, cool efficiency and organization will take them a certain distance, but will not carry them to the very top. Capricorns need to cultivate their social graces, to develop a social style, along with charm and an ability to get along with people. They need to bring beauty into their lives and to cultivate the right social contacts. They must learn to wield power gracefully, so that people love them for it – a very delicate art. They also need to learn how to bring people together in order to fulfil certain objectives. In short, Capricorns require some of the gifts – the social graces – of Libra to get to the top.

Once they have learned this, Capricorns will be successful in their careers. They are ambitious hard workers who are not afraid of putting in the required time and effort. Capricorns take their time in getting the job done – in order to do it well – and they like moving up the corporate ladder slowly but surely. Being so driven by success, Capricorns are generally liked by their bosses, who respect and trust them.

Love and Relationships

Like Scorpio and Pisces, Capricorn is a difficult sign to get to know. They are deep, introverted and like to keep their own counsel. Capricorns do not like to reveal their innermost thoughts. If you are in love with a Capricorn, be patient and take your time. Little by little you will get to understand him or her.

Capricorns have a deep romantic nature, but they do not show it straight away. They are cool, matter of fact and not especially emotional. They will often show their love in practical ways.

It takes time for a Capricorn – male or female – to fall in love. They are not the love-at-first-sight kind. If a Capricorn is involved with a Leo or Aries, these Fire types will be totally mystified – to them the Capricorn will seem cold, unfeeling, unaffectionate and not very spontaneous. Of course none of this is true; it is just that Capricorn likes to take things slowly. They like to be sure of their ground before making any demonstrations of love or commitment.

Even in love affairs Capricorns are deliberate. They need more time to make decisions than is true of the other signs of the zodiac, but given this time they become just as passionate. Capricorns like a relationship to be structured, committed, well regulated, well defined, predictable and even routine. They prefer partners who are nurturers, and they in turn like to nurture their partners. This is their basic psychology. Whether such a relationship is good for them is another issue altogether. Capricorns have enough routine in their lives as it is. They might be better off in relationships that are a bit more stimulating, changeable and fluctuating.

Home and Domestic Life

The home of a Capricorn – as with a Virgo – is going to be tidy and well organized. Capricorns tend to manage their families in the same way they manage their businesses. Capricorns are often so career-driven that they find little time for the home and family. They should try to get more actively involved in their family and domestic life. Capricorns do, however, take their children very seriously and are very proud parents – particularly should their children grow up to become respected members of society.

Horoscope for 2022

Major Trends

Pluto has been in your own sign for the past twenty years. He's almost finished with you, but not just yet: he will be in and out of your sign next year but in 2024 he will leave for good. Most of you are not feeling the effects of this too strongly, but those of you born late in your sign – from January 14 to 19 – are feeling it intensely. Pluto's long transit has brought many personal dramas into your life – surgeries, near-death kinds of experiences and psychological encounters with death. You are giving birth to a new you – the you that you've always aspired to, the you that you wanted to become. This has already happened for most of you, but for those born late in Capricorn it is happening this year. A new birth can be a gory kind of business, but the end result is good.

Late in 2020 Saturn, the ruler of your Horoscope, moved into your money house. He will be there for the rest of the year ahead. This is fortunate for financial matters as it shows focus. But you will work harder for finances this year. Also, you need to resolve conflicts with the money people in your life. More on this later.

Your 3rd house of communication and intellectual activities has been strong for many years. Neptune, the ruler of the house, has set up shop there. This year the 3rd house is even more important as Jupiter will spend approximately half the year here. This is wonderful for students below the college level. They are focused on their studies and seem very successful. It is good for those of you in sales, marketing and teaching and for writers. Your communication and intellectual abilities are very much enhanced.

Jupiter spends the rest of the year in your 4th house of home and family. This indicates a likely move, or the fortunate purchase or sale of a home. Women of childbearing age are more fertile than usual. More on this later.

Uranus has been in your 5th house of fun and creativity for some years now and will be there for some more to come. Thus children and children figures in your life have been more difficult to handle. They seem rebellious and unusually independent. But this transit also brings very original personal creativity and more joy in the way you make money.

Health is basically good this year, though it needs more attention after May 11. Mars will spend an unusual amount of time in your 6th house, from August 20 onwards. This shows a need for good emotional health – also exercise becomes more important. More on this later.

Your most important interests this year are the body, image and appearance; finance; communication and intellectual interests; home and family (from May 11 to October 29 and from December 21 onwards); children, fun and creativity; and health and work (from August 20).

Your paths of greatest fulfilment will be communication and intellectual interests (until May 11 and from October 29 to December 21); home and family (from May 11 to October 29 and from December 21 onwards); and children, fun and creativity.

Health

(Please note that this is an astrological perspective on health and not a medical one. In days of yore there was no difference, both these perspectives were identical. But these days there could be quite a difference. For a medical perspective, please consult your doctor or health practitioner.)

Health looks good this year. As the year begins there is only one long-term planet – Pluto – in stressful alignment with you, and most of you are not feeling this – only those of you born late in your sign. On May 11 Jupiter moves into an adverse aspect, but Jupiter's influences tend to be mild. Health and energy are basically good. Sure, there will

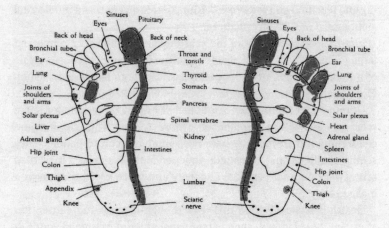

Important foot reflexology points for the year ahead

*Try to massage all of the foot on a regular basis – the top of the foot as well as
the bottom – but pay extra attention to the points highlighted on the chart.
When you massage, be aware of 'sore spots' as these need special attention.
It's also a good idea to massage the ankles and below them.*

be periods in the year where health and energy are less good than
usual. These periods come from the transits of short-term planets and
are temporary, not trends for the year. When they pass, your naturally
good health and energy return.

Your 6th house of health is basically empty until August 20 – another
positive signal. You take good health for granted. You have no need to
overly focus on it as nothing is wrong. On August 20 Mars will enter
your 6th house and spend the rest of the year there. This brings more
emphasis on health, but it seems more related to the family and family
members than your personal health.

Good though your health is you can make it even better. Give more
attention to the following – the vulnerable areas of your Horoscope –
this year (the reflex points are shown in the chart above):

- The heart. This has been important for more than twenty years,
  and this year especially so for those of you born January 14–19,
  late in the sign of Capricorn. (The reflex is shown above.) Chest

massage – especially of the breastbone and upper rib cage – will be beneficial too. The important thing with the heart is to avoid worry and anxiety, the two emotions that stress it out.

- The spine, knees, teeth, bones and overall skeletal alignment are always important areas for you. Regular back and knee massage should be part of your normal health regime. Regular visits to a chiropractor or osteopath would be good too. The vertebrae need to be kept in right alignment. A good regime for dental hygiene is also important. Make sure you get enough calcium for bone health. Yoga and Pilates are excellent exercises for the spine.

- The lungs, arms, shoulders, and respiratory system. Again, these are always important for you. Regular arm and shoulder massage should be part of your health regime. Tension tends to collect in the shoulders and needs to be released. Plain old fresh air is a natural healing tonic.

- The head and face gain in importance from August 20. Regular scalp and face massage will be beneficial, as you not only strengthen the scalp but the entire body as well. Craniosacral therapy is very good for the head. If you're out in the sun use a good sunscreen.

- The adrenals. This area too only becomes important from August 20, and the reflex points are shown above.

- The musculature is another area that becomes important after August 20. Good muscle tone and regular physical exercise, according to your age and stage in life, are important, although you don't need to become a bodybuilder. Weak muscles can knock the spine and skeleton out of alignment and this could cause all kinds of other problems.

Mars is your family planet. So, as we mentioned, your focus on health seems to be more about the health of family members than your own health. It would also show the need for good emotional health. Moods need to be kept positive and constructive.

There are many short-term health trends in your chart, because your health planet, Mercury, is very fast moving. He travels through your entire Horoscope in the course of a year, so health can vary depending on where Mercury is and the kinds of aspects he receives. This will be covered in the monthly reports.

Home and Family

This is a strong – and happy – home and family year. Not only is your 4th house strong for half the year, but all the long-term planets are below the horizon of your chart – in the night side of the Horoscope. Your 10th house of career, by contrast, is basically empty – only short-term planets will move through there and their effect is mostly short term. Now Capricorn is always ambitious, but this year less so than usual. Family and emotional issues – the foundation upon which the career is based – are taking priority. You haven't lost your ambition, but you're preparing the foundation for a future career push. The higher the edifice, the deeper the foundation needs to be.

Jupiter's move into your 4th house (and it's an on-and-off thing) from May 11 to October 29, and then from December 21 onwards, often shows a move – a happy one. Sometimes it's not a literal move; sometimes an additional home is acquired, sometimes you get access to additional homes even if you don't own them. Sometimes you buy expensive items for the home or renovate it. The whole effect is 'as if' you have moved. You live in a more comfortable home.

Jupiter's transit also shows that your family circle expands this year. Usually this happens through birth or marriage, but sometimes you meet people who are like family to you – who fulfil that function. As we mentioned, women of childbearing age become more fertile than usual. (This will be the case all next year too.)

But there is more happening here this year. Jupiter is your spiritual planet. His move into your 4th house shows that the family as a whole – and especially a parent or parent figure – is becoming more spiritual. They are all under intense spiritual influences. Their dream lives are active (as is yours). Their ESP faculties are more finely tuned. They are experiencing all kinds of supernatural phenomena. I wouldn't be surprised if the home was used to hold spiritual meetings, lectures or charity events.

A parent or parent figure will travel more this year. If this is a woman of childbearing age, she is more fertile than usual. Whether this parent is male or female there are many financial changes happening, but there is prosperity – next year too. He or she is having a stable kind of family year – moves are not likely.

Siblings and sibling figures are having a good year overall. There is prosperity and fertility (if of childbearing age). Moves are not likely but siblings could be renovating the home. Children and children figures in your life have been moving around a lot. They seem unsettled, but a formal move is not seen. Grandchildren, if you have them, or those who play that role in your life, are having a status quo home and family year.

Finance and Career

Finance is a major focus in the year ahead. Saturn, the ruler of your Horoscope (and thus an important and friendly planet), occupies your 2nd money house. This shows prosperity. You spend on yourself. You adopt the image of wealth, you dress expensively. People see you as a money person and this opens all kinds of doors and opportunities to you. Your personal appearance and demeanour are big factors in your earnings and this is probably why you spend on yourself. You consider yourself the best investment there is.

But finance is a bit complicated. You seem in disagreement with the money people in your life. There is some conflict there. You (and they) will have to work harder to reach a consensus. Somewhere there is a middle point of compromise and you need to find it.

But these are minor issues. Uranus, your financial planet, has been in your 5th house for some years now. The 5th house is a fortunate house, and it tends to prosperity. But not just prosperity as we understand it in the mundane world – it points to a happy prosperity. The act of earning is pleasurable. You earn while you are having fun or involved in some leisure activity. Perhaps an important deal is made while you are at the theatre or resort or sitting by the pool drinking pina coladas. Perhaps your job involves entertaining clients in posh clubs or with lavish dinners. You are lucky in speculations. (Every investment has some degree of risk to it – but some are riskier than others.)

You make money in happy ways and you spend it on happy things – things that bring you joy. This is happy wealth. You are enjoying the wealth that you have.

Your personal creativity is more marketable these days. You spend on children and children figures but you also earn from them. When they are young, they serve as inspiration to earn more. Often they have profitable ideas. Many a fortune was built by someone observing the behaviour of their child. When they are older, they can be materially supportive.

Industries that cater to the youth market – especially of an electronic nature – are interesting. Video games, digital music, streaming services – high-tech entertainment geared to young people seems fun and profitable. There are companies involved with online gaming which would be interesting as businesses or investments. You have a feeling for these things.

Career, as we mentioned, is not a big issue this year. You're building the infrastructure for the future this year. Building your base. Your 10th house is basically empty. And, as we mentioned, the night side of your chart is far stronger than the day side. This shouldn't alarm you. Some years are like that. Career is quiet and stable. The problem is not talent or ability – just lack of interest.

Venus is your career planet. As regular readers know, she is a very fast-moving planet who will move through your entire chart in any given year. Thus there are many short-term career trends that depend on where Venus is and the kinds of aspects she receives. These are best dealt with in the monthly reports.

Love and Social Life

Your 7th house of love is empty this year. So, as in many past years, love seems stable. You seem content with things as they are and have no need to make dramatic changes or give it unusual focus. Those who are married will tend to stay married, and singles will tend to stay single.

However, if love problems arise it could be because of this lack of attention. You will have to focus more. Two lunar eclipses this year will force you to focus here. The first happens on May 16 and the second on November 8. These will be times for course corrections in love – eliminating the bugs and imperfections.

The status quo situation applies to those in or working on first or second marriages. Those in or working on the third marriage have better love and social aspects. If you are single, love will find you.

Someone is pursuing you. If you are married, there is closeness in the relationship and the beloved is very supportive and devoted.

The Moon is your love planet and is the fastest of all the planets. Where the other fast-moving planets, the Sun, Mercury and Venus, take a year to cycle through your chart, the Moon does this every month. Thus love can happen for you in many ways and through many venues depending on where the Moon is and the aspects she receives. These are best dealt with in the monthly reports.

In general we can say that love will go better for you as the Moon waxes (grows larger). You have more energy, enthusiasm and social grace during those periods. The new and full Moons tend to be active social days (if these occur under good aspects they bring happiness; if they occur under adverse aspects they bring challenges).

A parent or parent figure is having a fabulous love and social year – from May 11 onwards (with a brief hiatus from October 29 to December 21). If he or she is single there can be a marriage or serious relationship happening.

Siblings and sibling figures are having a prosperous year, but love seems quiet.

Children and children figures probably shouldn't marry this year (or in the next few years as well). They seem too unstable to get into anything serious. They are better off with serial love affairs.

Grandchildren, if you have them (or those who play that role in your life), are having a fabulous love and social year. Much depends on their age. If they are very young, they are making friends and seem popular. Older ones can marry or be involved in a relationship that is 'like' a marriage.

Self-improvement

Neptune has been in your 3rd house for many years now. Spiritually understood, he is elevating the mind, the intellect, the mental faculties to a higher, more spiritual plane – a higher vibration. We have written of this in past reports. But this year, this process is much accelerated, because your spiritual planet, Jupiter, is also in the 3rd house for half the year. This is elevation on steroids.

The first thing that is happening is that your taste in reading is much more refined. You have a taste now for spiritual-type literature. Regular mundane reading seems boring to you and lacks relevance or meaning. You want something deeper.

Also, the way you communicate is becoming very inspired. Many fine writers were (and are) Capricorns. I'm thinking of Jack London, Edgar Allen Poe, Rudyard Kipling and J. R. R. Tolkien. Those of you who already write will be inspired from on high. 'All writing,' says Emerson, 'is by the grace of God.' You are in that grace right now. Some of you might decide to take it up these days. Poetry also seems appealing for Capricorn.

Your speech and written words have a musical quality to them. Normally Capricorn speaks bluntly and to the point. Now you are more cognizant of tone, rhythm, nuance. This is so in your mental process as well. It's not just about what is said or written. You're aware of what is not said, or the way something is said – what was emphasized, what was glossed over; this gives you a deeper insight into what you're reading.

With Uranus, the planet of change, in your 5th house of creativity, you're ready to explore new avenues of creativity these days – writing might be just the right thing. (Music also looks interesting.)

Dealing with rebellious children has been an issue for some years now. You are learning how to handle this through direct practical experience. By the time Uranus is finished with you, you'll be an expert. Capricorn likes authority and likes to exert it. But too much authoritarianism won't work with the kids. In fact, it can incite them even further. Uranus prides himself on 'bucking' authority. He likes 'sticking it to the man'. But Uranus also loves truth. So, if you need to limit the children (and they do need limits) don't be authoritarian about it, take the time to explain why. They need to understand this.

Mars will be in your 6th house of health from August 20 onwards. We have discussed the physical health implications of this, but the real, deeper, message is the need for emotional healing. Mars, as you know, is your family planet, ruling your moods, emotions and memories. So this will be a time to get more involved in emotional healing – healing of the past, healing of the memory body. It will be a good time to embark on psychological-type therapies. But you can do much to clear the memory body on your own, through meditation. (My book *A*

Technique for Meditation gives techniques for doing this.) If anything bothers you or throws you off your game, that is a signal to clear the issue. You can do 'touch and let go' as outlined in my book, or do the writing out exercise. There is much additional information on this subject on my website, www.spiritual-stories.com.

Month-by-month Forecasts

January

Best Days Overall: 2, 3, 11, 12, 21, 22, 29, 30
Most Stressful Days Overall: 8, 9, 16, 17, 23, 24
Best Days for Love: 2, 3, 11, 12, 16, 17, 21, 22, 23, 29, 30
Best Days for Money: 2, 3, 4, 5, 6, 11, 12, 16, 21, 22, 25, 29, 30, 31
Best Days for Career: 2, 3, 11, 12, 21, 22, 23, 24, 29, 30

A happy and prosperous month, Capricorn, enjoy.

The action this month is in your 1st house. It is easily the strongest house in the chart: at least half the planets, and sometimes more, are either there or moving through there. You're in the midst of a yearly personal pleasure peak and the maximum period of personal independence. It is a 'me, me, me' kind of month. It's time to take responsibility for your own happiness – to create your own happiness. Personal initiative matters now. The time will come to cultivate the social graces, but not yet. Make the changes that need to be made to perfect your happiness. You have a lot of cosmic support. If you are happy, there is that much less suffering in the world.

This is a month for having things your way. You know what's best for you – you know it better than others. So, as the saying goes, follow your path of bliss.

This is not an especially strong love month. Your 1st house is chock-full of planets while your 7th house of love is empty – only the Moon visits there on the 16th and 17th. Relationships *can* work, as long as the beloved gives in to you.

On the 20th the Sun joins Saturn in your money house and you begin a yearly financial peak. This is a good period to take on debt or to pay it down – depending on your need. It is also good for tax and insurance planning and, if you are of an appropriate age, for estate planning. If you have good business ideas, it is a good period for attracting outside investors for your projects.

Health looks excellent this month. You have the energy of ten people. Your health planet, Mercury, will go retrograde on the 14th, so this is not a good time to undergo medical tests or procedures. If you must do these things do them before the 14th.

Jupiter and Neptune in your 3rd house of communication shows an excellent month for students – and the next few months will be that way too.

February

Best Days Overall: 7, 8, 17, 18, 26, 27
Most Stressful Days Overall: 5, 6, 12, 13, 19, 20
Best Days for Love: 1, 7, 8, 9, 10, 12, 13, 17, 18, 22, 23, 27
Best Days for Money: 1, 2, 3, 7, 8, 12, 13, 17, 18, 21, 22, 26, 27, 28
Best Days for Career: 7, 8, 17, 18, 19, 20, 27

Mars entered your sign on January 25 and will remain there for the rest of the month ahead. Mars and Pluto in your own sign is a very dynamic aspect. Sex appeal is stronger than usual. You excel in exercise regimes. You get things done in a hurry. The downside of this is rush and hurry, which can lead to accidents or injury. Also, you could come across as 'combative' these days – spoiling for a fight. People can see you this way. So you need to be careful about this.

Your 1st house is still strong this month, while your 7th house of love is still empty – only the Moon visits there on the 12th and 13th. So the month ahead, like last month, is a 'me' oriented month. You're working to set up the conditions for your personal happiness. Personal independence and personal initiative matter now. It's all up to you now.

Venus, your career planet, has been in your sign for all the year so far. Last month she was retrograde, but now she is moving forward. This shows career opportunities coming to you – they seek you out.

You look very successful as well. People see you this way. The only problem is that career doesn't seem a big issue right now. All the planets are below the horizon of your chart and you are in the night-time of your year. The opportunities are there, but the problem is lack of interest.

Career might not be strong but finances are. You remain in the midst of a yearly financial peak until the 18th. You might be working harder for your earnings, but they come.

Your 3rd house has been strong (and fortunate) all this year so far, but it gets even stronger after the 18th. There are many signals here. Siblings and sibling figures are prospering. Students are doing well in school. Sales and marketing people are having a banner month. A new car or communication equipment (or both) is coming to you. The money people in your life get even richer.

Love doesn't seem a big issue this month. Like last month, your 7th house is empty (apart from the Moon's visit on the 12th and 13th). This tends to the status quo. You seem focused on getting your personal goals in order rather than on partnerships.

March

Best Days Overall: 6, 7, 8, 16, 17, 25, 26
Most Stressful Days Overall: 4, 5, 11, 12, 13, 18, 19
Best Days for Love: 2, 3, 9, 11, 12, 13, 18, 19, 23, 27, 28
Best Days for Money: 1, 2, 3, 6, 7, 11, 12, 16, 17, 21, 22, 25, 26, 27, 28, 30, 31
Best Days for Career: 9, 18, 19, 27, 28

All the planets are moving forward this month and the Sun moves into Aries on the 20th. You are in the best starting energy of the year. This is a time to launch those new projects or products into the world. You have a lot of cosmic 'oomph' behind you.

Though you are not in a yearly financial peak, finances look good. Your money house is strong and it should be a prosperous month. Mars and Venus move into the money house on the 6th. Mars, your family planet, shows good family support for finances. Venus's position indicates spending on the children or children figures in your life, and perhaps earning from them as well. It also shows the support of bosses and elders. They seem in sync with your financial goals. Sometimes this aspect leads to a pay rise – official or unofficial.

Your 3rd house is still strong this month – especially until the 20th. The mental faculties are stronger than usual, so it is a good time to take courses in subjects that interest you. It is also good to teach in your areas of expertise. The Sun travels with Jupiter from the 4th to the 6th and this brings a nice payday for the spouse, partner or current love.

Mars travels with Pluto from the 2nd to the 4th. This is a dynamic aspect so be more mindful on the physical plane. This applies to parents or parent figures as well. A parent or parent figure can be having surgery. Mars will make dynamic aspects with Uranus from the 20th to the 22nd. Be more mindful on the physical plane during that period too.

On the 20th the Sun enters your 4th house of home and family. You are in the midnight hour of your year. This is a time for sleeping, withdrawing from outer consciousness and focusing on inner things. During sleep the outer consciousness is inactive, but tremendous things are happening within. Cell repair is taking place. The patterns for the next day are being set. The forces are being built up for the next day. There is much activity but behind the scenes.

Capricorn is always ambitious, but now it is time to focus on the home – the foundation upon which a successful career is based.

Health is still good, but it needs more attention after the 20th.

April

Best Days Overall: 3, 4, 13, 14, 21, 22, 30
Most Stressful Days Overall: 1, 2, 8, 9, 15, 16, 28, 29
Best Days for Love: 1, 2, 8, 9, 12, 13, 17, 18, 21, 22, 25, 26, 27
Best Days for Money: 3, 4, 8, 9, 13, 14, 17, 18, 21, 22, 23, 24, 26, 27, 30
Best Days for Career: 8, 15, 16, 17, 18, 25, 26, 27

Your 3rd house is still very powerful this month. Both Mars and Venus will enter there – Venus on the 5th and Mars on the 15th. This is an excellent month for siblings and sibling figures. They are very prosperous these days – especially from the 1st to the 17th. They are doing well careerwise too. Students, writers, teachers, and sales and marketing people are also doing well now.

Health still needs watching until the 20th. There is nothing serious amiss, just the short-term stresses caused by short-term planets. Make sure to get enough rest. Enhance the health with head, face and scalp massage, physical exercise and massage of the adrenal reflexes until the 11th. After the 11th neck and throat massage will be beneficial. Health will improve dramatically after the 20th.

A solar eclipse on the 30th only affects you mildly, but it won't hurt to reduce your schedule a bit anyway. Since this eclipse occurs in your 5th house, children and children figures should stay out of harm's way. A reduced schedule for them would be wise. Children and children figures are redefining themselves these days. They are changing the way they think of themselves and how they want others to think of them. A parent or parent figure has to make important financial changes. There is some financial shake-up going on. The Sun is the ruler of your 8th house of regeneration, so every solar eclipse impacts this area. There can be confrontations with death (psychological confrontations, usually) or near-death experiences. If you have outside investors there can be disturbances with them. The spouse, partner or current love has financial shake-ups.

In spite of the eclipse a happy career opportunity comes to you on the 30th and children or children figures in your life have a good financial day.

Your 4th house is still powerful until the 20th, so the focus is on home, family and your emotional wellness. On the 20th, as the Sun enters your 5th house, you begin a yearly personal pleasure peak. It is time to enjoy life. Time to take a vacation from all cares and worries.

May

Best Days Overall: 1, 10, 11, 19, 25, 26
Most Stressful Days Overall: 5, 6, 12, 13, 25, 26
Best Days for Love: 5, 6, 7, 8, 10, 11, 20, 30, 16, 17
Best Days for Money: 1, 6, 10, 11, 16, 19, 21, 25, 27, 28
Best Days for Career: 7, 8, 12, 13, 16, 17

An eventful month, Capricorn. The planetary power shifts decisively from the East to the West – from the sector of self to the sector of others. Jupiter makes a major move into your 4th house on the 11th. Three planets have their solstices this month (which is highly unusual). And, last but not least, we have a lunar eclipse on the 16th that affects you strongly.

Health needs some attention this month, from the 11th onwards. It's nothing serious, just short-term stress caused by short-term planets. The good news is that you are focused on health this month and you're on the case. Hopefully, you're not too much on the case. Mercury, your health planet, is retrograde from the 10th and this is not a time for medical tests or procedures (especially if they are elective). You can enhance the health with arm and shoulder massage, massage of the lung and bronchial reflexes and with plain old fresh air from the 1st to the 24th. After the 24th enhance the health with neck and throat massage.

With the planetary power now mostly in the social Western sector, the month ahead is more about other people than yourself. The Cosmos wants you to develop your social skills, and it will arrange things so that your good will come through others and their good graces. Personal skills, initiative or self-assertion won't do much for you. Your social grace will.

Venus has her solstice from the 4th to the 8th. This brings a pause in your career affairs and then a change of direction. Mars, your family planet, has his solstice from May 27 to June 2. So there is a pause in your family life and then a change of direction.

Jupiter's solstice goes on for a long time – he is a very slow-moving planet. His solstice begins on the 12th and continues to June 11. This brings a pause and then a change of direction in your spiritual life.

The lunar eclipse of the 16th occurs in your 11th house of friends. So, there are dramas with friends and friendships can get tested. Friends can have life-changing kinds of dramas. Your current relationship will get tested as well: the Moon, the eclipsed planet, is your love planet. Usually such an eclipse brings up repressed material – grievances, etc. – that needs to be processed. Good relationships survive these things and get even better. It's the essentially flawed relationships that are in danger. You go through two lunar eclipses every year, however, so by now you know how to handle them.

June

Best Days Overall: 6, 7, 15, 16, 23, 24, 25
Most Stressful Days Overall: 1, 2, 3, 9, 10, 21, 22, 28, 29, 30
Best Days for Love: 1, 2, 3, 6, 7, 9, 10, 16, 18, 26, 28, 29, 30
Best Days for Money: 4, 6, 7, 13, 15, 16, 17, 18, 21, 23, 24
Best Days for Career: 6, 7, 9, 10, 16, 26

Family remains important, now that Jupiter is in your 4th house. Mars, your family planet, is also there. There is happiness and prosperity in the family. The family circle expands. Capricorns of childbearing age are very fertile now. A parent or parent figure is prospering.

Your 6th house of health and work is powerful until the 21st. Mercury, your health planet, moves forward again on the 3rd so it is now safer to undergo those tests or medical procedures. Health is basically good until the 21st. After that you need to rest and relax more and enhance the health with arm and shoulder massage and massage of the lung and bronchial reflexes. Make sure to get plenty of fresh air.

Jobseekers have good fortune until the 21st (and even afterwards). Even those already employed have opportunities for overtime or second jobs. Those of you who employ others also have good fortune.

On the 21st the Sun enters your 7th house and you begin a yearly love and social peak. Love is very erotic these days, and you're attracted to wealthy people. It is not clear which is more alluring – wealth or good sexual magnetism. Both are important.

The spouse, partner or current love is prospering this month. He or she is enjoying financial windfalls and happy opportunities.

Saturn, the ruler of your Horoscope, goes retrograde on the 4th. This, I feel, is perhaps a good thing. It weakens self-esteem and self-confidence and brings a need to review personal goals and directions. But with the social Western sector of your chart very powerful now, you don't need too much self-confidence. You need social grace. You need to get on with others. Let others have their way, so long as it isn't destructive.

July

Best Days Overall: 4, 5, 12, 13, 21, 22, 31
Most Stressful Days Overall: 6, 7, 18, 19, 20, 26, 27
Best Days for Love: 6, 7, 8, 9, 15, 17, 26, 27, 28, 29
Best Days for Money: 1, 2, 4, 5, 10, 11, 12, 13, 14, 15, 18, 19, 21, 22, 28, 29, 31
Best Days for Career: 6, 7, 15, 26

Planetary retrograde activity is steadily increasing this month, and by the end of the month 40 per cent of the planets will be moving backwards. Life is slowing down. Events need more time to develop.

Still, none of this affects the love and social life, which is going great guns this month. Your 7th house of love is the most powerful in your chart at the moment. Singles are dating more and have abundant love opportunities. Even those who are married are going out more and attending more social functions. Will singles marry? Maybe. Maybe not. But you meet people you would consider marriage material.

The spouse, partner or current love was prosperous last month and is even more prosperous in the month ahead. He or she will enter a yearly financial peak on the 23rd.

Mars makes dynamic aspects with Pluto on the 1st and 2nd. You and a parent or parent figure need to be more mindful on the physical plane. At the end of the month – the 30th and 31st – Mars travels with Uranus, which is also a dynamic aspect for you and the parent or parent figure. The good news is that he or she is active – and helpful – in your financial life.

Your 7th house is stronger than your 1st house. Most of the planets are in the West right now as well. So, let others have their way so long as it isn't destructive. The planetary momentum is running towards others and away from self.

Health still needs watching until the 23rd, after which you will see a dramatic improvement. In the meantime, enhance health through arm and shoulder massage, and massage of the lung and bronchial reflex until the 5th. After the 5th diet is important. Good health for you means good social health. So, if problems arise restore harmony with friends and the beloved as quickly as possible. After the 19th chest massage and massage of the heart reflex will be important. Spiritual healing is unusually effective on the 22nd and 23rd.

Finances are good this month but more complicated after the 23rd. There are more challenges after that date, and probably there's more work involved in earnings after then. The spouse, partner or current love is very generous on the 30th and 31st.

August

Best Days Overall: 1, 9, 10, 17, 18, 27, 28
Most Stressful Days Overall: 2, 3, 15, 16, 22, 23, 29, 30
Best Days for Love: 4, 5, 7, 8, 15, 16, 22, 23, 25, 26
Best Days for Money: 1, 7, 9, 10, 11, 12, 15, 17, 18, 25, 27, 28
Best Days for Career: 2, 3, 4, 5, 15, 25, 26, 29, 30

The night side of your Horoscope still dominates your chart. However, the day side – the side that deals with outer events and achievement – is as strong as it will ever be this year. You can't ignore home, family or your emotional wellness but you can divert some attention to the career.

The month ahead is happy. Health is good. Energy seems high. There will be a Grand Trine in the Earth signs from the 4th onwards. This is another positive for you. Earth is your native element and your practical gifts are appreciated by others. Your always strong management skills are even stronger now.

Your family planet Mars moves into your 6th house of health on the 20th and will spend the rest of the year there. This gives various messages. Good health for you means good family health – a healthy domestic and emotional life. Probably you are more involved with the health of family members than with your own. Exercise seems important for the rest of the year. You need good muscle tone. Your health planet, Mercury, moves quickly this month, flying through three signs and houses of your chart. This is a positive signal for health. There is confidence. You cover much ground. But the health needs change quickly. Until the 4th good heart health is important. From the 4th to the 19th good intestinal health is important. Abdominal massage is good. After the 26th, hip massage and massage of the kidney reflex become important.

Finances will improve after the 23rd. They're OK before then, but there seems to be more work and more challenge involved with them.

The month ahead seems sexually active, but love seems to tend to the status quo. Your 7th house is empty – only the Moon moves through there on the 22nd and 23rd. Generally, if the sex life is active we presume that love is going well. But sex and love are two different things.

Mars makes dynamic aspects with Saturn on the 6th and 7th. So be more mindful on the physical plane. Be more patient with a parent or parent figure. You seem in conflict.

September

Best Days Overall: 5, 6, 13, 14, 15, 23, 24
Most Stressful Days Overall: 11, 12, 18, 19, 20, 26, 27
Best Days for Love: 4, 5, 6, 13, 14, 15, 18, 19, 20, 25, 26
Best Days for Money: 3, 5, 6, 7, 8, 11, 14, 15, 21, 23, 24, 30
Best Days for Career: 4, 5, 13, 14, 15, 26, 27

You are entering – on the 23rd – your strongest career period of the year, Capricorn. You've had stronger periods in past years, certainly, and you will have stronger periods in the future. But for this year, this is the peak. Your 10th house is strong and so is your 4th house. The night side of the Horoscope is still dominant. So your challenge is to balance a healthy domestic life with a successful career. You go from one to the other.

Venus, your career planet, has her solstice from the 30th to October 3. She pauses in the heavens – in her latitudinal motion – and then changes direction. So it is with your career. There is a brief pause and then a change of direction.

Health is good this month, but after the 23rd it will need keeping an eye on due to the short-term stresses caused by short-term planets. It doesn't seem serious. You can enhance the health with more rest as usual, but also through chest massage and massage of the heart reflex. Hip massage and massage of the kidney reflex is important until the 24th. After the 24th massage of the lower abdomen and the small intestine reflex will be helpful. Your health planet Mercury is retrograde from the 10th onwards. (Retrograde activity in general is at the maximum extent for the year, so this Mercury retrograde will be stronger than the previous ones this year. There is a cumulative effect.) Again, this is not a time for having tests, scans, etc., or procedures. The tendency for error is increased. If you must have these things, try to arrange for them to be done before the 10th, or wait till next month.

Career-related travel is likely this month, but it would be best if you can avoid it or delay it. If this is not possible, try to space out any connecting flights. Insure your tickets. Allow more time to get to and from your destination.

Finances are good this month, although keep in mind that your financial planet, Uranus, is still retrograde. So earnings are happening – Uranus is receiving good aspects until the 23rd – but there can be glitches and delays.

Love doesn't seem a big deal. Your 7th house is empty – only the Moon visits there on the 18th, 19th and 20th. This tends to the status quo.

October

Best Days Overall: 2, 3, 11, 12, 21, 22, 30
Most Stressful Days Overall: 9, 10, 16, 17, 23, 24
Best Days for Love: 4, 5, 13, 14, 16, 17, 25
Best Days for Money: 2, 3, 4, 5, 8, 9, 11, 12, 18, 21, 22, 26, 27, 30
Best Days for Career: 4, 5, 13, 14, 23, 24, 25

Health still needs watching until the 23rd. But afterwards you should see a dramatic turnaround. In the meantime enhance the health with chest massage and massage of the heart reflex; abdominal massage and massage of the small intestine reflex (until the 11th); and hip massage and massage of the kidney reflex from the 11th to the 30th. Mercury starts moving forward again on the 2nd (and in general retrograde activity is lessening this month), so it is safer now to have those tests, scans and procedures.

You remain in the midst of a yearly career peak until the 23rd. So keep the balance between home and family and the career. You won't be able to ignore home and family issues, but you can shift some attention to the career.

Venus, your career planet, is still having her solstice until the 3rd. So there is a pause in the career and then a change of direction.

Finances are better before the 23rd than after. Your financial planet, Uranus, is still retrograde to boot. After the 23rd you have to work harder for your earnings – but if you put in the work, they will happen.

After the 23rd you enter a strong social period. It is not necessarily a romantic period but more about friendships and group activities. Children and children figures are having a very strong social period. Marriage is not advisable for them right now – though the opportunities are there.

A solar eclipse on the 25th occurs in your 11th house of friends. This eclipse is relatively benign for you (however, if it hits something in your personal Horoscope – cast especially for you – it can be powerful indeed). This eclipse will test friendships. There are shake-ups and disturbances in trade or professional organizations that you're involved with. There can be dramas in the lives of friends – perhaps they are having surgery or near-death kinds of experiences. Bosses and parents or parent figures are making important financial changes. Likewise with the spouse, partner or current love. Financial course corrections are necessary. Children and children figures are having love dramas. A current relationship gets tested.

November

Best Days Overall: 7, 8, 17, 18, 26, 27
Most Stressful Days Overall: 5, 6, 12, 13, 19, 20
Best Days for Love: 3, 4, 12, 13, 14, 23, 24
Best Days for Money: 1, 2, 4, 7, 8, 14, 17, 18, 23, 26, 27, 28, 29
Best Days for Career: 3, 4, 13, 19, 20, 23, 24

Although your health is excellent this month (and will get even better next month), a very powerful lunar eclipse on the 8th is going to shake up your life and the world at large. This is a total lunar eclipse (the most powerful there is) but, in addition, it impacts three other planets in your chart – Mercury, Uranus and Venus. So take it nice and easy over that period. Things that need to be done should be done, but anything non-essential is better off rescheduled – especially if it's stressful.

This eclipse occurs in your 5th house of children, impacting children and children figures in your life. They need to redefine themselves, how they think of themselves – their self-concept – and how they want others to think of them. Because this eclipse affects Venus, the impact on them is even stronger. If they haven't been careful in dietary matters, this kind of eclipse can trigger a detox of the body. This can seem like sickness but it isn't. It's just the body getting rid of things that don't belong there.

The impact on Venus, your career planet, shows that career changes are afoot. There can be shake-ups in your corporate hierarchy, dramas in the lives of bosses and superiors, and perhaps a change in the rules and regulations that govern your industry. You have to pursue your career in a different way. Sometimes people actually change their career paths.

A parent or parent figure has a personal drama. Another parent or parent figure is making important financial changes.

The impact on Uranus, your financial planet, shows financial shake-ups for you personally. You need to make course corrections in your financial planning and strategy. The events of the eclipse will reveal where your financial assumptions are unrealistic.

Every lunar eclipse tests your current relationship. As you know, this happens twice a year and by now you are used to it. Generally dirty laundry – repressed grievances – rise to the surface to be dealt with. In addition, the spouse, partner or current love is having personal dramas and these can be the cause of the problem. He or she should reduce his or her schedule during this period.

The impact of the eclipse on Mercury, your health planet, can bring a health scare. Because health is excellent right now, however, this is not likely to be anything more than a scare. But it will lead to important changes in your health regime in the coming months. A lot of these changes are very normal. We are evolving beings. Health needs change and health regimes should change along with them. Job changes can happen too – this can be within your present situation or with a new one. Since Mercury also rules your 9th house there are shake-ups in your place of worship and dramas in the lives of worship leaders. Probably not a good idea to travel during this period. If you must, try to schedule your trip around the eclipse period.

December

Best Days Overall: 4, 5, 6, 14, 15, 16, 23, 24
Most Stressful Days Overall: 2, 3, 9, 10, 11, 17, 18, 29, 30
Best Days for Love: 2, 3, 9, 10, 11, 13, 14, 22, 23, 24
Best Days for Money: 1, 4, 5, 11, 14, 15, 20, 21, 23, 24, 25, 26, 29
Best Days for Career: 2, 3, 14, 17, 18, 23, 24

On November 22 you entered a very spiritual period, and this goes on until the 22nd of this month. This is good; spiritual practice is perhaps the best way to deal with all the shake-ups that eclipses bring. Altruism and spiritual understanding will help the career as well. Good to be involved in charities or altruistic kinds of activities – especially until the 10th. On the 10th your career planet Venus moves into your own sign and stays there for the rest of the month. This is a happy transit. It brings career opportunities to you without you even having to try. They pursue you. This transit brings glamour and style to the image.

On the 22nd the Sun moves into your sign and you begin a yearly personal pleasure peak. It is time to enjoy all the pleasures of the senses and the body. Time to pamper the body and show appreciation for all the yeoman service it has given you over the years. There is a tendency to take the body for granted. But periodically we need to show it some appreciation.

The Sun's move into your 1st house on the 22nd favours weight-loss and detox regimes. So, on the one hand Venus is urging you to binge, while on the other the Sun is urging you to slim down! My feeling is that you will be doing both. You will binge and then diet and binge and diet. Back and forth.

Health is good this month. Even Jupiter's move into an adverse aspect with you on the 21st is not enough to cause problems. There are too many short-term planets that are supporting you. You can enhance the health further with thigh massage and massage of the liver reflex until the 7th, and with back and knee massage afterwards. Don't forget to exercise as well.

Jupiter moves into your 4th house again for the long haul on the 21st. This can bring moves, the expansion of the family circle and the fortunate purchase or sale of a home. There is happiness with the family.

The month ahead is prosperous – especially from the 22nd onwards. Uranus receives very nice aspects. However, keep in mind that Uranus is still retrograde (one of the few planets retrograde this month) so there can be delays and glitches in finances. Earnings will still happen, however.

Aquarius

~~~

THE WATER-BEARER

Birthdays from
20th January to
18th February

Personality Profile

AQUARIUS AT A GLANCE

Element – Air

Ruling Planet – Uranus
   Career Planet – Pluto
   Love Planet – Sun
   Money Planet – Neptune
   Planet of Health and Work – Moon
   Planet of Home and Family Life – Venus
   Planet of Spirituality – Saturn

Colours – electric blue, grey, ultramarine blue

Colours that promote love, romance and social harmony – gold, orange

Colour that promotes earning power – aqua

Gems – black pearl, obsidian, opal, sapphire

Metal – lead

Scents – azalea, gardenia

Quality – fixed (= stability)

Qualities most needed for balance – warmth, feeling and emotion

Strongest virtues – great intellectual power, the ability to communicate and to form and understand abstract concepts, love for the new and avant-garde

Deepest needs – to know and to bring in the new

Characteristics to avoid – coldness, rebelliousness for its own sake, fixed ideas

Signs of greatest overall compatibility – Gemini, Libra

Signs of greatest overall incompatibility – Taurus, Leo, Scorpio

Sign most helpful to career – Scorpio

Sign most helpful for emotional support – Taurus

Sign most helpful financially – Pisces

Sign best for marriage and/or partnerships – Leo

Sign most helpful for creative projects – Gemini

Best Sign to have fun with – Gemini

Signs most helpful in spiritual matters – Libra, Capricorn

Best day of the week – Saturday

Understanding an Aquarius

In the Aquarius-born, intellectual faculties are perhaps the most highly developed of any sign in the zodiac. Aquarians are clear, scientific thinkers. They have the ability to think abstractly and to formulate laws, theories and clear concepts from masses of observed facts. Geminis might be very good at gathering information, but Aquarians take this a step further, excelling at interpreting the information gathered.

Practical people – men and women of the world – mistakenly consider abstract thinking as impractical. It is true that the realm of abstract thought takes us out of the physical world, but the discoveries made in this realm generally end up having tremendous practical consequences. All real scientific inventions and breakthroughs come from this abstract realm.

Aquarians, more so than most, are ideally suited to explore these abstract dimensions. Those who have explored these regions know that there is little feeling or emotion there. In fact, emotions are a hindrance to functioning in these dimensions; thus Aquarians seem – at times – cold and emotionless to others. It is not that Aquarians haven't got feelings and deep emotions, it is just that too much feeling clouds their ability to think and invent. The concept of 'too much feeling' cannot be tolerated or even understood by some of the other signs. Nevertheless, this Aquarian objectivity is ideal for science, communication and friendship.

Aquarians are very friendly people, but they do not make a big show about it. They do the right thing by their friends, even if sometimes they do it without passion or excitement.

Aquarians have a deep passion for clear thinking. Second in importance, but related, is their passion for breaking with the establishment and traditional authority. Aquarians delight in this, because for them rebellion is like a great game or challenge. Very often they will rebel strictly for the fun of rebelling, regardless of whether the authority they defy is right or wrong. Right or wrong has little to do with the rebellious actions of an Aquarian, because to a true Aquarian authority and power must be challenged as a matter of principle.

Where Capricorn or Taurus will err on the side of tradition and the status quo, an Aquarian will err on the side of the new. Without this virtue it is doubtful whether any progress would be made in the world. The conservative-minded would obstruct progress. Originality and invention imply an ability to break barriers; every new discovery represents the toppling of an impediment to thought. Aquarians are very interested in breaking barriers and making walls tumble – scientifically, socially and politically. Other zodiac signs, such as Capricorn, also have scientific talents. But Aquarians are particularly excellent in the social sciences and humanities.

Finance

In financial matters Aquarians tend to be idealistic and humanitarian – to the point of self-sacrifice. They are usually generous contributors to social and political causes. When they contribute it differs from when a Capricorn or Taurus contributes. A Capricorn or Taurus may expect some favour or return for a gift; an Aquarian contributes selflessly.

Aquarians tend to be as cool and rational about money as they are about most things in life. Money is something they need and they set about acquiring it scientifically. No need for fuss; they get on with it in the most rational and scientific ways available.

Money to the Aquarian is especially nice for what it can do, not for the status it may bring (as is the case for other signs). Aquarians are neither big spenders nor penny-pinchers and use their finances in practical ways, for example to facilitate progress for themselves, their families, or even for strangers.

However, if Aquarians want to reach their fullest financial potential they will have to explore their intuitive nature. If they follow only their financial theories – or what they believe to be theoretically correct – they may suffer some losses and disappointments. Instead, Aquarians should call on their intuition, which knows without thinking. For Aquarians, intuition is the short-cut to financial success.

Career and Public Image

Aquarians like to be perceived not only as the breakers of barriers but also as the transformers of society and the world. They long to be seen in this light and to play this role. They also look up to and respect other people in this position and even expect their superiors to act this way.

Aquarians prefer jobs that have a bit of idealism attached to them – careers with a philosophical basis. Aquarians need to be creative at work, to have access to new techniques and methods. They like to keep busy and enjoy getting down to business straight away, without wasting any time. They are often the quickest workers and usually have suggestions for improvements that will benefit their employers. Aquarians are also very helpful with their co-workers and welcome responsibility, preferring this to having to take orders from others.

If Aquarians want to reach their highest career goals they have to develop more emotional sensitivity, depth of feeling and passion. They need to learn to narrow their focus on the essentials and concentrate more on the job in hand. Aquarians need 'a fire in the belly' – a consuming passion and desire – in order to rise to the very top. Once this passion exists they will succeed easily in whatever they attempt.

Love and Relationships

Aquarians are good at friendships, but a bit weak when it comes to love. Of course they fall in love, but their lovers always get the impression that they are more best friends than paramours.

Like Capricorns, they are cool customers. They are not prone to displays of passion or to outward demonstrations of their affections. In fact, they feel uncomfortable when their other half hugs and touches them too much. This does not mean that they do not love their partners. They do, only they show it in other ways. Curiously enough, in relationships they tend to attract the very things that they feel uncomfortable with. They seem to attract hot, passionate, romantic, demonstrative people. Perhaps they know instinctively that these people have qualities they lack and so seek them out. In any event, these relationships do seem to work, Aquarian coolness calming the more passionate partner while the fires of passion warm the cold-blooded Aquarius.

The qualities Aquarians need to develop in their love life are warmth, generosity, passion and fun. Aquarians love relationships of the mind. Here they excel. If the intellectual factor is missing in a relationship an Aquarian will soon become bored or feel unfulfilled.

Home and Domestic Life

In family and domestic matters Aquarians can have a tendency to be too non-conformist, changeable and unstable. They are as willing to break the barriers of family constraints as they are those of other areas of life.

Even so, Aquarians are very sociable people. They like to have a nice home where they can entertain family and friends. Their house is usually decorated in a modern style and full of state-of-the-art appliances and gadgets – an environment Aquarians find absolutely necessary.

If their home life is to be healthy and fulfilling Aquarians need to inject it with a quality of stability – yes, even some conservatism. They need at least one area of life to be enduring and steady; this area is usually their home and family life.

Venus, the generic planet of love, rules the Aquarian's 4th solar house of home and family, which means that when it comes to the family and child-rearing, theories, cool thinking and intellect are not always enough. Aquarians need to bring love into the equation in order to have a great domestic life.

Horoscope for 2022

Major Trends

Health and energy need more attention this year: two powerful, not-to-be-toyed-with long-term planets are in stressful alignment with you all year. This in itself is not the problem. It's when the short-term planets also join the party that problems can happen. More details later.

In spite of your lower than usual energy, many nice things are happening in the year ahead, Aquarius. You are super prosperous. Your money house is prominent, and beneficent Jupiter will spend half the year here. More on this later.

On May 11 Jupiter will move into your 3rd house and will spend the other half of the year here. This is a wonderful transit for students below the college level. They succeed in their studies. It is also great for writers, journalists, teachers, sales and marketing people. They should have a good financial year.

Saturn has been in your 1st house since December 2020, a transit which has good points and difficult points. The good points are a serious attitude to life. It shows someone who takes responsibility for things – perhaps too much. It shows a person with good management and organizational skills. But there is a dark side to this. Saturn in your own house can make you overly pessimistic. You feel your age and physical limitations very acutely. There can be a tendency to be 'over serious' and this can impact your marriage and love life. More on this later.

Pluto has been in your 12th house for twenty years or so. This shows a complete transformation happening in your spiritual life. This is still going on this year, but Pluto will leave in 2024 and the strongest effects of the transit are over with now.

Uranus has been in your 4th house for some years now, signalling a focus on the family and family instability. The emotional life can also be highly unstable. More details later.

Your most important interests this year are the body, image and personal appearance; finance; communication and intellectual interests (from May 11 to October 29 and from December 21 onwards); home and family; and spirituality.

Your paths of greatest fulfilment will be finance (until May 11 and from October 29 to December 21); communication and intellectual interests (from May 11 to October 29 and from December 21); and home and family.

Health

(Please note that this is an astrological perspective on health and not a medical one. In days of yore there was no difference, both these perspectives were identical. But these days there could be quite a difference. For a medical perspective, please consult your doctor or health practitioner.)

Health, as we mentioned, needs keeping an eye on this year. The problem is that your 6th house of health is not prominent – not a house of power – and thus your tendency is to ignore things. You sort of take good health for granted. You could do this in the past but not since last year. You will need to force yourself to pay attention.

Since your energy levels are not up to their usual standard, your first line of defence is to maintain high energy levels. If you feel tired, rest. If you're working out and feel some discomfort, there's no need to push things; rest and return to your workout later – or perhaps reduce it to a comfortable level. Listen to the messages of your body.

Also, you can give more attention to the following areas – the vulnerable areas of your Horoscope this year (the reflex points are shown in the chart below). Since problems are most likely to begin here, keeping them healthy and fit is sound preventive medicine.

- The heart became an important area since March 2019, when Uranus moved into stressful aspect with you. It became even more important last year as Saturn joined the party in making a stressful aspect. The reflex is shown above. I have found that chest massage

Important foot reflexology points for the year ahead
Try to massage all of the foot on a regular basis – the top of the foot as well as the bottom – but pay extra attention to the points highlighted on the chart. When you massage, be aware of 'sore spots' as these need special attention. Also, pay special attention to the ankles.

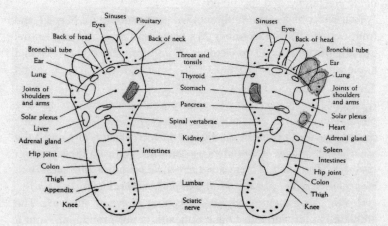

– massage of the breastbone and upper rib cage – strengthens the heart. On a more metaphysical level, avoid worry and anxiety, the two emotions that stress out the heart. Replace worry with faith. Meditation is a big help for this.

- The ankles and calves are always important for Aquarius. Both the ankles and calves should be regularly massaged. Feel for sore spots and massage them out. It should be a regular part of your normal health regime. A weak ankle can knock the spine and skeleton out of alignment and this will cause all kinds of other problems. Give the ankles more support when exercising.

- The stomach and breasts. These areas are always important for Aquarius too, as the Moon is your health planet. The reflexes are shown above. Diet is always an issue with you (not so for everyone, by the way). *What* you eat is important, and should be checked with a professional, but *how* you eat is just as important. Work to elevate the act of eating from mere animal appetite to an act of worship. Grace should be said (in your own words) before and after meals. Food should be blessed (in your own words). A good idea to have nice soothing music playing while you eat. These practices will not only elevate the energy vibrations of the food but of your body and digestive system as well. You will get only the highest and best from the food you eat and what you eat will digest better. Regular breast check-ups for women is a good idea.

The Moon also rules your emotional life. So, good emotional health is very important. There is a need to keep the moods and emotions constructive and happy. If health problems (God forbid) arise, restore harmony in the family as quickly as possible. Regular meditation will help keep your moods positive.

Your health planet is the fastest-moving planet in the zodiac, moving through your whole chart in any given month. Thus, there are many short-term health trends that depend on where the Moon is and the aspects she receives. These are best dealt with in the monthly reports.

Home and Family

Your 4th house of home and family has been prominent ever since March 2019 when Uranus moved in there, and it will remain prominent for some years to come (next year especially). The good news is that you are focused here in a very personal way. This ensures that you will get 'best case' scenarios.

The family situation is ultra-volatile these days. There are many dramas and crises in the family. There can be splits in the family circle as well. It will take all of your focus to hold things together.

Mood swings, in yourself and perhaps in family members, are very extreme as well. Meditators can keep this under control with meditation, but others might have to medicate.

The problem with these mood swings is that you don't know where you stand with family members from one moment to the next. You never know when they will erupt. You have to be on your toes all the time. These are not things you can figure out logically.

Uranus in the 4th house signals multiple moves or much renovation in the home. The home is a continuous work in progress. We have written of this in past reports and it still applies in the year ahead. It's as if you are searching for your dream home and every time you think you've got it, a new idea, a new vision comes to you and you start again. Little by little you are being led to your dream home and dream family situation.

You seem very devoted to a parent or parent figure, but he or she seems restless and unstable. He or she has a passion for personal freedoms these days – and wants to shed him or herself of all burdens and responsibilities.

Two eclipses in the coming year occur in your 4th house. One is a solar eclipse on April 30 and the other is a lunar eclipse on November 8. These will further shake up the family situation. But the good news is that they force much-needed course corrections in the home and family life.

Renovations or construction work in the home can happen all year, but if you have the choice July 4 to August 20 will be a good time. If you're beautifying the home in a cosmetic kind of way – or buying art objects for the home – May 28 to June 23 is a good time.

One of the parents or parent figures in your life is moving around a lot – perhaps staying in different places for long periods of time. But a formal move is not likely. (There is nothing against it, however.)

Siblings and sibling figures are prospering this year. If they are of childbearing age, they are more fertile than usual, but a move doesn't seem likely. Children and children figures in your life are having a quiet, stable home and family year, likewise grandchildren (if you have them).

Finance and Career

As we mentioned, the year ahead is very prosperous. Your money house is not only prominent but contains beneficent Jupiter. Jupiter, the planet of abundance and expansion, is more munificent than usual. For a start, he will be in his own sign and house for half the year. He is comfortable in Pisces and acts strongly. But he is also travelling with Neptune, your financial planet for a good part of the year. You will end the year much richer than you began.

Jupiter rules your 11th house. This gives many messages. First it is another signal of Jupiter's beneficence as the 11th house is a beneficent house. But it would also show earnings from the online world, from social networking and technology. Whatever you actually do, the online world and your technological expertise is important. You spend more on technology but will earn from it as well. Your friends are rich and they seem to provide opportunity. Fondest financial hopes and wishes are coming true this year. (And, once that happens, you will most likely formulate a new set of 'fondest hopes and wishes'.)

Aside from technology, you have a good feeling for industries that involve water – water utilities, water bottlers and purifiers, shipping, shipbuilders, fisheries, the seafood business, oil, natural gas and certain pharmaceuticals (makers of aesthetic and mood enhancers). These are all interesting as jobs, businesses or investments.

Jupiter will move into your 3rd house on May 11. This will bring a new car and communication equipment – it could happen next year too.

Pluto, your career planet, has been in your spiritual 12th house for a couple of decades now. He will still be there in the year ahead, but next year he will begin (on and off) to transition into your 1st house. So career changes will be happening and you're getting prepared for them. Two eclipses in your 10th house of career will also spur you to alter things. The lunar eclipse of May 16 and the solar eclipse of October 25 both occur in your 10th house. These changes will be positive.

For the past twenty years your success has been hidden – behind the scenes. Soon, in the next couple of years or so, your success will be more overt – out there for all to see.

In the meantime, you still favour not-for-profit organizations and altruistic kinds of careers. You've needed a career that was meaningful to you and to the world. We have written about this in past reports and the trend continues in the year ahead.

Those of you born early in the sign – January 20–22 – are feeling Pluto's influence in your 1st house even now. You are adopting the image of success. People see you this way. Career opportunities seek you out and there's not much you need to do.

Love and Social Life

Your 7th house of love hasn't been prominent in years and neither is it this year. It is practically empty – only short-term planets will move through there and their effect is temporary. This shows a status quo kind of love year. Singles will tend to stay single and those who are married will tend to stay married. In a way this is good. You seem content with things as they are and have no need to give it undue focus.

There is another issue here that reinforces what we say. Almost all the long-term planets (with the exception of Uranus) are in the Eastern sector of your chart – the sector of self. Your 1st house of self is prominent, while your 7th house is empty. So, this is a 'me' kind of year. It is about getting your personal desires and interests in order, about finding personal happiness rather than pleasing others, about asserting your independence. You are more self-contained this year.

The Western social sector of your chart will strengthen as the year progresses, but it will never be stronger than the East. The Eastern sector will always dominate.

The Sun is your love planet. He is a fast-moving planet and will cycle through your entire horoscope every year, initiating many short-term love trends that depend on where the Sun is and the kinds of aspects he receives. These are best dealt with in the monthly reports.

Two solar eclipses this year (this is pretty much the norm for every year) will shake up the love life and bring course corrections in love. There is a solar eclipse on April 30 and another one on October 25. We will discuss them more fully in the monthly reports.

So far we've been discussing those of you in or working on your first marriage. But the same holds true for those of you who are in or working on their second marriage – the situation is stable. Those working on their third marriage have good romantic aspects this year. Your social grace is very strong. This could involve a wealthy person or someone who is involved in your financial life. He or she could be 'just a friend' up till now, but it could develop into something more.

The area of friendships seems more active than romance. While Jupiter is in Pisces, your money house (until May 11 and from October 29 to December 21), you meet friends and have social opportunities as you pursue your financial goals and with people involved in your finances. From May 11 to October 29 and from December 21 onwards you find friends in the neighbourhood and in educational-type settings.

Parents and parent figures are having their marriages tested these days. If they are single, marriage is not advisable. In contrast, siblings and sibling figures are having a quiet love and social year. They too seem more into a 'me' kind of year.

Children and children figures in your life are having a good love and social year. They are focused on this and will tend to be successful. They are attracted to people of status and prestige, and they are meeting these kinds of people this year. Grandchildren, if you have them, have great romantic opportunity from May 11 onwards. Much depends on their age. If they are old enough, serious romance can happen – even marriage. Younger grandchildren are making new and significant friends.

Self-improvement

With Neptune, the most spiritual of the planets, as your financial planet, intuition and the spiritual laws of prosperity are always important to you – a lifelong interest. Ever since Neptune moved into Pisces in 2012 this interest has deepened and we have written of this in past reports. This year, the interest strengthens further as Jupiter moves into Pisces and travels with your financial planet for a good part of the year. This transit signals financial intuition on steroids. Not only will you have good financial intuition this year, but many of your past intuitions will be shown to be true. There is natural money – money that is earned in seemingly natural ways, through our work, parents, spousal support, investments, etc. – and there is 'miracle money', money that comes out of the blue, in ways that you never imagined. (Now even natural money is really 'miracle money' only it is disguised – all affluence comes from the spirit.) This is a year for miracle money. Natural money is very wonderful, and we should be grateful for it. But miracle money is much more joyful.

Most of you already know much about spiritual affluence, but there's always more to learn. And this is a year for it. You will know, without a doubt, that there is a power that cares about you and supplies you. No matter what is going on in the world, or how much money you have or don't have in the bank – its supply is unfailing, so long as we operate its laws.

You will receive financial guidance in dreams, through hunches, so-called 'gut feelings', psychics, tarot readers, spiritual channels and ministers.

You are generally a charitable person, and this year even more so. But it's probably wise to keep your giving proportional – a certain percentage of earnings. Tithing is an excellent practice (and this has been the case for many years now). Proportionate giving will keep you from getting carried away and doing too much. Giving opens the spiritual doors of supply. There is a lot more information on this subject on my website, www.spiritual-stories.com.

Saturn, your spiritual planet, has been in your sign since 2020, as we've mentioned. This is a great transit for many things. You have good management and executive ability. You are able to get the body and image in the right shape: you are more disciplined about this. This is an excellent year for losing weight if you need to. However, and we wrote about this last year too, it is not great for love and social relationships. You tend to be cool and detached by nature. But these days perhaps more so. This is not a conscious thing. You're under Saturn's influence. It's as if you took a drug and this is one of the side effects. People can be put off by feelings of coldness and distance. They feel there are barriers around you that can't be penetrated. They feel it is difficult to get close to you. The good news is that this is easily correctable. Make it your mission to project warmth and love to others. Do this every day and watch the social life improve.

Month-by-month Forecasts

January

Best Days Overall: 4, 5, 13, 14, 23, 24, 31
Most Stressful Days Overall: 11, 12, 18, 19, 25, 26
Best Days for Love: 2, 3, 11, 12, 18, 19, 21, 22, 23, 29, 30
Best Days for Money: 6, 7, 16, 17, 25, 26
Best Days for Career: 3, 12, 22, 25, 26, 30

Prosperity is ultra-strong this month – and will get even better next month. With prosperity comes the freedom to pursue your spiritual interests. This is the main headline of the month.

Your 12th house of spirituality is chock-full of planets: 60 per cent of the planets are there or moving through there. This is a lot of power. Your ESP and spiritual faculties are unusually strong. You are making all kinds of spiritual types of breakthroughs – and when these happen it is a most joyous thing. It's like being let out of prison. There is a great sigh of relief. All kinds of supernatural experiences will happen. Your dream life is probably more interesting and exciting than your everyday life. Saturn, your spiritual planet, has been in your sign for over a year now and will be here for the rest of the year ahead. So you are seen as spiritual, altruistic and philanthropic. You are being given spiritual teaching to help you mould and shape the body by spiritual means. The truth is that the body is totally subservient to spirit.

On the 20th the Sun moves into your sign and you begin a yearly personal pleasure peak. A good time to indulge in the pleasures of the body and senses – a good time to pamper the body. Also an excellent time to get the body and image into the shape that you want it.

Almost all – 90 per cent – of the planets are in the independent Eastern sector of your chart this month (dropping to 80 per cent from the 11th to the 26th, when the Moon visits the Western sector). So you are in a period of maximum personal independence. The month ahead is all about 'me' – and there's nothing wrong with that. Your self-interest, your happiness is as important as anyone else's. So this is a time to make the changes necessary for your personal happiness. Later on in the year, when the planetary power shifts to the West, this will be more difficult to do.

Love is also happy this month. You are having love on your terms. The spouse, partner or current love is eager to please and puts you first. For singles there is nothing much you need to do to attract love. It will find you. Just go about your daily business. Before the 20th love and romantic opportunities happen in spiritual-type settings – at meditation seminars or lectures, spiritual study groups, and charitable or altruistic kinds of events.

People are catering to you these days, rather than the other way around.

February

Best Days Overall: 1, 9, 10, 11, 19, 20, 28
Most Stressful Days Overall: 7, 8, 14, 15, 16, 21, 22, 23
Best Days for Love: 1, 7, 8, 9, 10, 14, 15, 16, 17, 18, 22, 23, 27
Best Days for Money: 2, 3, 12, 13, 21, 22, 23
Best Days for Career: 8, 18, 21, 22, 23, 27

Spirituality is still very important. Though your 12th house is not as prominent as last month, it is still very strong. So, review our discussion of this last month – much of what we said still applies now.

Health is excellent this month. Though there are two long-term planets in stressful alignment with you, the short-term planets are giving you support. You can enhance the health further in the ways mentioned in the yearly report. In general, from the 1st to the 16th you will be more enthusiastic about health issues than after the 16th. From the 16th onwards, detox regimes are favourable. Until the 16th, therapies and treatments that build up the body are good.

The planetary power is still mostly in the East this month and the sector of self. So it's still all about you. Your personal initiative, your personal skill and abilities are what matter. Others are catering to you these days rather than vice versa. You are having your way – as well you should. You know what's best for you. So, it is still a good month to make those changes that need to be made for your happiness. You don't need to consult with others.

You remain in the midst of a yearly personal pleasure peak until the 18th. This might even last a little longer, as the ruler of your 5th house of fun and creativity, Mercury, enters your sign on the 15th. With Saturn in your sign for over a year now, this lightens things up a bit. Your tendency is to be too serious.

On the 18th the Sun enters the 2nd money house and you begin a yearly financial peak. For many of you this will be a lifetime peak as well. (Much depends on your age.) Friends, social contacts and the beloved are very involved and helpful in finance. Your financial intuition is supercharged. You are always a generous person, and this month even more so. Tithing is an excellent financial practice for everyone, but especially for you – and especially this month. Your love planet in the money house often brings partnership or joint venture opportunities. Although you're very independent these days, you can't abandon the social graces completely. Especially when it comes to finance. Your likeability plays an important role in money matters.

Until the 18th love seeks you out and there's not much you need to do to find it. Just show up. After the 18th singles find love as they pursue their financial goals and with people who are involved with their finances.

March

Best Days Overall: 1, 9, 10, 18, 19, 27, 28
Most Stressful Days Overall: 6, 7, 8, 14, 15, 21, 22
Best Days for Love: 2, 3, 9, 11, 12, 14, 15, 18, 19, 23, 27, 28
Best Days for Money: 2, 3, 11, 12, 21, 22, 30, 31
Best Days for Career: 8, 18, 21, 22, 26

All the planets are moving forward this month. Both your personal and the universal solar cycles are waxing (growing). And, on the 20th, the Sun moves into Aries – the best starting energy of the zodiac. So we have a clear message. Now is the time (especially after the 20th) to launch those new projects of yours, or to release new products into the world. There is much cosmic momentum behind you.

It is still a good time – if you haven't done it already – to make the changes that need to be made for your personal happiness and well-being. Next month the Eastern sector of self won't be as strong.

Health is still excellent this month – this in spite of two long-term planets being in stressful alignment with you. The short-term planets are supporting you. You can enhance the health even further in the ways mentioned in the yearly report. You will have more enthusiasm for health matters from the 2nd to the 18th as your health planet waxes. This period is good for doing things that build up the body. After the 18th is better for detox or weight-loss regimes (where you want to get rid of things in the body).

You are still in the midst of a yearly financial peak – and from the 10th to the 20th it is even stronger than last month. We see prosperity in other ways too. The Moon will visit your money house twice this month – usually it is only once.

Both Mars and Venus enter your own sign on the 6th. Venus in your sign brings beauty and social grace. Mars in your sign brings energy and dynamism. These are happy transits as they lift some of the pessimism of Saturn in your sign.

Love is happy this month. You are attracted to wealthy people. Wealth is a romantic turn-on. Singles find love opportunities as they pursue their financial goals and with people involved in their finances. The Sun in the money house often shows the opportunity for a partnership or joint venture. (Those of you who invest can profit from mergers and acquisitions.)

On the 20th the love planet moves into your 3rd house, and the love attitudes change. Love is found close to home, in your neighbourhood or perhaps with neighbours. Mental compatibility becomes very important in love – much more so than mere wealth. You gravitate to people who are easy to talk to, with whom you can share ideas. After the 20th you are more of a 'love at first sight' kind of person.

April

Best Days Overall: 5, 6, 15, 16, 23, 24
Most Stressful Days Overall: 3, 4, 10, 11, 17, 18, 30
Best Days for Love: 1, 2, 8, 10, 11, 17, 18, 20, 21, 22, 25, 26, 27, 30
Best Days for Money: 8, 9, 17, 18, 25, 26, 27
Best Days for Career: 4, 14, 17, 18, 22

Health needs more attention from the 20th onwards. So enhance the health in the ways mentioned in the yearly report. You have more enthusiasm for health matters from the 1st to the 16th. That period is good for building up the body. From the 16th to the 30th is a good period for detox and weight-loss regimes, for getting rid of things from the body that don't belong there.

Though overall energy could be better, the month ahead is generally happy and prosperous. Your money house is still very powerful. Jupiter and Neptune have been there all year so far, and on the 5th Venus moves in. On the 15th Mars also joins the party. So there is much financial power these days. From the 1st to the 17th Jupiter travels with your financial planet Neptune – increasing earnings. Friends are also prospering. Venus in the money house shows that family support is good. Mars in the money house shows earnings from writing, teaching, sales, marketing and trading.

A solar eclipse on the 30th occurs in your 4th house of home and family. This often brings disturbances or shake-ups in the family circle. (By the way, good things can be just as disruptive as bad things – and good things are happening in the family that day.) Often repairs are needed in the home. Siblings and sibling figures are making important financial changes. Children and children figures are experiencing spiritual changes – they should drive more carefully during this period.

With the Sun as your love planet, every solar eclipse tests the love life – and this one is no different. You have these tests twice a year and by now you know how to handle these things. Generally, these eclipses bring up repressed grievances. These need to be dealt with. Sometimes the relationship gets tested because of some dramatic personal event in the life of the beloved. He or she could be having important career changes.

You're still very much a 'love at first sight' kind of person until the 20th. Perhaps you jump into relationships too quickly and impulsively. But no matter, you're developing courage in love. After the 20th you become more conservative. Love is close to home. Family and family connections are important in love.

May

Best Days Overall: 2, 3, 4, 12, 13, 21, 30, 31
Most Stressful Days Overall: 1, 7, 8, 9, 14, 15, 27, 28
Best Days for Love: 7, 8, 9, 10, 11, 16, 17, 20, 30
Best Days for Money: 6, 15, 16, 23, 24, 25
Best Days for Career: 1, 11, 14, 15, 20, 28

The money house decreases in importance this month. On the 3rd Venus leaves the 2nd house, and on the 11th Jupiter leaves it. Mars leaves the money house too, on the 25th. Prosperity has been incredibly strong this year and by now your short-term financial goals should have been achieved and you can change your focus to intellectual interests – reading, studying and learning. This is a great month for students below college level. They are successful in their studies and even receive prizes and honours. It is good for intellectual workers as well – teachers, writers, sales and marketing people. Your communication skills are always strong, but now even more so.

Love is still close to home until the 21st. There is more socializing from home and with family members. A quiet, romantic evening at home is more alluring than a night out on the town. Emotional intimacy is as important as physical intimacy. In fact, the sharing of feelings is a kind of foreplay during this period.

This changes after the 21st as your love planet moves into your 5th house of fun and creativity. Now, a night out on the town is far more preferable than staying at home. You're attracted to people who can show you a good time. Love has to be fun. The responsibilities of love are not taken into consideration. This position favours love affairs rather than serious committed love.

A lunar eclipse on the 16th affects you strongly, especially those of you born late in the sign of Aquarius (from February 14–18); take it nice and easy over that period. This eclipse occurs in your 10th house of career and signals career changes. Sometimes people actually change their careers with this kind of eclipse, but not usually. Usually the rules of the game change. Adjustments need to be made because of changes in your corporate hierarchy or in your industry. Job changes can also happen – sometimes within your current situation, but sometimes with another company. If you hire others there can be employee turnover, either now or in the coming months. There can also be health scares, as the eclipsed planet, the Moon, is your health planet. But your health is basically good over this period and any such scares are likely to remain just that – scares – and not be anything of substance. However, there will be changes to your health regime – major changes – in the coming months.

June

> Best Days Overall: 9, 10, 17, 18, 26, 27
> Most Stressful Days Overall: 4, 5, 11, 12, 23, 24, 25
> Best Days for Love: 4, 5, 6, 7, 9, 10, 16, 18, 26, 28, 29
> Best Days for Money: 2, 3, 4, 12, 13, 19, 20, 21, 29, 30
> Best Days for Career: 7, 11, 12, 16, 25

Students are still doing well this month and are achieving much in their studies. Siblings, sibling figures and neighbours are kindly disposed to you and bring good fortune. In addition, they are personally prospering. The money people in your life get richer. New cars and communication equipment come to you – this is a good time to buy these things.

Health is much improved over last month and improves even further as the month progresses. You can enhance the health further in the ways mentioned in the yearly report.

The month ahead is happy, Aquarius. On May 21 you began one of your yearly personal pleasure peaks. This will go on until the 21st of this month. So, it's time to enjoy life. Even if life seems drab for some of you, find things that you can enjoy. You not only lift your spirits, but many problems will dissolve of their own accord.

Enjoying life will also help the love life. The romantic people in your life are looking for fun – light-heartedness. You've been too serious of late. Love should be happy, but, like last month, these are not the aspects for marriage, more like love affairs. Mental compatibility with the beloved is very important. Good communication – the exchange of ideas – is a form of foreplay. Love attitudes change once again after the 21st, as the Sun moves on into your 6th house. Emotional intimacy can be just as important as physical intimacy now – perhaps it is the prelude to physical intimacy. You are attracted to therapists and health professionals and perhaps to people involved in your health. Co-workers also seem alluring. Jobseekers have good fortune after the 21st and the social aspects of the job are probably given as much weight as wages, hours and benefits.

Health is good this month, yet you seem focused here after the 21st. Hopefully this is more about prevention and healthy lifestyles. Be careful not to magnify little things into bigger things.

Finances are not what they were for the first four months of the year, but they are still good – especially after the 21st.

July

Best Days Overall: 6, 7, 14, 15, 23, 24
Most Stressful Days Overall: 1, 2, 8, 9, 21, 22, 28, 29
Best Days for Love: 1, 2, 6, 7, 8, 9, 17, 15, 26, 28, 29
Best Days for Money: 1, 2, 9, 10, 11, 16, 17, 18, 19, 27, 28, 29
Best Days for Career: 5, 8, 9, 13, 22

On the 5th the preponderance of planetary power shifts to the social Western sector of your Horoscope, and on the 23rd your 7th house of love, social activities and 'others' becomes powerful. You are in a social period now. Personal gifts and abilities are less important than social grace – your ability to get on with others. Your social skills will carry the day, not your personal abilities or initiative. Let others have their way, so long as it isn't destructive. Your way is probably not the best way now. Your good will come through others.

Mars enters your 4th house on the 5th and stays there for the rest of the month. This is a good time for undertaking major renovations in the home. (Some of you might be thinking of building a home.) A sibling or sibling figure prospers. He or she seems focused on finances. A parent or parent figure seems impatient and argumentative. Passions run high at home.

Health needs more attention from the 5th onwards, and so it is good that you have a strong focus on health this month. This is a good sign. You can enhance the health in the ways mentioned in the yearly report. As always, make sure to get enough rest.

On the 23rd as the Sun, your love planet, enters your 7th house, you begin a yearly love and social peak. This should be marvellous for those of you who are single as the Sun is powerful in his own sign and house. The social grace and magnetism are much stronger than usual. Singles have choices this month: there are opportunities for serious, committed love and for 'fun and games' love – love affairs.

Finances are good this month – but keep in mind that your financial planet, Neptune, is now in retrograde motion (and will be for many more months). So, though your financial intuition is very sharp, it does need verification these days. The 16th and 17th are especially good financial days – both you and the current love prosper. On the 30th and 31st the beloved prospers, and this is also a good love and social period.

August

Best Days Overall: 2, 3, 11, 12, 20, 21, 29, 30
Most Stressful Days Overall: 4, 5, 17, 18, 25, 26
Best Days for Love: 4, 5, 7, 8, 15, 16, 25, 26
Best Days for Money: 5, 7, 13, 14, 15, 23, 25
Best Days for Career: 1, 4, 5, 10, 18, 28

Mars began to travel with Uranus on July 31, and they remain travelling together on the 1st and the 2nd. This brings a closeness between you and a sibling or sibling figure in your life. Your communication skills are especially strong during this period. However, you should be more mindful on the physical plane, and especially when driving. Avoid arguments and confrontations.

We have a Grand Trine in the Earth signs this month. Your communication skills and mastery of ideas might not be appreciated just now. People seem more focused on practical things.

Health still needs watching until the 23rd. There is nothing serious afoot; this is short-term stress caused by short-term planets. In the meantime, make sure to get enough rest. Perhaps you can schedule more massages or natural treatments where possible. Enhance the health in the ways mentioned in the yearly report. By the 23rd you will see a dramatic improvement.

You're still in the midst of a yearly love and social peak until the 23rd. Don't let hyper-pessimism detract from your appeal. Happiness and an uplifting manner will draw love to you. One can be serious, but also maintain joy and optimism.

Planetary retrograde activity increases this month. There will never be less than 40 per cent of the planets in retrograde motion and, after the 24th, 50 per cent of the planets are retrograde. So the pace of life is slower. There is much indecision both in you and others. It's OK. It's natural. It's the astrological weather.

Finances are more challenging than last month. Neptune, your financial planet, is still retrograde, and he receives stressful aspects after the 23rd. Earnings will come, but there will be more work involved (and delays and glitches).

Mars moves into your 5th house on the 20th and will stay there for the rest of the year ahead. Children and children figures seem more combative now. They lose their temper too easily. They can be involved in fights.

September

Best Days Overall: 7, 8, 16, 17, 26, 27
Most Stressful Days Overall: 1, 2, 13, 14, 15, 21, 22, 28, 29
Best Days for Love: 4, 5, 6, 13, 14, 15, 21, 22, 25, 26
Best Days for Money: 2, 3, 9, 10, 11, 19, 20, 21, 29, 30
Best Days for Career: 1, 2, 10, 18, 28, 29

Retrograde activity reaches its zenith this month. From the 10th onwards, 60 per cent of the planets are retrograde. Life seems to stand still. Nothing seems to be happening (at least, not outwardly). There is much personal and worldly indecision. We are on a precipice and we wait. What we read in the newspaper or see on TV is probably not accurate and should be taken with many grains of salt. Our job is to enjoy this time and make it work to our benefit. For, make no mistake, big things are happening beneath the surface – we just don't know exactly what. Sometimes we need to go backwards in order to go forward.

Your love planet, the Sun, never goes retrograde. So love at least is moving forward. It seems happy this month. The Sun is making nice aspects to Uranus, the ruler of your Horoscope, so there is romantic opportunity for singles. The problem in love is you. You're not sure what you want. You're indecisive.

Love is erotic until the 23rd. Sexual magnetism seems the primary allurement at the moment, and romantic opportunities happen in strange places and ways – at funerals or funeral parlours, or as you attend a wake or comfort a bereaved person. On the 23rd this will change, as your love planet enters Libra. Love becomes more romantic and not just sexual. There is a need for philosophical compatibility – a similar world view. Romantic opportunities are likely at college or college functions, at your place of worship or at religious functions. People at your place of worship can play Cupid. There is an allurement to foreigners and romantic opportunities can also happen in foreign lands.

The spouse, partner or current love is having a banner financial month, but after the 10th he or she needs to do more homework, more due diligence, before making important financial decisions.

Health is much improved over last month and will get even better after the 23rd.

Though your financial planet, Neptune, is still retrograde, finances should improve after the 23rd. Before the 23rd there is more work involved – more challenge.

October

Best Days Overall: 4, 5, 13, 14, 23, 24
Most Stressful Days Overall: 11, 12, 18, 19, 25, 26
Best Days for Love: 4, 5, 13, 14, 18, 19, 25
Best Days for Money: 6, 7, 8, 9, 17, 18, 26, 27
Best Days for Career: 3, 12, 22, 25, 26

Retrograde activity among the planets decreases dramatically this month, and by the end of October only 30 per cent of the planets will still be retrograde (compared to 60 per cent last month). Things are starting to move forward again. Part of it is due to the solar eclipse of the 25th which will blast away obstructions to progress.

In addition, three planets are having their solstices this month. They pause in the heavens and then change direction (in their latitudinal motion). This too is playing a role in unblocking things. A change in direction is happening in various departments of life.

The day side of your Horoscope, though far from dominant, is as strong as it will ever be this year. Home and family – and emotional wellness – are still your major interests, but you can shift some attention to the career. This is not a very strong career year, but you are in your peak for the year from the 23rd.

The solar eclipse of the 25th has a strong effect on you, so take it nice and easy over this period. Also, your health in general needs more watching after the 23rd as well. Make sure to get enough rest and enhance the health in the ways mentioned in the yearly report.

The solar eclipse of the 25th occurs in your 10th house of career, signalling career changes. Generally, people don't change their actual career paths (although sometimes they do) but instead the way they pursue their existing path. Often upheavals in their company or industry cause this. Sometimes government regulations change the rules by which your company or industry operates. Sometimes there are dramas in the lives of bosses and elders that cause change. There are dramas in the lives of parents or parent figures.

Every solar eclipse impacts your love life and this one is no different. A current relationship gets tested. This doesn't necessarily mean a break-up. You go through these eclipses a minimum of twice a year – so this is not strange. But it shows that it is time to deal with dirty laundry and repressed grievances. Good relationships survive these things, but flawed ones can be in trouble. Sometimes the testing happens because of personal dramas in the life of the spouse, partner or current love. The relationship itself is not the problem.

November

Best Days Overall: 1, 2, 10, 11, 19, 20, 28, 29
Most Stressful Days Overall: 7, 8, 15, 16, 22, 23
Best Days for Love: 3, 4, 13, 14, 15, 16, 23, 24
Best Days for Money: 3, 4, 13, 14, 23, 30
Best Days for Career: 8, 9, 18, 22, 23, 27

You've had better career years in your life and will have better ones in the future, but this month is the pinnacle of the current year. You're in the midst of a yearly career peak until the 22nd.

The main headline this month is the total lunar eclipse of the 8th, which has a very strong effect on you personally and on the world at large. Take it nice and easy during that period.

This eclipse occurs in your 4th house of home and family but also impacts three other planets – Uranus, Mercury and Venus. So there are dramas at home and in the lives of family members. There are shake-ups in the family. Repairs might be needed in the home. There are personal dramas in the lives of family members and of parents or parent figures. You also seem personally affected too. You need to redefine yourself and your self-concept, to update and refine it. Otherwise, others will define you in not so pleasant ways. This redefinition will lead to wardrobe changes and changes in the image and presentation in the coming months. The dream life is apt to be overactive and not pleasant at this time, but pay it no attention – it is just psychic debris stirred by the eclipse. It has no other significance.

Since Mercury is affected by the eclipse, children and children figures are affected. They should take it easy and reduce their schedules at this time too. The impact on Mercury can show psychological confrontations with death or near-death kinds of experiences. Your spiritual practice (which will be strong later in the month) will help you deal with this. Bosses, parents and parent figures have their marriages or serious relationships tested. Siblings and sibling figures are forced to make important financial changes.

The eclipsed planet, the Moon, is your health planet. So, there can be health scares. If this happens, wait a couple of weeks and get a second opinion. Scans and tests done during an eclipse period, when the planetary energies are all roiled up, might not be accurate. Have them rechecked. There will be important changes in your health regime in the coming months. Job changes are also likely. If you employ others there is instability in the workforce and staff turnover is likely.

You're still in a yearly career peak, but the eclipse brings distractions to your focus.

Health needs watching until the 22nd, but you should see a dramatic improvement afterwards. Enhance the health in the ways mentioned in the yearly report.

December

Best Days Overall: 7, 8, 17, 18, 25, 26
Most Stressful Days Overall: 4, 5, 6, 12, 13, 19, 20
Best Days for Love: 2, 3, 12, 13, 14, 22, 23, 24
Best Days for Money: 1, 10, 11, 20, 21, 27, 28, 29
Best Days for Career: 6, 15, 16, 19, 20, 24

Last month's monster eclipse must have changed certain trends in the world. Suddenly it seems in vogue to think and act 'outside the box' – to go outside the normal boundaries. Three planets are 'out of bounds' this month (which is highly unusual). Mars has been 'out of bounds' since October 24 and remains so all this month. Mercury is 'out of bounds' from the 1st to the 22nd and Venus from the 2nd to the 24th.

Usually when a planet is 'out of bounds' it means there are no answers to be found within the normal boundaries and so one must look elsewhere – explore the unknown. This is what is happening with a parent or parent figure, in your religious and philosophical life, with children and children figures in your life, with the finances of a parent or parent figure, with siblings, sibling figures and in your intellectual tastes. But as we mentioned, it seems trendy in the world at large.

Health is much improved over last month and events in the world are moving forward as well. The pace of life quickens. Once again, the planetary power is mostly in the East and the time for 'people pleasing' is over with. (They should always be treated respectfully.) You go your own way now. You run your own race. If there are changes to be made that enhance your personal happiness, by all means make them. Let the world adapt to you rather than vice versa.

The month ahead is happy. The power is in your 11th house of friends until the 22nd and this is your favourite house. The planetary power pushes you to do what you love to do – to be involved with friends and groups, to study science, astronomy, astrology and technology, to be involved with networking and online activities.

On the 22nd, as the Sun enters your spiritual 12th house, your spiritual practice becomes important. (You will feel this even before the 22nd.) Your 12th house is almost as strong as it was when the year began. So, you can expect a hyper-charged dream life and one that is significant and meaningful. Your ESP and spiritual faculties are also supercharged. Your challenge will be to keep both feet on the ground.

Finances are good this month. There is prosperity happening.

Pisces

⊬

THE FISH

Birthdays from
19th February to
20th March

Personality Profile

PISCES AT A GLANCE

Element – Water

Ruling Planet – Neptune
  Career Planet – Jupiter
  Love Planet – Mercury
  Money Planet – Mars
  Planet of Health and Work – Sun
  Planet of Home and Family Life – Mercury
  Planet of Love Affairs, Creativity and Children – Moon

Colours – aqua, blue-green

Colours that promote love, romance and social harmony – earth tones,
  yellow, yellow-orange

Colours that promote earning power – red, scarlet

Gem – white diamond

Metal – tin

Scent – lotus

Quality – mutable (= flexibility)

Qualities most needed for balance – structure and the ability to handle form

Strongest virtues – psychic power, sensitivity, self-sacrifice, altruism

Deepest needs – spiritual illumination, liberation

Characteristics to avoid – escapism, keeping bad company, negative moods

Signs of greatest overall compatibility – Cancer, Scorpio

Signs of greatest overall incompatibility – Gemini, Virgo, Sagittarius

Sign most helpful to career – Sagittarius

Sign most helpful for emotional support – Gemini

Sign most helpful financially – Aries

Sign best for marriage and/or partnerships – Virgo

Sign most helpful for creative projects – Cancer

Best Sign to have fun with – Cancer

Signs most helpful in spiritual matters – Scorpio, Aquarius

Best day of the week – Thursday

Understanding a Pisces

If Pisces have one outstanding quality it is their belief in the invisible, spiritual and psychic side of things. This side of things is as real to them as the hard earth beneath their feet – so real, in fact, that they will often ignore the visible, tangible aspects of reality in order to focus on the invisible and so-called intangible ones.

Of all the signs of the zodiac, the intuitive and emotional faculties of the Pisces are the most highly developed. They are committed to living by their intuition and this can at times be infuriating to other people – especially those who are materially, scientifically or technically orientated. If you think that money, status and worldly success are the only goals in life, then you will never understand a Pisces.

Pisces have intellect, but to them intellect is only a means by which they can rationalize what they know intuitively. To an Aquarius or a Gemini the intellect is a tool with which to gain knowledge. To a well-developed Pisces it is a tool by which to express knowledge.

Pisces feel like fish in an infinite ocean of thought and feeling. This ocean has many depths, currents and undercurrents. They long for purer waters where the denizens are good, true and beautiful, but they are sometimes pulled to the lower, murkier depths. Pisces know that they do not generate thoughts but only tune in to thoughts that already exist; this is why they seek the purer waters. This ability to tune in to higher thoughts inspires them artistically and musically.

Since Pisces is so spiritually orientated – though many Pisces in the corporate world may hide this fact – we will deal with this aspect in greater detail, for otherwise it is difficult to understand the true Pisces personality.

There are four basic attitudes of the spirit. One is outright scepticism – the attitude of secular humanists. The second is an intellectual or emotional belief, where one worships a far-distant God-figure – the attitude of most modern church-going people. The third is not only belief but direct personal spiritual experience – this is the attitude of some 'born-again' religious people. The fourth is actual unity with the divinity, an intermingling with the spiritual world – this is the attitude of yoga. This fourth attitude is the deepest urge of a

Pisces, and a Pisces is uniquely qualified to pursue and perform this work.

Consciously or unconsciously, Pisces seek this union with the spiritual world. The belief in a greater reality makes Pisces very tolerant and understanding of others – perhaps even too tolerant. There are instances in their lives when they should say 'enough is enough' and be ready to defend their position and put up a fight. However, because of their qualities it takes a good deal to get them into that frame of mind.

Pisces basically want and aspire to be 'saints'. They do so in their own way and according to their own rules. Others should not try to impose their concept of saintliness on a Pisces, because he or she always tries to find it for him- or herself.

Finance

Money is generally not that important to Pisces. Of course they need it as much as anyone else, and many of them attain great wealth. But money is not generally a primary objective. Doing good, feeling good about oneself, peace of mind, the relief of pain and suffering – these are the things that matter most to a Pisces.

Pisces earn money intuitively and instinctively. They follow their hunches rather than their logic. They tend to be generous and perhaps overly charitable. Almost any kind of misfortune is enough to move a Pisces to give. Although this is one of their greatest virtues, Pisces should be more careful with their finances. They should try to be more choosy about the people to whom they lend money, so that they are not being taken advantage of. If they give money to charities they should follow it up to see that their contributions are put to good use. Even when Pisces are not rich, they still like to spend money on helping others. In this case they should really be careful, however: they must learn to say no sometimes and help themselves first.

Perhaps the biggest financial stumbling block for the Pisces is general passivity – a *laissez-faire* attitude. In general Pisces like to go with the flow of events. When it comes to financial matters, especially, they need to be more aggressive. They need to make things happen, to create their own wealth. A passive attitude will only cause loss and missed opportunity. Worrying about financial security will not provide that security. Pisces need to go after what they want tenaciously.

Career and Public Image

Pisces like to be perceived by the public as people of spiritual or material wealth, of generosity and philanthropy. They look up to big-hearted, philanthropic types. They admire people engaged in large-scale undertakings and eventually would like to head up these big enterprises themselves. In short, they like to be connected with big organizations that are doing things in a big way.

If Pisces are to realize their full career and professional potential they need to travel more, educate themselves more and learn more about the actual world. In other words, they need some of the unflagging optimism of Sagittarius in order to reach the top.

Because of all their caring and generous characteristics, Pisces often choose professions through which they can help and touch the lives of other people. That is why many Pisces become doctors, nurses, social workers or teachers. Sometimes it takes a while before Pisces realize what they really want to do in their professional lives, but once they find a career that lets them manifest their interests and virtues they will excel at it.

Love and Relationships

It is not surprising that someone as 'otherworldly' as the Pisces would like a partner who is practical and down to earth. Pisces prefer a partner who is on top of all the details of life, because they dislike details. Pisces seek this quality in both their romantic and professional partners. More than anything else this gives Pisces a feeling of being grounded, of being in touch with reality.

As expected, these kinds of relationships – though necessary – are sure to have many ups and downs. Misunderstandings will take place because the two attitudes are poles apart. If you are in love with a Pisces you will experience these fluctuations and will need a lot of patience to see things stabilize. Pisces are moody, intuitive, affectionate and difficult to get to know. Only time and the right attitude will yield Pisces' deepest secrets. However, when in love with a Pisces you will find that riding the waves is worth it because they are good, sensitive people who need and like to give love and affection.

When in love, Pisces like to fantasize. For them fantasy is 90 per cent of the fun of a relationship. They tend to idealize their partner, which can be good and bad at the same time. It is bad in that it is difficult for anyone to live up to the high ideals their Pisces lover sets.

Home and Domestic Life

In their family and domestic life Pisces have to resist the tendency to relate only by feelings and moods. It is unrealistic to expect that your partner and other family members will be as intuitive as you are. There is a need for more verbal communication between a Pisces and his or her family. A cool, unemotional exchange of ideas and opinions will benefit everyone.

Some Pisces tend to like mobility and moving around. For them too much stability feels like a restriction on their freedom. They hate to be locked in one location for ever.

The sign of Gemini sits on the cusp of Pisces' 4th solar house of home and family. This shows that Pisces likes and needs a home environment that promotes intellectual and mental interests. They tend to treat their neighbours as family – or extended family. Some Pisceans can have a dual attitude towards the home and family – on the one hand they like the emotional support of the family, but on the other they dislike the obligations, restrictions and duties involved with it. For Pisces, finding a balance is the key to a happy family life.

Horoscope for 2022

Major Trends

A happy and prosperous year ahead, Pisces. Health and energy are good. There are no long-term planets in stressful alignment with you. All the others are either helping you or leaving you alone. More on this later.

Jupiter makes an unusually short transit through your sign. He will spend approximately six months in Pisces. Usually he will stay in a sign for eleven or twelve months. Probably he doesn't need to spend that much time there. He can do his work quickly. He will be in your sign until May 11 and from October 29 to December 21. Women of childbearing age are unusually fertile at these times. Older Pisceans will need to watch the weight. You are living the 'good life' this year, and this is often the price we pay.

There is prosperity happening too. Jupiter in your sign until May 11 elevates the standard of living. Regardless of how much you have, you live as if you had more. But after May 11, Jupiter moves into your money house and stays there until October 29, before re-entering the 2nd house on December 21. This is a classic signal for prosperity. Jupiter is not just bringing prosperity and fruitfulness, but as your career planet, career success as well. More on this later.

Pluto has been in your 11th house for the past twenty or so years. He is there in the year ahead, but is getting ready to leave. Your friendships have been transformed. Many have gone down the tubes. In many cases friends have died or have had near-death kinds of experiences. This has been a factor in the transformation as well.

Saturn has been in your 12th house since late in 2020 and he will remain there all this year. This transit shows a more down-to-earth kind of spirituality. It is not all 'pie in the sky' – though it sometimes seems that way. It has many practical applications. More on this to come.

Uranus has been in your 3rd house for some years now, and will be there for some more to come. Students below college level seem most affected by this. There are changes of schools, of educational plans and disruptions in school.

Mars will spend an unusual amount of time in your 4th house this year – from August 20 onwards. (Generally he stays in a sign and house for around six weeks, so he is camping out here.) He will be the only long-term planet in stressful alignment with you. This transit would indicate renovations or construction work in the home. More on this later.

Your most important areas of interest in the year ahead are the body, image and personal appearance; finance (from May 11 to October 29 and from December 21 onwards); communication and intellectual interests; home and family (from August 20 onwards); friends, groups and group activities; and spirituality.

Your paths of greatest fulfilment this year will be the body, image and personal appearance (until May 11 and from October 29 to December 21); finance (from May 11 to October 29 and from December 21 onwards); and communication and intellectual interests.

Health

(Please note that this is an astrological perspective on health and not a medical one. In days of yore there was no difference, both these perspectives were identical. But these days there could be quite a difference. For a medical perspective, please consult your doctor or health practitioner.)

As we mentioned above, health will be good this year. No really long-term planets are in stressful alignment this year; only Mars will be in such an alignment, and that after August 20. All the other long-term planets are either helping you or leaving you alone. Your empty 6th house (only short-term planets move through there) is another positive for health – you have no need to pay too much attention here as all is well. After August 20 you might want to pay a bit more attention though.

Two solar eclipses this year will force changes in the health regime, but this happens twice a year (the Sun being your health planet) and by now you know how to handle things. This year the solar eclipses are on April 30 and October 25.

Of course, there will be periods where health and energy are less easy than usual – perhaps even stressful. These things come from the transits of the short-term planets. They are temporary and not trends for the year. When they pass, your normal good health and energy return.

With energy levels higher, pre-existing conditions should be in abeyance this year.

Good though your health is you can make it better. Give more attention to the following – the vulnerable areas of your Horoscope this year (the reflex points are shown in the chart opposite):

- The heart. This is always an important area for Pisces as the Sun, the ruler of the heart, is your health planet. The reflex is shown above. Chest massage and massage of the breastbone and upper

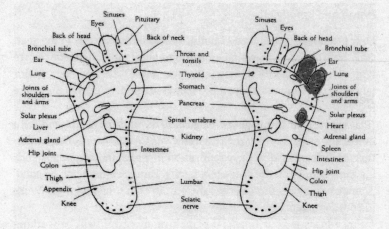

Important foot reflexology points for the year ahead

*Try to massage all of the foot on a regular basis – the top of the foot as well as
the bottom – but pay extra attention to the points highlighted on the chart.
When you massage, be aware of 'sore spots' as these need special attention.
It's also a good idea to massage the ankles and below them.*

rib cage will strengthen the heart as well. As our regular readers
know, it is good to avoid worry and anxiety: the two emotions that
stress the heart. Meditation will help you cultivate faith rather than
worry.

- The feet too are always important for Pisces as Pisces rules the
  feet. Regular foot massage will always be wonderful for you. You
  not only strengthen the feet but the whole body as well.

Your health planet, the Sun, is a fast-moving planet. During the year
he moves through your entire Horoscope. Thus there are many short-
term health trends that depend on where the Sun is and the kinds of
aspects he receives. These are best dealt with in the monthly reports.

Jupiter will be in your sign on and off from January 1 to October 29.
While this is a happy transit – it brings all the pleasures of the body
and senses to you – too much of a good thing can be a problem. You
can put on the pounds this year if you're not careful.

Home and Family

Your 4th house of home and family is not prominent early in the year. Only short-term planets move through there and their effects are temporary. This tends to the status quo. Moves are not likely. Major family changes are not happening. Things are pretty much as they were last year.

However, all this changes on August 20 as Mars moves into your 4th house and stays there for the rest of the year. As we mentioned earlier, this can bring a major house renovation. It would indicate you spending more money on the home and family. Family support will be good. There could be conflicts in the family unit – passions run high. Work to cool down tempers.

Since Mars is your financial planet, many of you will be working from home – remotely. Many of you will be installing home offices or enlarging them. Some will be starting home-based businesses. The home is as much a place of business as a home.

Mars camping out in your 4th house would also show you installing gym and workout equipment, perhaps athletic equipment, in the home.

Your family planet, Mercury, is a very fast-moving planet. He will move through every sign and house of your Horoscope in any given year. (This year he will move through your 11th house twice.) Thus, there are many short-term family trends that depend on where Mercury is and the kinds of aspects he receives. These are best covered in the monthly reports.

Wait till after August 20 to make important repairs or renovations to the home (if you have the liberty to wait). If you're beautifying the home – redecorating – June 23 to July 18 seems a good time.

A parent or parent figure could move in the year ahead. He or she is having a strong career year. If this parent is a woman of childbearing age, pregnancy could happen. She seems very fertile.

Siblings and sibling figures are nomadic these days. They could move multiple times. But even if they don't formally move, they could be living in different places for long periods of time.

Children or children figures could have moved in recent years. The year ahead, however, is quiet. (More moves could happen in a few years.) Grandchildren, if you have them, could have moved last year.

This year it is not advisable. Let them stay put and make better use of the space that they have.

Finance and Career

A prosperous year ahead, as we mentioned. You won't escape the good fortune. Jupiter, the planet of wealth, abundance and expansion, will spend approximately half the year in your own sign and half the year (approximately) in Aries. In Pisces, Jupiter is said to be 'dignified'. In Aries he is said to be 'in his joy'. Suffice it to say that he is strong in both these signs. This signals an expansion of earnings and happy earning opportunities coming to you. Assets you already own will increase in value.

As we mentioned, while Jupiter is in your sign you will be living at a higher standard than usual. You will travel, eat in the good restaurants, and pamper the body. You will dress better than usual too.

Those who are the superiors in your life – bosses, elders, parents, authority figures – all seem devoted to you. If you have issues with the government this is a good time to resolve them. You should achieve 'best case' scenarios.

Jupiter is not just the planet of wealth. In your chart he is your career planet. Thus career opportunities – and good ones – are coming to you. You don't even need to seek them out; they will find you. You will have the image of a successful person. You will dress the part and project this kind of aura. People will see you this way. People will look up to you.

Your career planet in your own sign shows that regardless of what you actually do, your real mission is your body and image: you need to get them into right shape and model it for others. Your personal appearance and overall demeanour is a big factor in career success.

Jupiter moves into Aries from May 11 to October 29 and from December 21 onwards, and earnings should increase even further. You not only have the devotion and support of the authority figures in your life, but they are also favourable to your financial plans. This transit would show pay rises – directly or indirectly. Your good career reputation brings earnings opportunities.

Mars, your financial planet, is an 'in between' kind of planet. He is faster than the long-term planets, but much slower than the fast-moving ones. Where the Sun, Mercury and Venus will move through your entire Horoscope in any given year, Mars will move through six or seven signs and houses. So, because of this, there are many short-term financial trends that depend on where he is and the kinds of aspects he receives. These are best dealt with in the monthly reports.

Your financial planet spends an unusual amount of time in your 4th house this year – more than four months. He will be there from August 20 onwards. This indicates the importance of family and family connections in finance. The transit would favour residential real estate, the food business, hotels, motels and businesses that cater to the homeowner. Since Mars will be in Gemini, it also favours telecommunications, transportation and media companies. Those of you who teach, write, sell or trade should have a successful period then.

Love and Social Life

Your 7th house of love is not a house of power this year, and this has been the case for many years now. It is basically empty (short-term planets will move through there, but their impact is also short term). In addition, the Western, social sector of your Horoscope is bereft of long-term planets. Though the Western sector will strengthen as the year progresses, it will never dominate. The Eastern sector of self, or personal independence, will always be stronger. So the year ahead is not a very social kind of year. It is more about getting your body, image and personal desires in order. It is about exercising your independence and pursuing your personal path to happiness. Once this is attained romance can happen from that place.

This tends to a stable, quiet romantic year. Singles will tend to stay single and those who are married will tend to stay married. It shows a feeling of contentment with things as they are. However, if love problems arise, your lack of attention and focus could be the root cause of the problem. You will have to pay more attention.

There is nothing against romance in this chart, only a lack of interest – a lack of 'fire in the belly'.

Those of you in or working on the first, second or third marriage are having a quiet kind of love year. But those working on the fourth marriage have beautiful love aspects. Romance is in the air.

Fast-moving Mercury is your love planet, and during the course of the year he will move through every sign and house of your Horoscope. (In fact, this year he will move through your 11th house twice.) So, there are many short-term trends in love that depend on where Mercury is and the kinds of aspects he receives. These are best dealt with in the monthly reports.

The spouse, partner or current love is having a very socially active kind of year. He or she is meeting new and significant people and enlarging his or her circle of friends.

Parents or parent figures in your life are having their marriages tested from August 20 onwards. It doesn't mean that they will fail; the Cosmos is just testing them. They have to work harder to keep things together. Siblings and sibling figures are also having their marriages tested. If they are single, marriage is not even advisable right now.

Children and children figures have had much social trauma over the past twenty years. Divorces could have happened. Things began to improve in 2020, and this year the love life is stable.

Grandchildren, if you have them, or those who play that role in your life, can marry this year – or be involved in a serious romantic relationship. If they are too young for this it will manifest as an active social life, meeting new friends.

Self-improvement

There are two fundamental attitudes to relationship. One view holds that one has to be complete in oneself before relationship can happen. One must already have one's personal centre and personal happiness and relationship flow from that point. The other attitude is that relationship completes the person. One cannot be happy unless they are in relationship. One must transcend all selfishness and cater to others and personal happiness will follow naturally. There are truths to both attitudes. Sometimes one is true, sometimes the other. This year – and for the past few years – you embrace the former view. Get your personal house in order. Learn to enjoy your own company and others will enjoy it too. Be comfortable in your own skin.

Pisces is spiritual by nature. With Neptune in your sign for many years now, this tendency has accelerated further. And now with Jupiter in your sign as well, it accelerates even further. Jupiter, as we've mentioned, is your career planet. Thus you need a spiritual-type career. You would be comfortable in a non-profit or charitable organization. You would be comfortable in a career that involved a spiritual organization. Another way to read this is that your spiritual practice, your spiritual growth, *is* the actual career – the actual mission in the year ahead (especially until May 11 and from October 29 to December 21).

Saturn has been in your spiritual 12th house since late 2020. Pisceans tends to be too fuzzy in spiritual matters: it is enough for you to transcend the physical world and live in bliss. But with Saturn in your 12th house you need a more practical approach. Your spirituality has to have an impact on the practical affairs of life. It must be organized and structured. It has to solve real-world problems. (And it does if we allow it.)

Month-by-month Forecasts

January

Best Days Overall: 6, 7, 16, 17, 25, 26
Most Stressful Days Overall: 1, 13, 14, 21, 22, 27, 28
Best Days for Love: 2, 3, 4, 5, 11, 12, 13, 14, 21, 22, 23, 29, 30
Best Days for Money: 1, 6, 8, 9, 16, 19, 25, 29
Best Days for Career: 1, 6, 16, 25, 27, 28

A happy month ahead, Pisces, enjoy.

You begin the year in excellent health. There is only one planet, Mars, in stressful alignment with you and he will move into harmony on the 25th. Only the Moon – and then only occasionally – will make stressful aspects, and these are very short lived. You have plenty of energy to achieve whatever you set your mind to. You can enhance the health even further with back and knee massage until the 20th and with calf and ankle massage after the 20th.

The planetary power is overwhelmingly in the Eastern sector of your chart – the sector of self. And this strength increases as the month progresses. So you are in a period of strong personal independence. Self-esteem and self-confidence are strong – and will get stronger in the coming months. The world needs to conform to you rather than the other way around. Take the steps – make the changes – needed for your happiness. Happiness is up to you these days.

Your 11th house of friends and groups is unusually powerful all month. At least half (sometimes more) of the planets are either there or moving through there. So the month ahead is very social. It is not necessarily romantic, but social. It's about being involved with friends and groups activities. Being around people with similar interests. Platonic kinds of relationships.

This is not an especially strong romantic month. Your love planet, Mercury, goes retrograde on the 14th. So romantic confidence could be better. Mercury will be in Aquarius from the 2nd to the 27th, which would also favour platonic love. A friend might want to be more than that. You gravitate to spiritual people who are unusual and a bit rebellious. You would favour scientists, inventors, astronomers, astrologers and people involved in technology. On the 27th Mercury retrogrades back into Capricorn and you become more cautious in love (as you should be). You're more traditional about it.

Finances are good. Jupiter in your sign shows good fortune and prosperity and this will get stronger in the coming months. Your financial planet Mars in your 10th house until the 25th signals increased earnings and the favour of bosses and parents or parent figures. Pay rises – official or unofficial – are likely.

February

Best Days Overall: 2, 3, 12, 13, 21, 22, 23
Most Stressful Days Overall: 9, 10, 11, 17, 18, 24, 25
Best Days for Love: 7, 8, 17, 18, 19, 20, 27, 28
Best Days for Money: 2, 3, 5, 6, 7, 8, 12, 13, 17, 18, 21, 22, 26, 27
Best Days for Career: 2, 3, 12, 13, 21, 22, 24, 25

You're still in a strong social month, but more involved with friends, groups and group activities. Being involved in these things can actually lead to romance in many cases and boosts the bottom line. Your 11th house is still very strong (though not as strong as last month) and there are many planets in the sign of Aquarius, which rules friends and groups.

On January 20 the Sun entered your spiritual 12th house and is there until the 18th. So this is a strong spiritual period. Yes, friends are nice, groups are nice, but find some alone time. Spiritual growth happens best in solitude.

Health is even better than last month. All the planets (with the exception of the Moon and then only temporarily) are in harmonious alignment with you. The Sun's entry into your sign on the 18th increases health and energy even further. Your challenge now is to use all this extra life force – which is like money in the bank – in wise and constructive ways. People who complain about 'lack of power' are really missing the point. Their problem is the misuse of the power that they already have.

The planetary power will be at its maximum Eastern position from the 18th onwards, and on into next month. So, you are in a period of maximum personal independence. You can and should have things your way. You know your path of happiness better than others. Now is the time to grasp it. Make the changes that need to be made for your happiness. The world will adapt to you rather than the other way around. Your personal skills, abilities and initiative are important now. You are practising positive self-assertion.

Your financial planet Mars moved into Capricorn on January 25 and will be there for the rest of this month. Mars is 'exalted' in this sign. He reaches the maximum extent of his power. So your earning power is 'exalted' now. (Three planets in your own sign, including the Sun and Jupiter, are also boosting earnings.) It is a prosperous month ahead.

The month is mostly about yourself and attaining personal desires. It's not really about others. So love and romance are not big deals right now. The tendency will be to the status quo.

March

Best Days Overall: 2, 3, 11, 12, 13, 21, 22, 30, 31
Most Stressful Days Overall: 9, 10, 16, 17, 23, 24
Best Days for Love: 1, 9, 11, 12, 16, 17, 18, 19, 22, 27, 28
Best Days for Money: 2, 3, 4, 5, 9, 11, 12, 18, 19, 21, 22, 27, 28, 30, 31
Best Days for Career: 2, 3, 11, 12, 21, 22, 23, 24, 30, 31

A happy, healthy and prosperous month ahead, Pisces.

Last month on the 18th, as the Sun entered your sign, you began one of your yearly personal pleasure peaks – for many of you this is a lifetime peak (much depends on your age). This peak continues until March 20. So it is time for taking care of number one; for enjoying all the pleasures of the body and the senses – the carnal delights; for pampering the body and rewarding it for the yeoman, selfless service it has given you all these years. This month personal pleasure is even stronger than last month as Mercury also enters your sign, on the 10th.

Personal independence is even stronger than last month too. So, once again, make the changes that need to be made for your happiness. Take the bull by the horns and create your own paradise. This is a month (like last month) for having your way in life. Others will adapt to you. With Mercury, your love planet, in your own sign from the 10th to the 27th, you even have love on your terms. There is a big improvement in the love life. Love pursues you rather than the other way around. If you are in a relationship the spouse, partner or current love is very devoted and eager to please.

Prosperity has been strong this year thus far, and gets even stronger in the month ahead as, on the 20th, the Sun enters your money house and you begin a yearly financial peak. (Prosperity will be even stronger over coming months.) Job opportunities are coming to you this month and there's not much you need to do to attract them. They seek you out. The 4th to the 6th seems especially good for that.

On the 20th as the Sun enters Aries you will be in the strongest starting energy of the zodiac. But it is even stronger than normal. Both the cosmic *and* your personal solar cycles will be waxing – growing – at this time. Also, and this is most significant, *all* the planets are in forward motion. If you have new projects to start or products to release on the market, this would be the time to do it. (Next month would also be good.) Anything you start now will have a lot of cosmic momentum behind it.

April

Best Days Overall: 8, 9, 17, 18, 25, 26
Most Stressful Days Overall: 5, 6, 13, 14, 19, 20
Best Days for Love: 1, 2, 8, 12, 13, 14, 17, 18, 21, 22, 25, 26, 27
Best Days for Money: 1, 2, 5, 6, 8, 9, 17, 18, 25, 26, 27, 28, 29
Best Days for Career: 8, 9, 17, 18, 19, 20, 26, 27

The starting energy for new projects or products is even stronger than last month! If you can do these things from the 1st to the 16th (when the Moon also waxes) you'll have the most super starting energy that I've seen in years.

The month ahead is very prosperous – perhaps even more so than last month. Mars, your financial planet, moves into your sign on the 15th. This brings windfalls and financial opportunities. The money people in your life are devoted to you. Money pursues you. You dress and live as a prosperous person. You spend on yourself. You invest in yourself.

Jupiter travels with Neptune, the ruler of your Horoscope, from the 1st to the 17th. This not only increases wealth, but brings career success, status and opportunity to you. And, let's not forget that you are still in the midst of a yearly financial peak until the 20th.

Health remains excellent all month. Mars in your sign not only brings financial windfalls but more personal energy and the 'can do' spirit. You excel in your exercise and athletic regimes (achieving personal bests). However, try to avoid rush and hurry and flare-ups of temper.

A solar eclipse on the 30th occurs in your 3rd house and is relatively mild in its effects on you. (If it hits a sensitive point in your personal Horoscope though – the chart cast personally for you – it can be powerful indeed.) It occurs in your 3rd house of communication and intellectual interests. Students below college level can experience disruptions at school and changes in their educational plans. It would be a good idea to drive more carefully at this time. Cars and communication equipment will get tested and often need repair or replacement. Siblings and sibling figures in your life are impacted and need to reassess themselves, redefine how they think of themselves and how they want others to think of them. This will lead to wardrobe changes and a whole new look and presentation in the coming months.

Since the Sun is your health and work planet, this kind of eclipse can bring health scares – an unfavourable result in a scan or test. But since health is so good this year, it is likely to be just a scare and nothing more. However, there will be changes in your health regime in the coming months. Job changes are also likely – these will be good. They can be within your present situation or with another company. Children and children figures have financial dramas.

May

Best Days Overall: 5, 6, 14, 15, 23, 24
Most Stressful Days Overall: 2, 3, 4, 10, 11, 16, 17, 30, 31
Best Days for Love: 2, 3, 4, 7, 8, 10, 11, 12, 13, 16, 17, 18, 19, 28
Best Days for Money: 6, 7, 8, 9, 16, 17, 18, 25, 26
Best Days for Career: 6, 16, 17, 25

An eventful month. Jupiter, your career planet, makes a major move into your money house on the 11th. He will also be in his solstice for a very long time – from the 12th to the 11th of June. He is pausing – practically stationary – at the same degree of latitude. Then he will change direction. It is a career pause that refreshes. You will pause and then change direction in the career. One of the important changes is that you will value money over status and prestige. Those things are nice, but whether you have status or not, you're still charged the same to get on the underground or bus. So, you are entering a super prosperity period – more so than you've had all year.

The planetary power is starting to shift – it's a nudge really – from the East to the West – from the sector of self to the sector of others. The sector of self still dominates, but not as it has thus far this year. Personal independence is a tad less than it has been.

A lunar eclipse on the 16th occurs in your 9th house. This eclipse is rather mild in its effect on you personally, but it won't hurt to reduce your schedule a little. Others might be less lucky. (Also keep in mind that if this eclipse hits a sensitive point in your personal Horoscope – cast personally for you – it can be very powerful.) College-level students are affected. There can be shake-ups in their school and in the curriculum. The hierarchy of the school can be shaken up. Often students change their courses of study, and sometimes even change institutions. It's not a good idea to be travelling around during the eclipse period. Your religious, philosophical and theological beliefs will get tested. This is probably a good thing: they get a reality check. Some of your beliefs will get discarded, some will get revised and updated. There are likely to be shake-ups in your place of worship and in the lives of worship leaders.

The Moon, the eclipsed planet, rules children, so they are affected by the eclipse. They should stay out of harm's way. If they are of the appropriate age a serious relationship gets tested. But even younger children or children figures in your life can have dramas with their friends.

This eclipse impacts Saturn, your planet of friends. So, there are dramas – often life-changing dramas – in the lives of friends. Friendships get tested and often take a new route. High-tech gadgetry and computers get tested as well. Often repairs or replacement is needed. Stay safe online and don't open suspicious emails.

June

Best Days Overall: 1, 2, 3, 11, 12, 19, 20, 28, 29, 30
Most Stressful Days Overall: 6, 7, 13, 14, 26, 27
Best Days for Love: 6, 7, 16, 17, 26, 27
Best Days for Money: 4, 13, 14, 21, 22
Best Days for Career: 4, 13, 14, 21

Health needs more attention this month, but there's nothing serious afoot – it's only short-term stress caused by the short-term planets. Energy levels are not what they have been so far this year. So, make sure to get enough rest. Enhance the health with massage of the heart reflex and chest massage. After the 21st right diet becomes important, and massage of the abdomen and stomach reflex would be useful. Health and energy will improve after the 21st.

The planetary power is mostly in the bottom half – the night side – of your chart; 70–80 per cent of the planets are there. Your 4th house of home and family gained power last month and becomes even more powerful this month. So the focus is on home, family and your emotional wellness. (Emotional wellness is a factor in health after the 21st as well.) You are building the foundations for future career success these days.

This is a month for making psychological progress, which will happen whether you are in formal therapy or not. The past is with you these days. And it is good to look at it from your present state of consciousness.

Finances are super this month. The two financial planets in your chart – Jupiter, the planet of abundance, and Mars, your actual financial planet – are both in your 2nd money house all month. This shows increased earnings. Pay rises – official or unofficial – can happen. Your good career reputation brings financial opportunities. If you have issues with the government this is a good month to deal with them.

Your financial planet Mars is still in his solstice until the 2nd. (It began on May 27.) So there is a pause in your financial affairs and then a change of direction. (Jupiter is still in his solstice until the 11th). Don't panic over this prolonged pause. Earnings will come pouring in afterwards.

Love is straightening out this month. Mercury goes forward on the 3rd and this brings more clarity in love. Until the 14th singles find love opportunities in educational settings – at school, in lectures, seminars, bookshops and the library. Intellectual compatibility is important. These things are important even afterwards, but something new is added from the 14th – a need for emotional intimacy. Family values seem important in love as well. Family and family connections are playing a role in love from the 14th onwards.

July

Best Days Overall: 8, 9, 16, 17, 26, 27
Most Stressful Days Overall: 4, 5, 10, 11, 23, 24, 31
Best Days for Love: 4, 5, 6, 7, 8, 16, 17, 15, 26, 28, 29, 31
Best Days for Money: 1, 2, 3, 10, 11, 12, 13, 18, 19, 20, 21, 22, 28, 29
Best Days for Career: 1, 2, 10, 11, 18, 19, 28, 29

A happy and prosperous month ahead, Pisces, enjoy.

Health is dramatically improved over last month, although last month's downturn was just a short-term blip in overall energy levels. In addition, when the Sun entered your 5th house on June 21 you began one of your yearly personal pleasure peaks. So this is a fun-filled month. Just having fun – enjoying life – has spectacular health benefits. (There is much anecdotal evidence about this.) You're enjoying your job and enjoying your health regime. You know how to make them fun.

The planetary power has shifted slightly to the Western sector – the social sector of your chart. In August one other planet (Mars) will cross over to the West. But the West is not the dominant sector. You're still very much in a 'me' period, but you are more social than usual. Once 'me' is satisfied you can indulge in relationships.

Your love planet Mercury moves breezily and speedily this month. This shows confidence and someone who covers a lot of territory. It also shows rapid shifts in the needs of love. Until the 5th emotional and mental compatibility are still important. After the 5th intellectual compatibility becomes less important and it's more about emotional intimacy. Additionally, you are attracted to people who can show you a good time. From the 5th to the 19th you don't seem too serious about love; it's more a form of entertainment. This is not especially conducive to serious committed love. Fun is still important after the 19th, but you seem more serious then. You show your love through practical service to the beloved, and this is how you feel loved in turn. You're attracted to people who 'do' for you – who serve your interests. After the 19th there are romantic opportunities at the workplace or as you pursue your health goals. People involved in your health can be very alluring.

Health is excellent this month, yet you seem very focused here from the 23rd. Hopefully this interest involves a healthy lifestyle. You could be so focused on health that you can tend, if you're not careful, to magnify little things into bigger things.

From the 23rd onwards jobseekers have great aspects and opportunities. Even those already employed can have job offers or opportunities for overtime and second jobs. You're in the mood for work. You work hard and play hard.

August

Best Days Overall: 4, 5, 13, 14, 22, 23
Most Stressful Days Overall: 1, 7, 8, 20, 21, 27, 28
Best Days for Love: 1, 4, 5, 15, 25, 26, 27, 28
Best Days for Money: 1, 7, 9, 10, 15, 16, 18, 19, 25, 29
Best Days for Career: 7, 8, 15, 25

Mars moves to the Western, social sector of your Horoscope on the 20th. The Western sector is as strong as it will ever be this year now, but it is still far from dominant. You still come first. You're not giving yourself over to others – except when it suits you. You're in the strongest social season of your year – especially from the 23rd onwards. Your challenge now is to balance your needs with those of others. Somewhere there is a balance point. If you are in a relationship, you and the beloved seem psychologically distant. You see things from opposite perspectives. If you can bridge the differences (and love can do that easily) things can work out.

Health will need some more attention from the 23rd. This is no big deal – only short-term stresses caused by the short-term planets. Don't panic if energy levels are not up to their usual standards. Enhance the health through massage of the heart reflex and chest massage until the 23rd and with massage of the small intestine reflex and the lower abdomen after then. As always, listen to the messages of the body and rest when tired.

On the 23rd you enter a yearly love and social peak. You become more attracted to health professionals and to people involved in your health. The workplace too seems more social. Family members and family connections are involved in love from the 4th to the 26th. There is more socializing with the family during this period as well.

Mars makes a major move on the 20th into your 4th house of home and family, and your financial planet will remain here for the rest of the year ahead. So, you are spending more on the home and the family. There is good family support. You earn money from home and from family connections. You can be too moody about finance. In a good mood the world is your oyster, and you feel rich. In a bad mood, everything is going to hell and you feel poor. It is important to develop a dispassionate attitude about finance. Also, financial experiences from the past will tend to rise to mind now. Past mistakes or disasters will surface so that you can look at them and absorb the lessons.

The good news here is that there is a Grand Trine in the Earth signs this month. This will give you a practical attitude to life and sounder financial judgement.

September

Best Days Overall: 1, 2, 9, 10, 18, 19, 20, 28, 29
Most Stressful Days Overall: 3, 4, 16, 17, 23, 24, 30
Best Days for Love: 4, 5, 7, 8, 13, 14, 15, 16, 24, 28, 29
Best Days for Money: 3, 7, 8, 11, 12, 16, 17, 21, 26, 27, 30
Best Days for Career: 3, 4, 11, 21, 30

Although personal independence is still strong, it is not as strong as it was earlier in the year. So if important changes need still to be made it might be better to wait until December, or even next year.

You're still in a yearly love and social peak this month. You've had stronger love highs in past years (and will have them again in the future), but this year you're at your peak. Like last month love is about balancing your personal desires and inclinations with those of the spouse, partner or current love. If you can bridge your differences love should go well. Love becomes further complicated by the retrograde of your love planet Mercury from the 10th onwards. Definitely more patience is needed. This particular retrograde of Mercury is a lot stronger than previous ones we've had this year. This is because five other planets are also retrograde – we are at the maximum extent of retrograde activity for the year – and the effect is cumulative. With Neptune also retrograde all month neither you nor the spouse, partner or current love are sure of what you want. There is a lot of indecision in both of you (and in the world at large).

Health still needs keeping an eye on until the 23rd. Enhance the health by getting enough rest and through massage of the small intestine reflex and the lower abdomen. After the 23rd enhance the health with hip massage and massage of the kidney reflex. Detox regimes are helpful after the 23rd as well. Health will dramatically improve after that date.

Your career planet Jupiter has his solstice from the 8th of this month to October 16. (He is a very slow-moving planet and his pauses are longer.) So don't be alarmed at a pause in your career and financial activities. A major reset is going on and it will lead to a new direction in both areas of life.

Mars is still in your 4th house all month, and many of the trends that we discussed last month are still in effect. Review our discussion of this last month.

On the 23rd, your 8th house of regeneration becomes powerful. The spouse, partner or current love is having a strong financial month. There are many delays and glitches but earnings are strong in spite of this. Love might be complicated, but the sex life seems active.

We have two Grand Trines this month – a rare occurrence. The Grand Trine in the Earth signs is a continuation from last month. It keeps you grounded and down to earth. Pisces needs that. The spouse, partner or current love – and friends in general – seem pragmatic as well and they are helping this process.

The Grand Trine in the Air signs boosts your mental and communication faculties. Ideas and inspiration come to you. It is a good month for teachers, writers and intellectual workers.

October

Best Days Overall: 7, 16, 17, 25, 26
Most Stressful Days Overall: 1, 13, 14, 21, 22, 27, 28
Best Days for Love: 2, 3, 4, 5, 13, 14, 21, 22, 23, 24, 25
Best Days for Money: 5, 8, 9, 10, 14, 15, 18, 24, 26, 27
Best Days for Career: 1, 8, 9, 18, 26, 27, 28

Three planets are having their solstice this month – Venus, Mercury and Jupiter. So a reset is happening in you and in the world at large. There is a pause and then a change of direction. Jupiter's solstice continues until the 16th. This shows the pause in your career. Venus began her solstice on September 30 and it continues to the 3rd. This would show a pause in your intellectual activities and the finances of the spouse, partner or current love. Mercury has his solstice from the 13th to the 16th. This shows a pause and then a reset in your love life. All of this is perfectly natural and good. It is the number of solstices in the same month that is unusual.

Mars, your financial planet, goes 'out of bounds' on the 24th and will remain so until the end of the year. This indicates that in financial matters you're outside your normal orbit – you're exploring outside your sphere. You don't see solutions in the normal places and must search in pastures new.

A solar eclipse on the 25th is relatively mild in its effect on you – but, as we have said before, it might not be so mild on others in your circle. So reduce your schedule a bit anyway. (Also, as has been mentioned, if this eclipse hits a sensitive point in your personal horoscope – the one cast specifically for you – it can impact you very strongly; you should consult with your personal astrologer about this.)

The eclipse occurs in your 9th house – the second eclipse in this house this year. So, once again, there are shake-ups in your place of worship and dramas in the lives of worship leaders. College-level students experience disruptions at their institutions and are forced to change their educational plans. Sometimes they just change plans; sometimes they actually change schools. Foreign travel is not advisable in this period. If you must travel, try to schedule your trip around the eclipse period.

Every solar eclipse impacts health and work, Pisces. This is because the eclipsed planet, the Sun, rules these areas in your chart. So there can be a health scare, but because health is basically good it is probably no more than that. (Should this happen to you – you get an unfavourable test result or scan, for example – have it redone in a couple of weeks and see what it shows then. Or get a second opinion.) There will be important changes to your health regime in the coming months. Job changes can happen too. The conditions of the workplace change. Employers can experience employee turnover in the coming months.

November

Best Days Overall: 3, 4, 12, 13, 22, 23, 30
Most Stressful Days Overall: 10, 11, 17, 18, 24, 25
Best Days for Love: 3, 4, 13, 14, 17, 18, 23, 24, 25
Best Days for Money: 1, 2, 4, 5, 6, 10, 11, 14, 19, 20, 23, 28, 29
Best Days for Career: 4, 14, 23, 24, 25

Retrograde activity is lessening now, as it was last month, and events are starting to move forward (I feel the eclipses – last month and this – are playing a role in this).

We have a very strong lunar eclipse on the 8th that impacts many planets. It's a total eclipse as well. So many areas of your life – and the world at large – are shaken up. Take it nice and easy over this period. Sensitive people like you can feel an eclipse two weeks before it happens, although usually the Cosmos will send you a personal message – some wild, unlikely event – that will tell you that the eclipse period has begun and that you need to start taking it easy.

This eclipse occurs in your 3rd house (the second eclipse in that house this year). Last month's solar eclipse affected college-level students. This one affects students below that level. There are disruptions at school. Educational plans will change. Sometimes there is a change of school. It would be a good idea to drive more carefully at this time. Cars and communication equipment get tested, and often repairs are needed. Siblings and sibling figures in your life are strongly affected. They need to redefine themselves for themselves. They need to upgrade their opinion of themselves. This will manifest as a change of wardrobe and presentation in the coming months. They will present a new look to others more in line with their present self-concept.

The impact on Uranus signals spiritual changes – changes of practice, teachings, teachers and attitudes. This is good, though not pleasant while it's happening. A spiritual reset is occurring. There are dramas in the lives of guru figures and shake-ups in spiritual or charitable organizations that you're involved with. Friends are making important financial changes.

The impact on Mercury will test your current relationship. In the case of singles, this kind of eclipse can lead to a desire to change their status and can lead to marriage in the future. There are personal dramas in the life of the beloved. There are dramas in the family and at home. Repairs could be needed in the home as well.

During this kind of an eclipse it is good to remember that we are not given more to cope with than we can handle.

December

Best Days Overall: 1, 9, 10, 11, 19, 20, 27, 28
Most Stressful Days Overall: 7, 8, 14, 15, 16, 21, 22
Best Days for Love: 2, 3, 14, 15, 16, 23, 24
Best Days for Money: 1, 2, 3, 7, 8, 11, 17, 18, 20, 21, 25, 26, 29, 30
Best Days for Career: 1, 11, 20, 21, 22, 29

Last month on the 22nd, the Sun entered your 10th house of career and you began a yearly career peak. In addition, your career planet Jupiter has been in your own sign since October 29. So, career is the major focus now and happy career opportunities are still coming to you. Jupiter started moving forward on November 24 and is travelling forward the entire month ahead. There is forward progress in your career. You have a good work ethic and employers are impressed.

Mercury, your love planet, moved into your 10th house on November 17 and is there until the 7th. This gives many messages. Your social contacts are helping boost the career. The family (and a parent figure) is very supportive. The family as a whole is raised in status through your career. The best way to serve your family and your current love is to succeed in your outer life.

Health needs some attention until the 22nd. So, as always, make sure to get enough rest. Enhance the health in the ways mentioned in the yearly report, but also add thigh massage and massage of the liver reflex until the 22nd. After then you can enhance the health with back and knee massage. Health will improve after the 22nd.

Your financial planet Mars is still retrograde all month. So though there is prosperity happening it is slower than usual. Try to be more perfect – handle all the details perfectly – in your financial dealings. This will minimize delays.

With Mercury in your 10th house (from November 17 to the 7th of this month) you find people of status and power alluring. But this changes somewhat after the 7th when Mercury enters your 11th house. Then you are more attracted by a relationship of equals. You want to be friends with your beloved as much as lover. As long as Mercury was in Sagittarius you were a love-at-first-sight kind of person and perhaps jumped into relationships too quickly. But Mercury in Capricorn from the 7th onwards tones this down. You become more cautious in love. You like to test it to see if it's real. You take your time falling in love. The overall social life becomes very active from the 7th onwards, but especially after the 22nd.